Home Woodworking Projects

Beautiful & Functional Items for Every Room

SHADY OAK PRESS

Home Woodworking Projects
Beautiful & Functional Items for Every Room

Shady Oak Press

Tom Carpenter
Director of Book Development

Jen Weaverling
Production Editor

Dan Cary
Photo Production Coordinator

Chris Marshall
Editorial Coordinator

Steve Anderson
Editor and Project Coordinator

Marti Naughton, Kate Opseth
Design, Art Direction and Production

Janice Thurs-Sherlock
Production Assistance

1 2 3 4 5 6 7 8 9 10 / 12 11 10 09 08 07
© 1999 North American Membership Group
ISBN: 978-1-58159-343-3

Distributed by:
Sterling Publishing Co., Inc.
387 Park Avenue South
New York, NY 10016-8810

For information about custom editions, special sales, premium and corporate purchases, please contact Sterling Special Sales Department at 800-805-5489 or specialsales@sterlingpub.com.

SHADY OAK PRESS

12301 Whitewater Drive
Minnetonka, MN 55343

Contents

Entry Bench **5**

Mission Table **11**

Display Coffee Table **19**

Workbench **25**

Double Rocker **31**

Kitchen Nook **37**

Beverage Bar **45**

Portable Desk **51**

Wainscot **57**

Quilt Rack **63**

Tool Cart **69**

Computer Desk **75**

Mantel **81**

Flower Bed **87**

Sink Board **93**

Radiator Cover **99**

Oval Frame **105**

Materials Cart **111**

Gardener's Bench **117**

Bathroom Vanity **123**

Corner Curio **129**

Building Custom Cabinets **137**

Triangular Table **145**

Treasure Chest **151**

INDEX **159**

Introduction

What better way to show off your woodworking talents than a home filled with your own project creations? From living room, den, dining room, bedroom and kitchen to deck, patio and garden (the outdoors are a "room" in their own right!), here are the project plans you've been looking for.

Create a beautiful mission table (page 11) for the kitchen. Build a workbench for your shop (page 25). Make a fun beverage bar (page 45) for any family room. Add wainscot to any room (page 57). Craft a beautiful mantel (page 81) for a fireplace. Cover up an old radiator (page 99). Put together a bathroom vanity (page 123) to be proud of. You can even master the art of cabinetmaking (page 137).

The secret to your success will be each project's exploded-view diagram, detailed cutting inventory, complete shopping list and clear instructions accompanied by detailed step-by-step photographs. There is never any guesswork involved when you use *Home Woodworking Projects* as your guide. Even if you're relatively new to the art, passion and pastime of woodworking, we know you'll be able to create these projects successfully.

Welcome to your personal guide to creating *Beautiful & Functional Items for Every Room*. This book makes the process easy, fun and rewarding.

SHADY OAK PRESS

Entry Bench

When the first snow of the season falls, our two small sons are quickly dressed in their snowsuits. An hour later, tired but elated, they trudge back inside, their winter boots covered in slush and sand.

In order to combat the inevitable flood in the foyer, and to eliminate messy trails across the hardwood floors, I decided to build a bench for the entryway with a boot rack and drip tray underneath. The rack was the key to the whole idea—a place to dry footwear without making a mess. It also provided a place to store bulky boots within easy reach of our 4-year-old.

Entry Bench

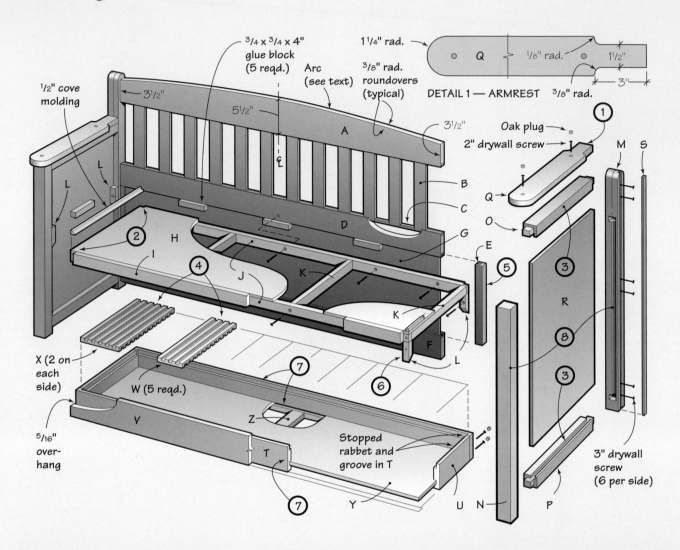

½" cove molding

¾ x ¾ x 4" glue block (5 reqd.)

Arc (see text)

1¼" rad.

⅜" rad. roundovers (typical)

1⅛" rad.   ⅛" rad.   1½"

DETAIL 1 — ARMREST   ⅜" rad.

3"

Q

3½"

5½"

A

3½"

B

C

D

G

Oak plug

2" drywall screw

Q

O

E

M   S

5

3

R

8

3

2

H

I

4

J

K

K

F

L

1

X (2 on each side)

W (5 reqd.)

Z

V

T

7

7

Y

6

⁵⁄₁₆" overhang

Stopped rabbet and groove in T

U   N   P

3" drywall screw (6 per side)

Entry Bench Cutting List*

Part/Description	No.	Size		Part/Description	No.	Size
A Back top rail	1	¾ × 5⅜ × 45 in.		**O** Side rail (top)	2	1½ × 1½ × 16½ in.
B Back slat	12	½ × 1½ × 10¾ in.		**P** Side rail (bottom)	2	1½ × 1½ × 16½ in.
C Fillet	26	⅜ × ½ × 2¹⁄₁₆ in.		**Q** Armrest	2	¾ × 2½ × 17½ in.
D Back middle rail	1	¾ × 3½ × 45 in.		**R** Side panel	2	½ × 15⅝ × 22⅝ in.
E Back panel cleat	2	¾ × ¾ × 11½ in.		**S** Leg fillet	2	³⁄₁₆ × ½ × 36 in.
F Back bottom rail	1	¾ × 3½ × 45 in.		**T** Tray (front/back)	2	¾ × 3½ × 44¼ in.
G Back panel	1	½ × 12⅛ × 44⅛ in.		**U** Tray (side)	2	¾ × 3½ × 12 in.
H Seat	1	½ × 15⅜ × 46½ in.		**V** Tray face	1	¾ × 4 × 44⅞ in.
I Seat face	1	¾ × 2 × 45 in.		**W** Small grate	6	¾ × 3½ × 12⅝ in.
J Seat frame (long)	2	¾ × 1½ × 46½ in.		**X** Large grate	4	¾ × 5½ × 12⅝ in.
K Seat frame (short)	4	¾ × 1½ × 13⅞ in.		**Y** Tray (bottom)	1	½ × 12⅝ × 43⅜ in.
L Seat cleat	4	¾ × ¾ × 3½ in.		**Z** Tray stretcher	1	¾ × 1½ × 12 in.
M Back leg	2	1½ × 1½ × 34 in.		***All parts red oak**		
N Front leg	2	1½ × 1½ × 26 in.				

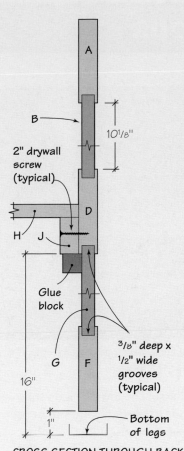

A

B

2" drywall
screw
(typical)

D

H

J

Glue
block

$^3/_8$" deep x
$^1/_2$" wide
grooves
(typical)

G F

10$^1/_8$"

16"

1"

Bottom
of legs

CROSS SECTION THROUGH BACK

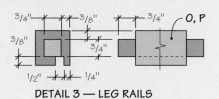

$^3/_4$"

$^3/_8$"

$^3/_4$"

DETAIL 2 — SEAT

$^3/_4$" $^3/_8$" $^3/_4$" O, P

$^3/_8$"

$^1/_2$" $^1/_4$" $^3/_4$"

DETAIL 3 — LEG RAILS

W, X $^1/_2$" (typical)

Front   Side
$^3/_8$"

DETAIL 4 — GRATE

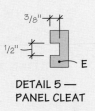

$^3/_8$"

$^1/_2$"

E

DETAIL 5 —
PANEL CLEAT

Counter-
sunk
hole

L

45°

DETAIL 6 —
SEAT CLEAT

$^3/_4$"

$^3/_8$"

T $^1/_2$"

DETAIL 7 —
TRAY RAIL

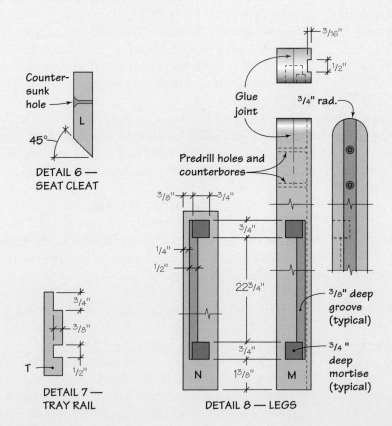

$^3/_{16}$"

$^1/_2$"

Glue
joint

$^3/_4$" rad.

Predrill holes and
counterbores

$^3/_8$" $^3/_4$"

$^3/_4$"

$^1/_4$"

$^1/_2$"

22$^3/_4$"

$^3/_8$" deep
groove
(typical)

$^3/_4$"
deep
mortise
(typical)

N $^3/_4$" M
1$^3/_8$"

DETAIL 8 — LEGS

Shopping List

- [ ] (1) $^3/_4$ × 1$^1/_2$ × 48-in. red oak
- [ ] (5) $^3/_4$ × 1$^1/_2$ × 72-in. red oak
- [ ] (1) $^3/_4$ × 3$^1/_2$ × 72-in. red oak
- [ ] (4) $^3/_4$ × 3$^1/_2$ × 96-in. red oak
- [ ] (1) $^1/_2$ × 5$^1/_2$ × 48-in. red oak
- [ ] (1) $^3/_4$ × 5$^1/_2$ × 48-in. red oak
- [ ] (2) $^3/_4$ × 5$^1/_2$ × 72-in. red oak
- [ ] (1) $^3/_4$ × 5$^1/_2$ × 96-in. red oak
- [ ] (1) $^1/_2$ × 48 × 96-in. red oak plywood
- [ ] (1) $^1/_2$ × 36-in. oak cove molding
- [ ] (8) $^1/_2$-in. oak plugs
- [ ] 2-, 3-in. drywall screws
- [ ] Wood glue
- [ ] Finishing materials
- [ ] Silicone caulk

Entry Bench: Instructions

PHOTO A: Lay out the back rail arc by flexing a hardboard strip as a guide. Spring clamps form stops at the ends.

We chose northern red oak for the entry bench, to match the woodwork in our home. This kind of furniture does not need to be heavy, so I settled on ½-in. five-ply plywood rather than the ¾-in. fiber core that my lumberyard stocks.

MILLING THE PARTS

Begin by gluing up pairs of ¾ × 1½-in. stock for each of the four legs and the side rails. These are the only parts requiring stock over ¾ in. thick. While the glue sets up, you can rip the rest of the parts to size.

Most of the joints depend on ½-in. dadoes either for strength or to conceal hardware. So, set up your table saw with a ½-in. dado cutter and your router table with a ½-in. straight bit. Mill a ⅜-in.-deep dado in the bottom edge of the back top rail, the top and bottom edges of the back middle rail, the top edge of the back bottom rail and on one edge of each of the back panel cleats.

Next, make the mortises that will join the rails to the legs. The glue joints on the legs should run front to back so the mortises are not cut into a joint.

Begin by laying out your cuts according to the detailed drawing. Then use a ⅝-in. spade bit to remove most of the waste to a depth of ¾ in. Square the edges with a sharp chisel.

To prevent splitting when chopping mortises, clamp a piece of scrap wood to each side of the leg to absorb the shock from the hammer impact. Use lighter hammer blows when paring along the grain than when chiseling across the grain. Once all four mortises are cut, the tenons can be cut on the four leg rails using the ½-in. dado insert in your table saw. The next step is to create the off-center stopped dado that houses the side panels. This is done on the router table. Begin by placing a strip of masking tape on the tool's fence alongside the bit and mark the edges of the bit on the tape. Mark the beginning of the stopped dado on each leg, then transfer those marks to the opposite side of the leg (the side that will face up as the cut is made). Set your fence and remove the waste in several passes, beginning and ending each cut according to the index marks. This is also a good time to run through-dadoes in the four side rails.

While the ½-in. bit is still in the router, run a ³⁄₁₆-in.-deep dado down the center on the outside of each of the back legs. Run dadoes ¾ in. up from the bottom of the tray sides and stopped dadoes ¾ in. up on the tray front and back, stopping the cuts ⅜ in. from the ends.

Finally, using the same bit and your router table fence, mill rabbets ⅜ in. wide by ¾ in. deep on the top inside edge of the tray sides and ends, stopping the dadoes on the sides ⅜ in. from the boards' ends.

CREATING THE ARC

Begin laying out the arc on the back top rail by locating the center of the board at 22½ in. Draw the centerline and place a mark on that line 5⅜ in. from the bottom of the board.

Clamp a scrap of wood 3½ in. from the bottom on each end. Then flex a strip of hardboard or ¼-in. plywood so the crest touches the 5⅜-in. mark, and trace the shape on the board (See Photo A).

Cut the arc with a band saw, scroll saw or jig saw, and finish the cut with a belt sander; then round off both sides of the arched edge with a ⅜-in.-radius roundover bit and a router. Be careful to avoid rounding the edges at the ends where they join the legs.

Cut the armrests on your band saw according to the pattern. A drum sander will make quick work of smoothing the inside curves. Then round over the top and bottom edges of each armrest, except the small section where the bottom will be aligned with the side rails. While your router is set up, round over the top and bottom front edges of the seat face.

Next, notch the seat and one end of the seat frame sides to fit around the inside of the back legs. The notch is ¾ in. along the seat and ⅜ in. front to back. Finally, round off the tops of the back legs with a belt sander.

ASSEMBLY

Assemble the two side panels first **(See Photo B)**, measuring diagonally to ensure they are square. Second, assemble the seat frame with 2-in. drywall screws and glue, predrilling and countersinking the screws. Next, glue and clamp the seat to the frame; then screw the end panels to the seat diagonally through the legs. The bottom of the seat frame should be 16 in. from the floor.

Screw the back top rail and the back middle rail into place next. These are attached with predrilled 3-in. screws countersunk into the bottom of the ³⁄₁₆-in. dado that we milled earlier in the outside faces of the back legs. The slats must be placed loosely in the dadoes while the top and middle rails are glued and screwed.

Get some help to hold everything in place during this operation. Glue the slat spacers, or fillets, into the middle rail dado and be aware that you may have to trim the spacers at either end to get a perfect fit **(See Photo C).**

Next, turn the bench upside down and glue the fillets into the top rail dado. Attach the two back panel cleats while the bench is upside down and drop the back panel into place **(See Photo D).** Install the bottom rail and then glue and screw the four seat cleats into the legs. Reinforce the seat with ¾ × ¾-in. glue blocks, and attach the seat face with glue and clamps.

When the glue is dry, turn the bench upright and install the armrests with glue and recessed screws, covering the screw heads with oak plugs you pare, and then sand flush. Finally, glue some ½-in. cove molding to the joints at the sides of the seat.

Assemble the tray with recessed screws and glue, plugging the holes in the back. Install the stretcher on-center under the bottom to prevent the tray from spreading. Finally, attach the face with glue and clamp the assembly while it dries.

PHOTO B: Glue the rail and leg joints. Do not glue the recessed panels when assembling the sides, to allow for expansion.

PHOTO C: Install fillets in the rail grooves between the loose slats. Glue the fillets but not the slats.

PHOTO D: With the bench inverted, secure the slotted cleats with glue and screws to hold the ends of the back panel.

PHOTO E: To create uniformly spaced dadoes in the grate, register the last cut against lines drawn on a piece of tape.

PHOTO F: The grates are made from short lengths of 1 × 4 and 1 × 6 oak to minimize waste. Finish them with marine varnish.

CUTTING THE GRATES

The large grates are milled from nominal 1 × 6 stock, the smaller ones from 1 × 4s. The two best features of the grates are that they can be removed easily for cleaning and that each piece can be cut quickly from a small piece of stock to minimize waste.

Begin by cutting the ⅜-in.-deep grooves across the grain, with the ½-in. dado head. Place a piece of masking tape across your table a few inches in front of the

Grate idea keeps mess in check

Wooden grates add an extra function to the bench's design. Each piece is removable, allowing quick cleanup of the messes that collect in the tray at the bottom. The attractive grid pattern is easily milled from a relatively small piece of stock, minimizing waste while it maximizes the likelihood of keeping your entryway clean and dry. A marine varnish finish helps them withstand repeated contact with snowy boots and rain-soaked footwear.

dado head and run a scrap through the cutter. Now mark the cut's path on the tape, then place another mark ½ in. to the right of the two sawcut marks.

Using your miter gauge and a backup fence, run the first piece of grate stock across the cutter with the right end touching the right-hand mark. For the second cut, line the left side of the first cut up to the right-hand mark and make the dado. Continue until all the bottom grooves are cut **(See Photo E).**

Make the top cuts with the grain so that no tearout is visible later. To make the first cut, set your rip fence ½ in. away from the dado head and raise the blade another 1/32 in. Move the fence as needed to create a new dado every inch (leaving ½ in. of stock between the grooves).

I used a sharp chisel to square the corners of the rabbet in the tray where the grates sit, but on reflection I think a better idea is to simply sand a radius on the outside corners of two of the larger grates.

FINISHING

I finished the bench with four coats of water-based clear polyurethane, sanding with 400-grit silicone carbide paper between coats. I also coated the outside of the tray with polyurethane, but on the grates and inside the tray I used three coats of marine varnish for water-resistance. I also sealed the joints inside the boot tray with non-yellowing caulk. With little snowmen like ours, I figured that I should give the piece as much protection as possible.

Mission Table

Working in a kitchen is a lot like working in a shop. No matter how many work surfaces and storage spaces you have, you can always use more. This Arts-and-Crafts-style rolling island fits the bill because it provides a nearly 2 × 4-ft. top, three drawers and a large shelf. It works equally well as a kitchen island, a baker's cart or a sideboard for the dining room.

Bakers will appreciate the granite top because it stays cool, which makes it ideal for rolling out pie crusts. Even if you don't bake, the top and shelf provide an extra 16 sq. ft. of surface area. With plenty of clearance, the shelf is particularly useful for storing large countertop appliances.

Mission Table

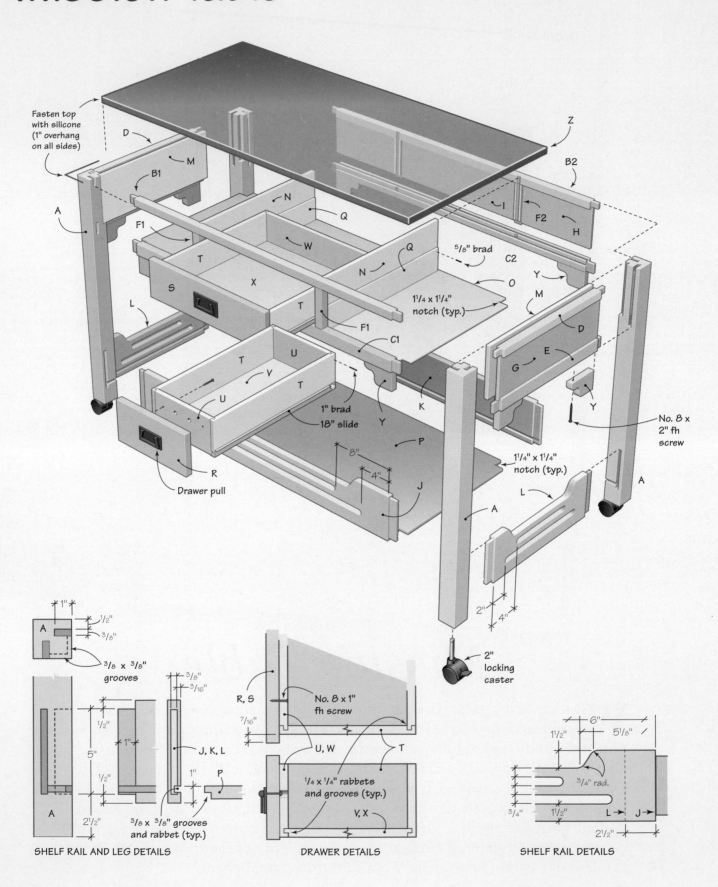

Fasten top with silicone (1" overhang on all sides)

D

M

B1

A

F1

T

S

X

L

N

Q

W

T

N

Q

O

Y

C2

⁵⁄₈" brad

M

D

G   E

Y

Z

B2

I

F2

H

1¼ x 1¼"
notch (typ.)

U

V

U

T

T

V

R

Drawer pull

U

C1

F1

K

Y

1" brad
18" slide

P

8"

4"

J

A

L

1¼" x 1¼"
notch (typ.)

No. 8 x 2" fh screw

A

2"   4"

2"
locking
caster

Shelf Rail and Leg Details

A

1"

½"

³⁄₈"

³⁄₈ x ³⁄₈"
grooves

³⁄₈"
³⁄₁₆"

½"

1"

½"

5"

2½"

A

J, K, L

1"

P

³⁄₈ x ³⁄₈" grooves
and rabbet (typ.)

SHELF RAIL AND LEG DETAILS

Drawer Details

R, S

No. 8 x 1"
fh screw

⁷⁄₁₆"

U, W

T

¼ x ¼" rabbets
and grooves (typ.)

V, X

DRAWER DETAILS

Shelf Rail Details

6"

5⅛"

1½"

³⁄₄" rad.

³⁄₄"

1½"

L   J

2½"

SHELF RAIL DETAILS

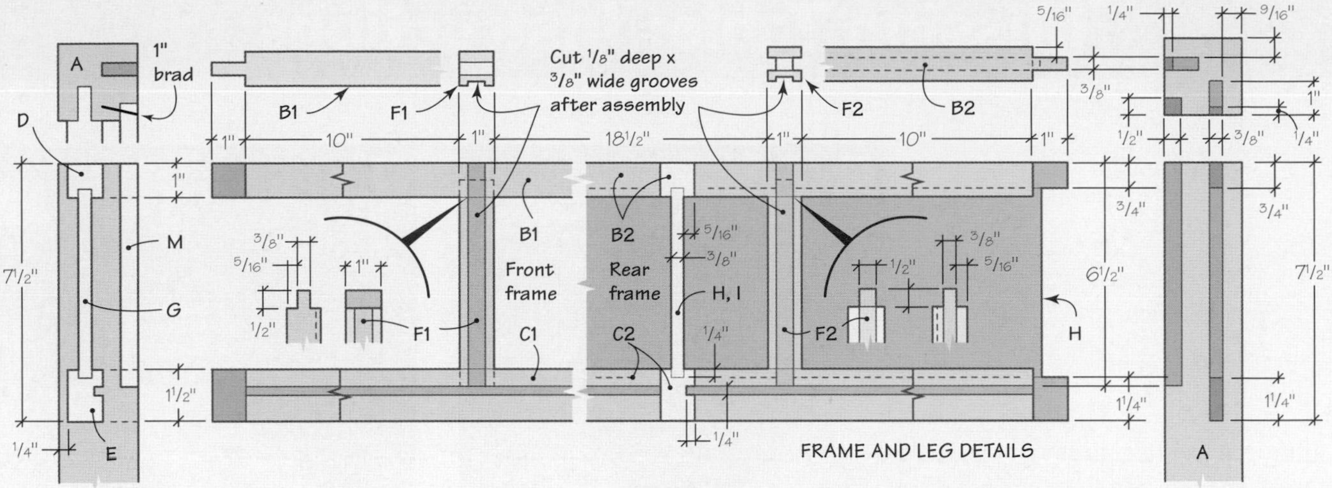

A
1" brad
D
M
G
E
7 1/2"
1"
1 1/2"
1/4"
B1
F1
Cut 1/8" deep x 3/8" wide grooves after assembly
F2
B2
1"
10"
18 1/2"
5/16"
1/4"
9/16"
3/8"
1/2"
Front frame
Rear frame
C1
C2
H, I
H
6 1/2"
3/4"
1 1/4"
FRAME AND LEG DETAILS

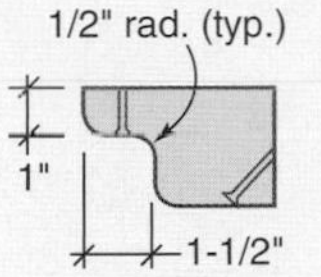

1/2" rad. (typ.)
1"
1-1/2"

BRACKET—Y

Shopping List

- ☐ 20 bf 6/4 quartersawn white oak
- ☐ 10 bf 8/4 quartersawn white oak
- ☐ ¼ × 24 × 48-in. birch plywood
- ☐ ¾ × 24 × 48-in. oak plywood
- ☐ (2) ½ × 30 × 60-in. Baltic birch plywood
- ☐ (1) ¾ × 23½ × 47-in. granite top
- ☐ (4) 2-in. locking casters
- ☐ (3) pairs 18-in. drawer slides
- ☐ (2) 3⅛-in. drawer pulls
- ☐ (1) 3¾-in. drawer pull
- ☐ (16) #8 × 2-in. flathead wood screws
- ☐ (7) #8 × 1-in. flathead wood screws
- ☐ ⅝-in. pneumatic brads
- ☐ 1-in. pneumatic brads
- ☐ Wood glue
- ☐ Polyurethane glue
- ☐ Finishing materials
- ☐ Silicone caulk

Mission Table Cutting List

Part/Description	No.	Size	Material
A Legs	4	2¼ × 2¼ × 31¾ in.	White oak
B1 Front top rail	1	1 × 1 × 42½ in.	"
B2 Rear top rail	1	1 × 1 × 42½ in.	"
C1 Front center rail	1	1 × 1½ × 42½ in.	"
C2 Rear center rail	1	1 × 1½ × 42½ in.	"
D Side top rails	2	1 × 1 × 19 in.	"
E Side center rails	2	1 × 1½ × 19 in.	"
F1 Front stiles	2	1 × 1 × 6 in.	"
F2 Rear stiles	2	1 × 1 × 6 in.	"
G End panels	2	⅜ × 5½ × 17½ in.	"
H Small back panels	2	⅜ × 5½ × 10½ in.	"
I Center back panel	1	⅜ × 5½ × 19 in.	"
J Front shelf rail	1	¾ × 6 × 42½ in.	"
K Rear shelf rail	1	¾ × 6 × 42½ in.	"
L Side shelf rails	2	¾ × 6 × 19 in.	"
M Drawer slide panels	2	½ × 6½ × 18 in.	Birch ply
N Dividers	2	½ × 6½ × 19¼ in.	"
O Dust cover	1	¼ × 19½ × 43 in.	"
P Shelf	1	¾ × 20 × 43½ in.	"
Q Spacers	4	¼ × 3 × 19 in.	"
R Small drawer faces	2	¾ × 4⅞ × 9⅞ in.	White oak
S Center drawer face	1	¾ × 4⅞ × 18⅜ in.	"
T Drawer sides	6	½ × 4¼ × 18 in.	Birch ply
U Small drawer fronts/backs	4	½ × 4¼ × 8½ in.	"
V Small drawer bottom	1	½ × 8½ × 17½ in.	"
W Center drawer front/back	2	½ x 4¼ x 17 in.	"
X Center drawer bottom	1	½ × 17 × 17½ in.	"
Y Corner brackets	8	¾ × 4 × 2½ in.	White oak
Z Top	1	¾ × 23½ × 47 in.	Granite

If our island design is too large for your kitchen, you can scale back the width and eliminate a drawer and still retain the look. However, if you have the urge to simplify the joinery—don't. The joinery was designed so that the island could withstand the rigors of being rolled around and worked on. Don't substitute stub tenons or biscuits for the island's 1-in.-long tenons or you'll sacrifice much of its durability.

LOCATING MATERIALS

Purchase all the materials—including the top and casters—before you start this project. To help keep costs down, I used the polished granite top from a cast-iron bistro table purchased at a home furnishings retail outlet. The price of the entire piece was less than what I would have paid at a local countertop supplier for just the granite. Other suitable top options include marble and solid-surfacing materials such as Corian.

Quartersawn white oak is the wood of choice for this project because it's the species most often associated with American Arts-and-Crafts furniture. You won't find this wood at your local home center, but rather at lumberyards that cater to the cabinetmaking trade.

Remember that the size of the

PHOTO A: To ensure plumb caster stem holes, use a drilling guide made from a piece of scrap leg stock and ¼-in. plywood.

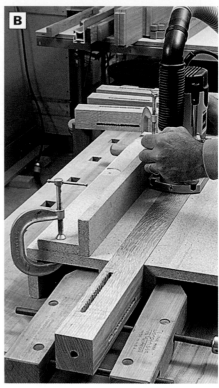

PHOTO B: A fence and two boxes clamped together provide accuracy and support for routing leg mortises.

casters will affect the height of the island. I used double-wheel, locking stem casters rated at 90 pounds each. Stem casters are less obtrusive than those that mount with a plate, and the locks prevent the island from wiggling when you perform certain kitchen functions, such as rolling dough. Also, the relatively small wheels of these casters don't look out of scale on the island's legs. If you have a wood or tile floor, casters with a soft urethane wheel (rather than nylon) will roll more smoothly and quietly with considerably less damage to the floor surface.

MILLING MATTERS

This project requires a fair amount of woodworking experience because the joinery is com-

plex and must be made precisely. You'll have to mill most of the parts to size from rough stock, so you'll need a jointer and a planer. They don't have to be particularly large machines; small benchtop models will do the job just fine.

Precision parts are the key to this project. Remember to mill all pieces of the same thickness at the same time. Even small variations in thickness and squareness can lead to big joinery and assembly problems later on.

To keep the distinctive quarter-sawn faces most visible, plan your milling operations carefully. On all the legs, matching quarter-sawn sides should face the front and back, giving the island a unified look and allowing for uniform staining.

PHOTO C: Define the rail tenon shoulders using a table saw cutoff box with a stopblock clamped to the rear fence.

PHOTO D: Cut the grooves in the rails for the dust cover and shelf with a router table and a straight bit.

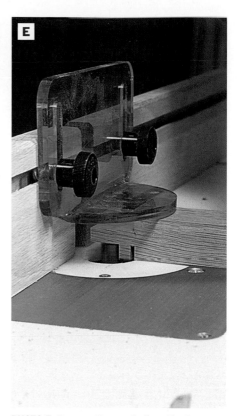

PHOTO E: Remove the waste from the tenon cheeks by pushing the work across the router bit with a miter gauge.

Because it's unlikely that you'll find ¹⁰⁄₄ or ¹²⁄₄ stock, you'll need to glue boards together to make the legs. To do this, mill ⁶⁄₄ rough stock that's at least 5 in. wide to 1¼ in. thick. Next, crosscut the milled boards so they're at least 1 in. longer than the finished leg; then rip them in half. Here's the trick to grain-matching the legs: Assemble the boards by simply folding them together along the cut line. Once the blanks are glued, you can joint and plane them to the finished size.

I was unable to get ⁴⁄₄ (1-in.-thick) rough stock to mill the ¾-in. parts, so I had to resaw ⁶⁄₄ stock (although milled ¾-in. stock is generally available, it is seldom flat enough). If you need to resaw stock, your band saw should have a 6-in. minimum resaw capacity and accept at least a ½-in. skip-tooth blade. Use a short, tall fence to guide the stock through the

blade. Even a wide, resawing blade may wander at times as it naturally tries to follow the wood grain. Minimize this action by holding the workpiece tightly against the fence. If you detect some flex in the blade, the board may require some planing after it has been cut.

LEG WORK

The legs are the hubs for most of the other parts, so start with leg joinery. First, cut the legs and all the other oak parts to length. To avoid confusion and mistakes, carefully lay out all the joints and label the parts. Don't cut any of the plywood parts yet; their size may require some minor tweaking to achieve a good fit.

Orient and label each leg for its position and grain direction. Once you've measured and marked one set of joints, transfer the layout to a story stick and use it to mark the

remainder of the like joints. This step prevents measuring errors.

Although there are several good ways to cut mortises, when working with a wood as hard as white oak, I prefer to remove most of the waste with a narrow bit and finish with a plunge router and a chisel. I restrain the workpiece on the drill press table with fences on both sides to prevent it from wandering. Then I rout the remaining waste in a few passes using a simple routing fixture (See Photo B). Make the mortises about ¹⁄₁₆ in. deeper than the length of the tenons to prevent the tenons from bottoming out and to provide a relief channel for excess glue.

Routing leaves the mortise ends radiused. Whether you square them with a chisel or leave them rounded makes no difference in the joint's strength. Of course, if you leave them rounded you'll have to round the corresponding

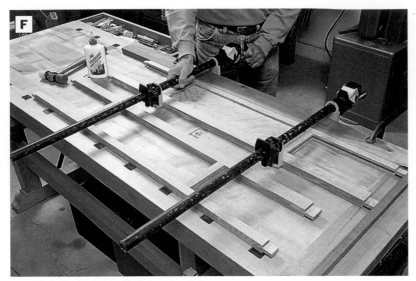

PHOTO F: Before routing grooves for the dividers, glue together the front and back rail assemblies.

PHOTO G: Gang the front and back rail assemblies to rout the centered grooves in the stiles.

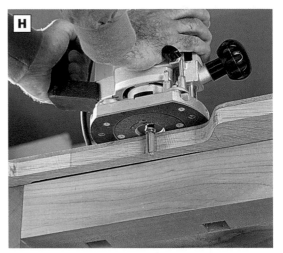

PHOTO H: Cut the shelf rail curve to within 1⁄16 in. of the pattern line; complete the cut using a template and a flush-trim bit.

tenon edges to fit. After you rout the mortises, leave the fence in the same position and rout the panel grooves.

Routing the grooves in the legs for the bottom shelf is a simple job, but it can be an awkward balancing act if your router is too big. A router with a small base and low center of gravity is less prone to tipping as you work across the leg. Clamp a fence to the leg to guide the router for these cuts.

TENON TACTICS

To be strong, tenons must fit just right—not too tight and not too loose. (The cure for a sloppy-fitting tenon is to glue veneer to both cheeks and then recut.) Of course, you should always cut the mortises first. Use some scraps to make test cuts so you can sneak up on the right size without sacrificing workpieces. When cutting tenons, abide by the rule of thirds: A tenon should be roughly one-third the thickness of the workpiece.

I usually cut the tenon shoulders on the table saw first **(See Photo C).** The saw provides a clean, square edge and defines which faces you must cut away later to make the tenon cheeks. The blade's cutting depth should be close to the level of the cheeks, but it doesn't have to be perfect.

Cutting the tenons on a router table produces smooth, uniform results. Guide the work with a miter gauge and make multiple full-depth passes across the bit **(See Photo E).** Use the router table fence as a stop to prevent the bit from cutting beyond the shoulder line.

ASSEMBLY STRATEGIES

Sand all the parts before you assemble them. It saves time, and the finished project looks better. You should only need to do touch-up sanding after assembly. Before you sand, fill voids and defects with a water-based wood putty, which will take stain better than a solvent-based product.

I prefer to remove mill marks and blemishes with a cabinet

scraper before I sand. It's faster, produces less dust and is more effective than sanding at removing planer marks. After scraping, I do a quick round of hand-sanding with 150-grit paper.

Assemble the front and back rail ladders first **(See Photo F).** Don't forget to install the center back panel in its grooves, and be sure the assembly is square by measuring its diagonals. Rout

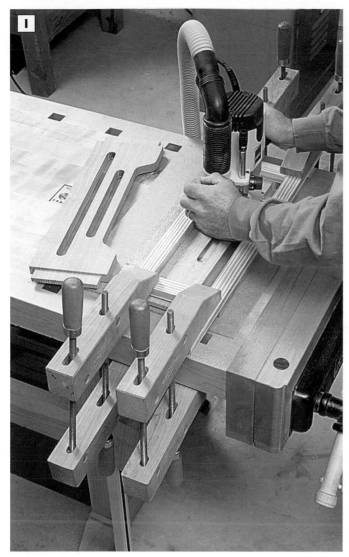

PHOTO I: Make successive passes to cut the decorative grooves. Two fences prevent the router base from drifting.

PHOTO J: Keep order by organizing parts and clamps. Use polyurethane glue for a longer open time.

the grooves for the dividers after assembling the ladders **(See Photo G).** You'll save time and end up with more consistent grooves if you gang-rout the assemblies.

I used wood glue to assemble the rail ladders because there were few parts. However, polyurethane glue, with its long open time, is a better choice for the complex main assembly **(See Photo J).** You'll need about 20 minutes to do the job. Polyurethane glue has the added advantage of acting as a lubricant when fitting tight joints, whereas wood glue will cause the wood to swell and grab. Regardless of the glue you use, dry-fit the parts with clamps first. Any joints that don't fit properly will be easy to spot.

Decorative shelf rails accentuate the Arts-and-Crafts design. After transferring the shape onto the workpiece, cut the curves using either a band saw or a jig saw (though the latter will have a difficult time

working through solid white oak). Be sure to cut $\frac{1}{16}$ in. outside the mark. This will allow you to complete the cut more accurately with a flush-trim bit in your router **(See Photo H).** The piloted bit rides along the edge of the template to ensure proper contours of consistent dimensions.

To highlight the style further, we added grooves to the shelf rails. Two fences secured the workpiece for this operation, while stopblocks at each end made sure I didn't go too far **(See Photo I).** Multiple passes are necessary in order to rout completely through the rails. Be sure to place a scrap piece below the rail to act as an auxiliary worksurface so you don't end up with an unwanted decorative groove in your bench as well.

DRAWERS & FINISHING

Assemble the island before you make the drawers

and cut the dividers to fit. To simplify drawer construction, I made all the parts out of ½-in. Baltic birch plywood and made the fronts and the backs the same. With only three drawers to make, I found the table saw to be the fastest and most accurate tool for cutting the grooves and dadoes.

The boxes are assembled with glue at each corner dado-rabbet joint. A carpenter's square can be a helpful guide to guarantee that each joint maintains a perpendicular relationship. Use clamps to hold the drawer together while it dries **(See Photo K)**, and measure diagonals to ensure a square assembly.

The drawer faces are flush to the frame, but require a ⅟16-in. gap on all sides. To achieve the necessary spacing, place shims at each corner. Hold the face securely while driving the screws from inside the drawer **(See Photo L).**

Finishing this project is easy because oak generally stains evenly without blotching. However, you should quickly wipe off excess stain to keep the wood from looking muddy. When you choose a stain, consider how the color will look with the granite top and the hardware. I used a brown-mahogany stain to get a look that's similar to that of traditional ammonia-fumed Arts-and-Crafts furniture. Any film finish (varnish, lacquer, water-based or shellac) will work as a topcoat. Keep in mind, as attractive as this piece looks, it is intended for use in the kitchen and will take a beating from time to time.

The final step is to glue down the top with a thin bead of silicone caulk along the edges. Be careful not to use too much or it can ooze onto the finished wood.

PHOTO K: Use clamps to draw the drawer box joints together before nailing and to adjust the sides until they're square.

PHOTO L: When installing the drawer face, use ⅟16-in.-thick shims to maintain even spacing around the front.

Display Coffee Table

Coffee tables are supposed to create an environment that invites conversation, so what better furniture project than a table that is itself a conversation piece? This design will not only showcase your woodworking talents, but also display collectibles or memorabilia where they can be studied and appreciated.

Don't be afraid to change the dimensions of the table. For instance, you can change the height of the tabletop to be level with or slightly below your sofa cushions. Or adjust the depth or overall size of the display box to accommodate whatever collection you might have.

Display Coffee Table

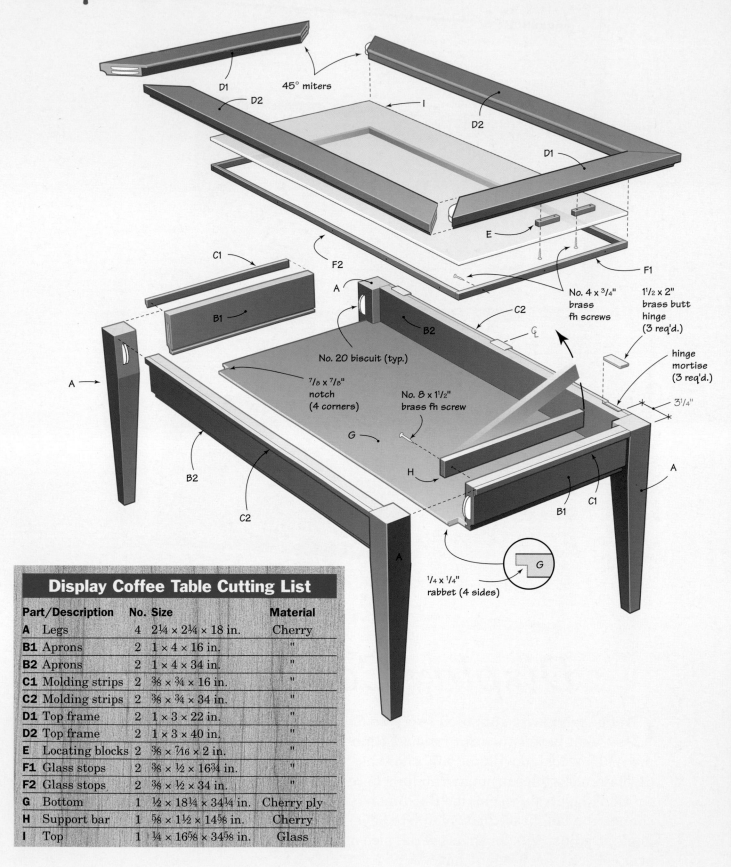

45° miters

D1

D2

D2

I

D1

E

F2

C1

B1

A

No. 20 biscuit (typ.)

⁷⁄₈ × ⁷⁄₈"
notch
(4 corners)

A

B2

C2

B2

G

C2

H

A

B2

C2

G

No. 4 × ³⁄₄"
brass
fh screws

F1

1¹⁄₂ × 2"
brass butt
hinge
(3 req'd.)

hinge
mortise
(3 req'd.)

3¹⁄₄"

No. 8 × 1¹⁄₂"
brass fh screw

B1

C1

A

A

G

¹⁄₄ × ¹⁄₄"
rabbet (4 sides)

Display Coffee Table Cutting List

Part/Description	No.	Size	Material
A Legs	4	2¼ × 2¼ × 18 in.	Cherry
B1 Aprons	2	1 × 4 × 16 in.	"
B2 Aprons	2	1 × 4 × 34 in.	"
C1 Molding strips	2	³⁄₈ × ¾ × 16 in.	"
C2 Molding strips	2	³⁄₈ × ¾ × 34 in.	"
D1 Top frame	2	1 × 3 × 22 in.	"
D2 Top frame	2	1 × 3 × 40 in.	"
E Locating blocks	2	³⁄₈ × ⁷⁄₁₆ × 2 in.	"
F1 Glass stops	2	³⁄₈ × ½ × 16¾ in.	"
F2 Glass stops	2	³⁄₈ × ½ × 34 in.	"
G Bottom	1	½ × 18¼ × 34¼ in.	Cherry ply
H Support bar	1	⁵⁄₈ × 1½ × 14⁵⁄₈ in.	Cherry
I Top	1	¼ × 16⁵⁄₈ × 34⁵⁄₈ in.	Glass

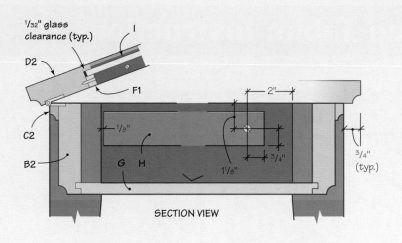

1/32" glass clearance (typ.)

I

D2

F1

C2

B2

1/8"

G   H

2"

3/4"

1 1/8"

3/4" (typ.)

SECTION VIEW

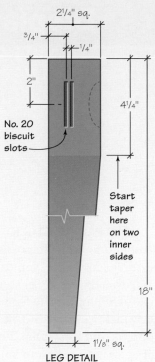

2 1/4" sq.

3/4"

1/4"

2"

4 1/4"

No. 20 biscuit slots

Start taper here on two inner sides

18"

1 1/8" sq.

LEG DETAIL

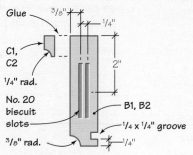

Glue

3/8"

1/4"

C1, C2

2"

1/4" rad.

No. 20 biscuit slots

B1, B2

1/4 x 1/4" groove

3/8" rad.

1/4"

APRON DETAIL

1/8" x 45° chamfer

D1, D2

No. 20 biscuit slots

3/4"

3/8"

3/8"

3/8" rad.

1/4"

FRAME DETAIL

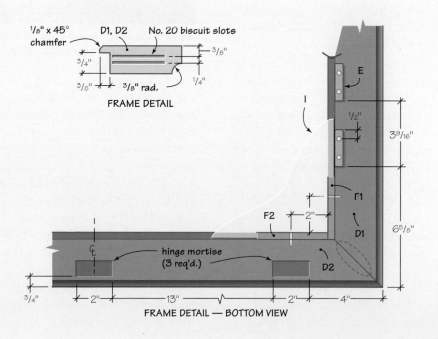

E

I

1/2"

3 9/16"

F1

F2

2"

D1

6 5/8"

D2

hinge mortise (3 req'd.)

3/4"

2"

13"

2"

4"

FRAME DETAIL — BOTTOM VIEW

Shopping List

- [ ] 6 bf of 10/4 cherry
- [ ] 10 bf of 5/4 cherry
- [ ] 3 bf of 4/4 cherry
- [ ] (1) 1/2 x 24 x 48-in. cherry-veneer plywood
- [ ] (1) 1/4 x 16 5/8 x 34 5/8-in. glass
- [ ] (24) #20 plate-joining biscuits
- [ ] (3) 1 1/2 x 2-in. brass butt hinges
- [ ] (20) #4 x 3/4-in. brass flathead wood screws
- [ ] (1) #8 x 1/2-in. brass flathead wood screw
- [ ] Wood glue
- [ ] 120- and 220-grit sandpaper
- [ ] Finishing materials

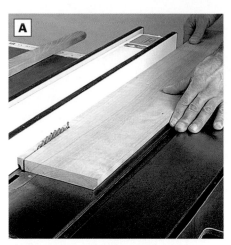

PHOTO A: Rip the molding strips from the board edges. Then plane the cut edges and repeat the molding/ripping process.

PHOTO B: Cut the molding strips to length; then attach them flush to the top of the apron with glue and spring clamps.

PREPARING STOCK

Although I chose cherry as the material for my table, you can use any hardwood. I used ¹⁰⁄₄ stock planed to 2¼ in. for the legs and ⁵⁄₄ stock, which I planed to 1 in., for the aprons and top frame. For the molding strips, stops and support bar, I used ⁴⁄₄ stock. The bottom is ½-in. cherry-veneer plywood.

Begin by milling your stock to thickness. If you don't have access to a thickness planer, ask your lumber supplier to plane the lumber or check with a local wood-working shop. Many small shops will do this for an hourly fee.

The safest and most efficient way to make the molding strips is to first rip a board that's at least 3 in. wide. Then, mold the board edges with a ¼-in. cove bit on the router table. Finally, rip the molded edges off the board on the table saw **(See Photo A)**.

Rip and crosscut the apron stock to the finished dimensions. While you're at it, crosscut the molding strips to the same length.

Use the router table and a ³⁄₈-in. cove bit to cut the molded edge along the bottom edge of each apron piece. Cut the grooves for the bottom in the apron stock with the table saw and a dado blade.

CASE JOINERY

The molding strips are more than just decorative details. The

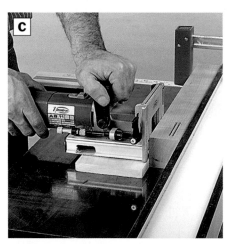

PHOTO C: The table saw and rip fence make a good worksurface and stop when cutting the biscuit slots in the legs.

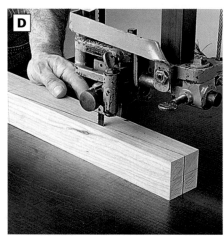

PHOTO D: Rough-cut the leg tapers on the band saw, keeping outside the line. Then, smooth the surface with a sander or a hand plane.

one attached to the back apron is mortised for the top hinges, so it's important that the glue joint between the apron and molding be strong.

Apply glue to one of the strips and to the edge of its matching apron. Position the strip so it's flush with the apron's top edge and apply clamps every 2 to 3 in. **(See Photo B)**. Repeat the procedure for the remaining pieces. Scrape off any squeezed-out glue from around the joint once it's dry.

The leg-to-apron joint is strong and easy to make. Rip and cross-cut the leg blanks to size, then lay out the plate-joining slots. Note that there are two #20 plate-joining biscuits, spaced ¼ in. apart, in each joint. Use the plate joiner to cut the slots in both the legs and apron ends. You can use your plate joiner's fence to locate the slots or make spacer blocks to use under the tool's base as I did **(See Photo C)**. The legs and aprons will require blocks of different

PHOTO E: Slide the bottom into the apron grooves; then glue and clamp the remaining leg/apron assembly in place.

PHOTO F: Locate the biscuit slots so they're not exposed by the glass rabbet or the ⅜-in. cove that are cut after assembly.

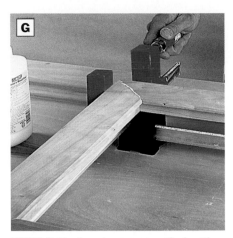

PHOTO G: Use bar clamps across the length and width of the top during glue-up. Adjust the clamps to align the miters.

thickness (your plate joiner's base-to-blade distance is also a factor). Use scrap lumber to test the locations of the slots and adjust the spacer thickness before cutting the actual table parts.

Lay out the leg tapers; then use the band saw to make the cuts (**See Photo D**). Be sure to saw on the waste side of the layout line. If you don't have a band saw, you can use either a table saw and a taper jig or a jig saw with a long blade.

Use a hand plane or belt sander to remove the saw marks and refine the leg profiles. Take care not to extend the taper into the top part of the leg where it joins the apron.

Cut the bottom panel to finished size. Lay out the notch in each corner for leg clearance; then make the cuts with a jig saw or back saw. Next, rout the rabbet on the bottom of the panel using an edge guide and straight bit.

It's a good idea to sand the parts with 120- and 220-grit paper before you assemble them. Although assembly inevitably causes some small scratches, touching up minor flaws is much easier than doing extensive sanding after assembly. Dust all parts thoroughly after sanding.

BASE ASSEMBLY

Begin the base assembly by joining leg pairs to the long aprons. Apply glue to both the biscuits and slots; then position the parts together and clamp. Check for square by measuring diagonally in both directions across the assembly.

Next, join the two short aprons to one of the long assemblies—the easiest way is upside down on your workbench. Slide the bottom panel into the apron grooves without glue (**See Photo E**), then install the second long apron/leg assembly. Check for square and make any necessary adjustments. Let the glue cure fully (six to 12 hours) before removing the clamps.

MAKING THE TOP

Rip the top frame stock to width, but leave the pieces several inches long. Use a straight bit and edge guide to rout the rabbet for the glass (you could also use a router table or a table saw). Make the cut in two or three passes so you don't overload the router or tear out the wood grain. Use a router table and a chamfer bit to cut the small bevel along the top inside edge of each piece.

Cut the frame parts to finished length with a miter saw or a table

saw and miter gauge. Lay out and cut the two biscuit slots in the ends of each frame piece. Position the slots so that they're not exposed when you cut the cove on the bottom outside edge of the frame (**See Photo F**).

Dry-fit the top frame to check for square before gluing and clamping (**See Photo G**). After the glue sets, rout the ⅜-in. cove around the bottom edge of the frame. Routing after assembly ensures that the coves will match perfectly at the corners.

HINGE INSTALLATION

Lay out the locations of the hinges on the top edge of the table base using a sharp utility knife. Remove most of the waste from each mortise with a router and straight bit. Guide the router by hand to within ¹⁄₁₆ in. of the layout lines; then clean the mortise with a sharp chisel (**See Photo H**). Or cut the mortise entirely with a chisel by making a series of closely spaced ⅛-in.-deep parallel cuts down the length of the mortise, then paring away the waste. Test the fit of the hinge in its mortise and adjust the depth of the recess until the hinge is flush with the surrounding wood. If you cut too deeply, use a veneer shim under

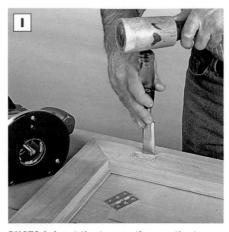

PHOTO H: Rout the butt-hinge mortises with a straight bit; then clean up the corners and edges with a sharp chisel.

PHOTO I: Inset the top mortises so the top has a uniform overhang. Use the same methods to cut these mortises.

PHOTO J: Use steel screws to test-fit the hinges and thread the pilot holes. Brass screws are soft and easily damaged.

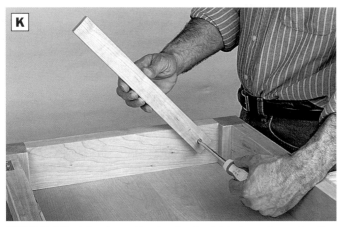

PHOTO K: Adjust the support bar tension by tightening or loosening the screw. Remove the bar for finishing.

PHOTO L: Bore clearance holes in the glass stops; then bore pilot holes in the frame before test-fitting the stops.

the hinge to achieve a flush relationship.

Mark the mortise locations in the tabletop; then cut them using the same techniques **(See Photo I).** Note that these mortises are set back from the top edge to allow the top to overhang the table base. This isn't a typical butt-hinge mortise, but it allows the top to open a full 90° for access to the interior.

Bore the screw holes and temporarily install the hinges using steel screws, which are less likely to strip out or snap **(See Photo J).** Save the brass screws for final assembly.

Finishing details

Cut the support bar. Then, bore a clearance hole and countersink for the screw. (Another way to support the top is to use a ¼-in.-dia. brass rod that's stored in a groove routed into the top edge of the apron.) Attach the bar to the side apron and adjust the tension by tightening the screw **(See Photo K).** Attach the locating blocks for the support bar to the underside of the top frame.

Remove the top frame from the base; then cut the glass stops. Drill clearance holes and countersinks in the stops for #4 × ¾-in. flathead wood screws. Then use a ¼-in. spacer to position the stops so you can bore pilot holes in the frame. Install the stops temporarily to check the fit **(See Photo L).** Don't install the glass yet—it's best to do this after finishing.

Sand the top frame to 220 grit. Dust off all surfaces thoroughly, then wipe them down with a tack rag before finishing.

I applied three coats of satin polyurethane, thinning the first coat with one part thinner to six parts finish. The next day I sanded lightly with 320-grit paper before applying an undiluted coat. I rubbed out the cured finish of the third coat with 0000 steel wool. When the finish is dry, reattach the top and the support bar and install the glass top.

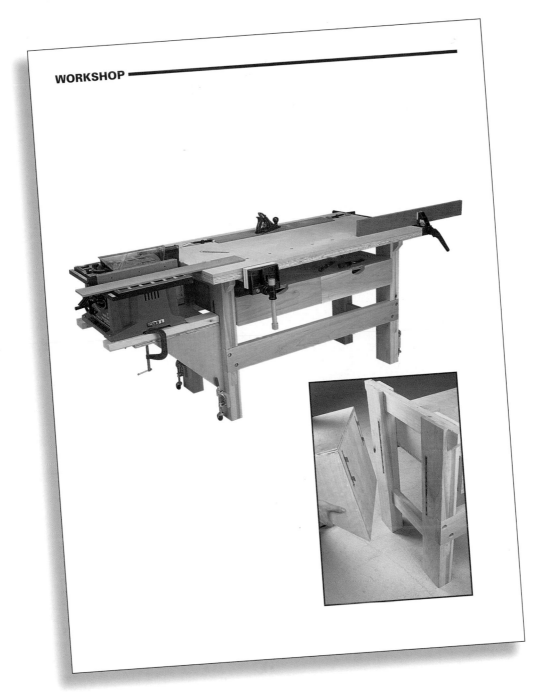

Workbench

Although a workbench is probably the most important tool in our shops, if it doesn't work well, it can be more hindrance than help. Building a bench is fairly easy, but designing a good one isn't. Whether you copy this plan precisely or merely adopt some of its features, you should end up with a bench that works great and doesn't cost a fortune to build.

Think of this project as a menu of elements. Choose and use the features you like and feel free to substitute different dimensions or materials to suit your work habits and budget. In short, make this bench work for you.

Workbench

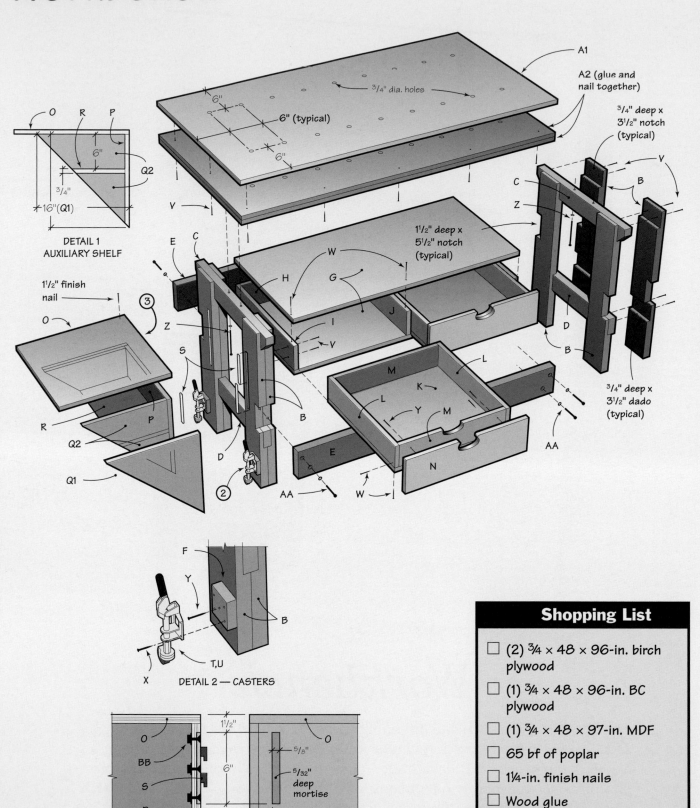

DETAIL 1 — AUXILIARY SHELF

O   R   P
6"
3/4"
16"(Q1)
Q2

DETAIL 2 — CASTERS

F
Y
B
T,U
X

DETAIL 3 — SHELF MORTISE

O
BB
S
P
1 1/2"
6"
5/8"
5/32" deep mortise
O
Q1
1 7/8"
P

A1
A2 (glue and nail together)
3/4" deep x 3 1/2" notch (typical)
3/4" dia. holes
6" (typical)
6"
6"
V
C
B
Z
D
B
3/4" deep x 3 1/2" dado (typical)
1 1/2" deep x 5 1/2" notch (typical)
W
H
G
I
J
V
M
L
K
Y
M
L
N
E
W
AA
1 1/2" finish nail
O
Z
S
R
P
Q2
Q1
D
E
C
B
AA

Shopping List

- ☐ (2) 3/4 × 48 × 96-in. birch plywood
- ☐ (1) 3/4 × 48 × 96-in. BC plywood
- ☐ (1) 3/4 × 48 × 97-in. MDF
- ☐ 65 bf of poplar
- ☐ 1 1/4-in. finish nails
- ☐ Wood glue
- ☐ Wood putty
- ☐ Hardware (see List)

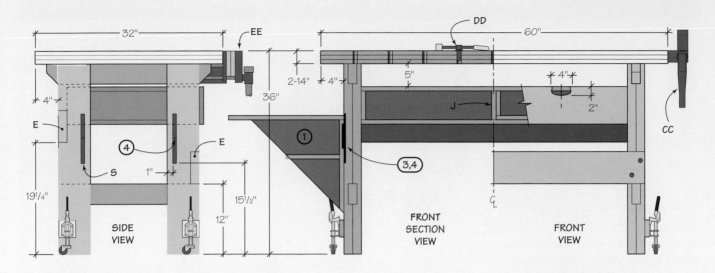

SIDE VIEW

FRONT SECTION VIEW

FRONT VIEW

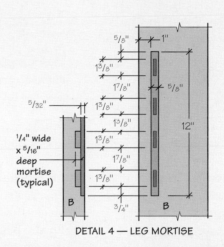

DETAIL 4 — LEG MORTISE

$^{1}/_{4}$" wide x $^{5}/_{16}$" deep mortise (typical)

Workbench Cutting List

Part/Description	No.	Size	Material
A1 Top	1	$^{3}/_{4}$ × 32 × 60 in.	MDF
A2 Top	2	$^{3}/_{4}$ × 32 × 60 in.	BC plywood
B Legs	8	$1^{1}/_{2}$ × $5^{1}/_{2}$ × $33^{3}/_{4}$ in.	Poplar
C Top rails	2	$1^{1}/_{2}$ × $3^{1}/_{2}$ × 28 in.	"
D Bottom rails	2	$1^{1}/_{2}$ × $3^{1}/_{2}$ × 24 in.	"
E Stretchers	2	$1^{1}/_{2}$ × $5^{1}/_{2}$ × 52 in.	"
F Caster blocks	4	1 × 3 × 3 in.	"

Drawers Cutting List

Part/Description	No.	Size	Material
G Frame top/bottom	2	$^{3}/_{4}$ × $22^{1}/_{2}$ × 46 in.	Birch ply
H Frame back	1	$^{3}/_{4}$ × 5 × $44^{1}/_{2}$ in.	"
I Frame sides	2	$^{3}/_{4}$ × 5 × $22^{1}/_{2}$ in.	"
J Frame divider	1	$^{3}/_{4}$ × 5 × $21^{3}/_{4}$ in.	"
K Drawer bottoms	2	$^{3}/_{4}$ × $21^{3}/_{4}$ × $21^{3}/_{4}$ in.	"
L Drawer sides	4	$^{3}/_{4}$ × $4^{1}/_{8}$ × $21^{3}/_{4}$ in.	"
M Drawer fronts/backs	4	$^{3}/_{4}$ × $4^{1}/_{8}$ × $20^{1}/_{4}$ in.	"
N Drawer faces	2	$^{3}/_{4}$ × $6^{1}/_{2}$ × 23 in.	Poplar

Auxiliary Shelf Cutting List

Part/Description	No.	Size	Material
O Top	1	$^{3}/_{4}$ × 20 × 20 in.	Birch ply
P Back	1	$^{3}/_{4}$ × 16 × $18^{1}/_{2}$ in.	"
Q1 Sides (outer)	2	$^{3}/_{4}$ × 16 × 16 in.*	"
Q2 Sides (inner)	2	$^{3}/_{4}$ × $15^{1}/_{4}$ × $15^{1}/_{4}$ in.*	"
R Shelf	1	$^{3}/_{4}$ × 9 × $18^{1}/_{2}$ in.	"

Hardware

Part/Description	No.
S $^{5}/_{8}$ x 6-in. bed-rail fasteners	(1 set of 4 required)
T In-line toggle clamps ($1^{1}/_{4}$-in. travel)	4
U $1^{1}/_{2}$-in.-dia. casters	4
V #10 × 2-in. flathead wood screws	50
W #8 × $1^{1}/_{2}$-in. flathead wood screws	75
X #8 × $1^{1}/_{2}$-in. roundhead wood screws	20
Y #6 × $1^{1}/_{4}$-in. drywall screws	15
Z $^{5}/_{16}$ × 5-in. lag screws and washers	4
AA $^{5}/_{16}$ × 3-in. lag screws and washers	8
BB $^{8}/_{32}$ × $1^{1}/_{4}$-in. machine screws, washers and nuts	6
CC Clamp	1
DD Bench dogs	2
EE Woodworking vise (9-in. capacity)	1

***Make two sides by cutting one piece of stock diagonally.**

Be sure to buy all of the hardware and vises before you design your bench so you don't end up with conflicts between mechanical fasteners, structural elements and accessories when you do your layout. Otherwise, you could end up with a dog hole in a leg or a vise that doesn't close. You can mount almost any type of clamp or vise hardware to this bench.

To custom-fit a bench, you need to resolve some basic design issues: height, size, structure, materials, storage and mobility. Begin by determining the right height and size for the work-surface. Next, consider the structural requirements of both the top and the base. The top must be strong, durable and free of obstructions. It also needs to accommodate a variety of clamps, dogs and vises. The base should be designed with mobility, stability and storage in mind.

BASE INSTINCTS

If your bench wobbles or scoots across the floor, it will be annoying and unsafe. The base members should be sufficiently rigid and large. As far as we're concerned, there's no such thing as a workbench that's too sturdy.

We made the base out of poplar and milled all of the pieces to standard dimensional lumber sizes so you could substitute

PHOTO A: Clamp the leg halves together; then gang-rout the dadoes and notches.

ordinary construction-grade fir 2 × 4s and 2 × 6s to speed construction and control costs. Milling parts from hardwood ensures straight, square, knot-free stock. But plan on spending more for the poplar than you would for dimensional lumber. To save money, we used affordable sheet goods, rather than hardwood, for the top.

Base storage is a plus, provided it stays clean and doesn't get in the way. We left an open space between the bench top and the drawer frame to facilitate clamping. The birch plywood drawer frame stiffens the base and prevents sawdust from getting into the drawers. Its top also provides a convenient place to keep tools handy, but out of the way, while you work.

The best height depends on your size and how you plan to use the bench. Between 32 and 36 in. works well for most people. Other factors include whether you will

PHOTO B: Roll glue on both plywood top pieces; then nail the pieces together.

use the bench to support tall workpieces or to plane broad ones. Ultimately, experience is the best guide for determining the optimum height.

Don't make your bench any longer or deeper than needed. If you can't reach your work or the bench leaves you with little room to move around your shop, it's too big. If you occasionally need a larger top, you can always throw a sheet of plywood on top of your bench.

TOP ISSUES

A laminated maple or beech top is ideal for woodworking and you could make one to fit this base. But you'll be better off with a sacrificial sheet goods top if you plan to use the bench for other tasks such as engine repair and crafts. Either way, the top should be rigid and should dampen vibration. A heavy top made of wood products will accomplish this naturally.

PHOTO C: After routing for the bed-rail fasteners, square the corners of the mortises with a chisel.

PHOTO D: Drill counterbores, then pilot holes for the lag screws that attach the stretchers.

PHOTO E: Clamp blocks to the legs to support the drawer frame during installation.

We designed this top with uniform thickness to make it easier to clamp workpieces and install the vise. Thinner tops with built-up edges found on inexpensive benches complicate clamping.

Avoid dark materials such as hardboard for your bench top. They make it more difficult to see your workpiece. Also, steer clear of materials that are too hard or too soft, or that will be prone to splinter or transfer color.

We made our top by gluing and nailing together two layers of ¾-in. BC plywood (See Photo B). It's okay to splice a layer if need be. Then, we screwed a layer of ¾-in. medium-density fiberboard (MDF) to the top from below for a smooth, light-colored worksurface that's easy (and inexpensive) to replace when worn.

If your plywood panels are bowed, butt the concave faces for gluing so the edges remain tight and the middles are drawn together. Orient the crowned side up before you attach the MDF top.

After all three top layers are assembled, bore ¾-in.-dia. holes for bench dogs in the top (See Photo H). Bench dogs allow you to clamp or brace large or irregular-shaped workpieces. You can make your own dogs out of dowels or buy commercially available ones. Use a drill guide to ensure perpendicular holes and slip a backup board under the top to prevent the exiting bit from splintering the plywood. Be sure to lay out the positions for all the hardware including vises, dog holes and fasteners before you fabricate the top or attach the base so they don't interfere with each other. Dog holes in the bench top and vise should be aligned. They typically are spaced 6 to 8 in. apart.

AUXILIARY TABLE

At times, it's helpful to have a lower or longer workbench surface. Consequently, this design incorporates an adjustable-height auxiliary table on one end. The side unit, actually a cantilevered shelf, can be used to support benchtop power tools at a more comfortable height. It also is ideal for drawing or working on delicate craft projects while seated. If you use the auxiliary table for a specific benchtop tool, be sure to size the top so it's large enough to fit the tool's base.

To permit quick and easy installation and removal, we attached the auxiliary table with

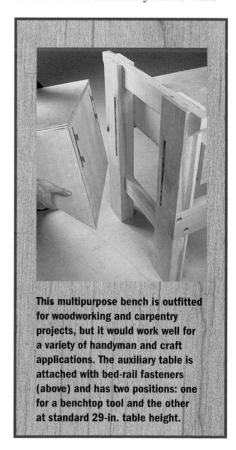

This multipurpose bench is outfitted for woodworking and carpentry projects, but it would work well for a variety of handyman and craft applications. The auxiliary table is attached with bed-rail fasteners (above) and has two positions: one for a benchtop tool and the other at standard 29-in. table height.

bed-rail fasteners. Gravity works in your favor with bed-rail fasteners—the greater the weight, the tighter they fit. We installed fasteners on the bench legs to support the table at two levels **(See Photo C).** One pair positions a benchtop table saw level with the main bench so it serves as an outfeed table. The other is at standard tabletop height (29 in.) for working while seated. To store the table and create extra shelf space, simply mount a mating set of fasteners to your shop wall.

We made the top of the auxiliary table flush with the triangular supports, but it would be even better if the top were as wide as the bench top so it over-hung the supports. That would have made it easier to clamp benchtop tools. The cantilevered design is a real plus because you don't have to level an extra set of legs and the top is always parallel to the bench top.

Accuracy is important when routing the mortises for the bed-rail fasteners. If your spans are off, the hooks won't mate in the slots. The easiest way to overcome this is to first lay out and cut the leg mortises on an assembled leg set. Then make a story stick (in this case, a piece of stock with the distance between the mortises accurately marked) and transfer the measurements from the stick to the back of the auxiliary table.

MOBILITY MATTERS

We used a modular design so this bench could be disassembled for moving. Both the top and the stretchers are fastened to the leg assemblies with lag screws **(See Photos D & G).** You also could use machine bolts with nuts, threaded inserts or T-nuts.

Even within the shop, moving a heavy bench can be difficult. So

PHOTO F: After the false drawer face has been accurately positioned, secure it with a clamp, then fasten it through the back.

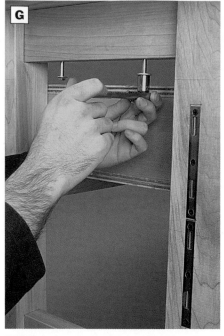

PHOTO G: Attach the bench top to the rails from below with lag screws and washers.

PHOTO H: Use a portable drill guide to bore bench-dog holes. This handy device maintains a perpendicular relationship with the workpiece, ensuring straight holes every time.

PHOTO I: To guarantee proper alignment when installing the casters, set them on the floor with the toggle levers up.

we designed lock-down caster mechanisms using in-line toggle clamps and small stem casters **(See Photo I).** Substitute larger casters and clamps if you plan to wheel your bench around a lot.

Double Rocker

W hen we first considered the idea of a double rocker for our new deck, what we wanted was a strong but lightweight piece that we could carry from the deck to the lawn. So I designed the rocker that is shown here.

It gets its weather resistance from the careful selection of joint hardware, wood species, finishes and glue. I made a conscious effort to minimize the cost when building the prototype. I chose pressure-treated southern yellow pine for the framework, which we later stained, and western red cedar for the slats.

Double Rocker

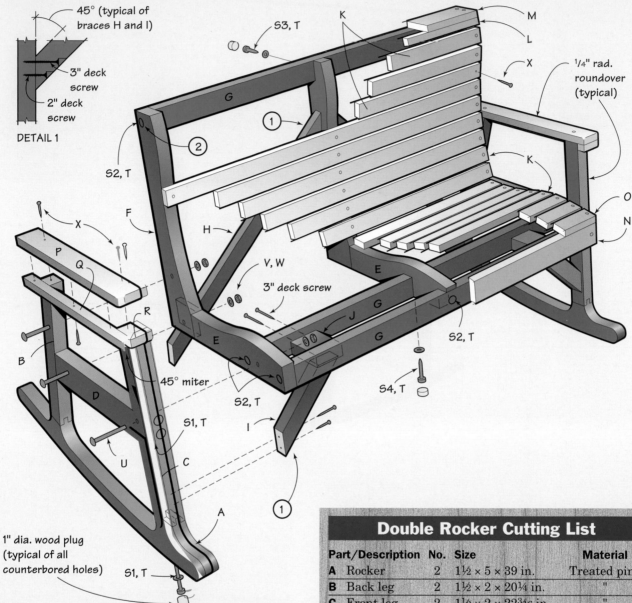

45° (typical of braces H and I)

3" deck screw

2" deck screw

DETAIL 1

S3, T

K

M

L

X

1/4" rad. roundover (typical)

G

1

2

S2, T

F

X

K

O

P

H

N

Q

V, W

3" deck screw

E

R

B

J G

E

G

45° miter

S2, T

D

S2, T

S1, T

C

S4, T

U

I

1

1" dia. wood plug (typical of all counterbored holes)

S1, T

A

Hardware*

Part/Description	No.
S1 5/16 × 6-in. lag screw	12
S2 5/16 × 3-in. lag screw	7
S3 5/16 × 1½-in. lag screw	1
S4 5/16 × 2½-in. lag screw	1
T 5/16-in. washer	21
U ¼ × 3½-in. carriage bolt	6
V ¼-in. washer	6
W ¼-in. nut	6
X 1½-in. screw	80

***Also see** Shopping List, next page.*

Double Rocker Cutting List

Part/Description	No.	Size	Material
A Rocker	2	1½ × 5 × 39 in.	Treated pine
B Back leg	2	1½ × 2 × 20¼ in.	"
C Front leg	2	1½ × 2 × 22³⁄₁₆ in.	"
D Rail	2	1½ × 3½ × 18 in.	"
E Seat brace	3	1½ × 4 × 22¾ in.	"
F Back brace	3	1½ × 4¾ × 30¼ in.	"
G Stretcher	2	1½ × 2½ × 47¾ in.	"
H Rear brace	2	1 × 2 × 36 in.	"
I Front brace	2	1½ × 2 × 12 in.	"
J Bridge	2	1½ × 3½ × 4¼ in.	"
K Slat	17	⅞ × 1⅞ × 47⅝ in.	Cedar
L Upper slat	1	⅞ × 1¹⁄₁₆ × 47⅝ in.	"
M Top	1	⅞ × 3¾ × 47⅝ in.	"
N Front	1	⅞ × 2⅞ × 47⅝ in.	"
O Lower slat	1	⅞ × 1¹⁄₁₆ × 47⅝ in.	"
P Arm top	2	⅞ × 2½ × 21⅜ in.	"
Q Arm side	2	⅞ × 1 × 21⅜ in.	"
R Arm front	2	⅞ × 1 × 2½ in.	"

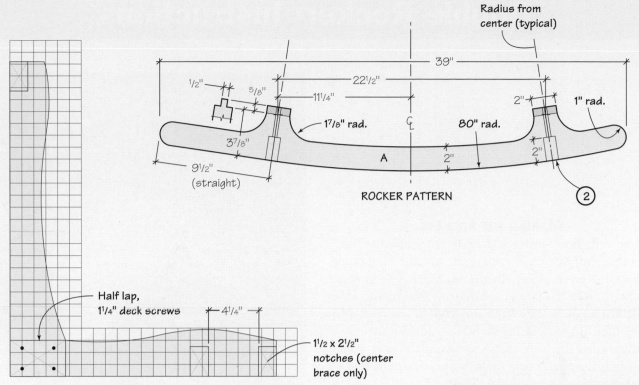

Radius from center (typical)

39"

22½"

½" 5/8"

11¼"

2" 1" rad.

1⅞" rad.

80" rad.

3⅞"

A

2"

2"

2"

9½" (straight)

ROCKER PATTERN

②

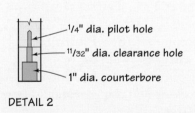

Half lap, 1¼" deck screws

4¼"

1½ x 2½" notches (center brace only)

BACK AND SEAT BRACE PATTERNS (Square = 1")

¼" dia. pilot hole

11/32" dia. clearance hole

1" dia. counterbore

DETAIL 2

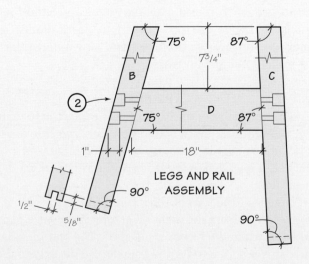

75° 87°

7¾"

B C

②

75° 87°

D

1" 18"

LEGS AND RAIL ASSEMBLY

½" 5/8"

90°

90°

Shopping List

- ☐ (2) 8-ft. 2 × 12 pressure-treated southern yellow pine
- ☐ (4) 8-ft. 1 × 8 western red cedar
- ☐ (12) 5/16 × 6-in. stainless-steel lag screws
- ☐ (1) 5/16 × 1½-in. stainless-steel lag screw
- ☐ (1) 5/16 × 2½-in. stainless-steel lag screw
- ☐ (7) 5/16 × 3-in. stainless-steel lag screws
- ☐ (21) 5/16-in. washers
- ☐ (6) ¼-in. washers
- ☐ (6) ¼ × 3½-in. carriage bolts
- ☐ (6) ¼-in. nuts
- ☐ (80) 1½-in. screws
- ☐ Moisture-resistant wood glue
- ☐ Finishing materials

Double Rocker: Instructions

MAKING THE ROCKERS

Use your best stock for the rockers. Examine the wood carefully to avoid imperfections that may cause checks and twists **(See Photo A).** The key is to make the bottoms of the two arcs uniform, square and identical. We made the arc from the front of the rocker to the center of the back leg an 80-in. radius and straightened the back ends to prevent the seat from tipping backward. For a little faster rocking action, you can reduce the radius to 72 in., but you'll need to adjust the leg posts.

To draw the arc, build an oversized trammel using a small scrap block and an 8-ft.-long furring strip **(See Photo B).** Drive a 6d finish nail into the scrap wood and clamp the scrap to your bench with the nail sticking up. Place another surface (at the same height) about 80 in. away and clamp the piece of stock for your first rocker onto it. Drill a ⅛-in. hole in one end of the furring strip and slip it over the nail. Then, measure out 80 in. from the nail and drill another hole in the strip to hold a pencil (use an elastic band if needed to secure the pencil). Draw the bottom arc of each rocker using the scaled drawing included in the technical art as a guide. Repeat the process for the second rocker. The rockers must have perfectly fluid arcs to function smoothly. Even the slightest flat spot will ruin the ride. Since it is difficult to achieve this with a band saw or a jig saw, don't even try. Instead, saw just outside the line **(See Photo C)** and finish up with a belt sander or an oscillating spindle sander until you get it perfect. Keep the sander moving—flat spots form quicker than you can say "Oops!"

To make sure that the two rockers are identical, clamp them together and sand them both simultaneously. If you use a belt sander, check for squareness with a small try square as you go.

The next step is to draw the cutting line for the top of the rockers. I attached a spring clamp 2 in. from

PHOTO A: Choose stock with tight grain and no splits for the rockers. Let the treated wood dry before you start.

the end of a piece of scrap wood, and with a pencil held against the end of the stick, I just followed the bottom arc **(See Photo D).**

Because weather resistance was very high on my list of priorities, I decided that the joints between the rockers and the legs should be elevated to discourage water from collecting. Transfer the scale drawing to your stock to lay out the posts. You can also use the drawing to sketch the 1-in. radius on both ends of each piece. Shape the tops of the rockers using a band saw, then round over the edges and sand the surfaces. Leave the tops of the four posts square, and move to your router table or hand saw to form the ⅝-in.-long tongue on the top of each post.

THE FRAME

The easiest way to think of this project is to visualize the seat assembly bolted between two side assemblies. Each side is made up of four elements—a rocker, a back leg, a front leg and a rail. Cut the legs a bit long.

Note that the tops of the legs are cut at different angles to support the arms. The tops of the back legs are 15°, while the fronts are just 3°. The bottom cuts are square so the weight is transferred directly to the

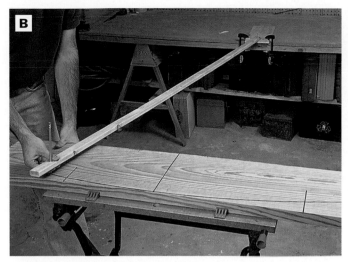

PHOTO B: Lay out the rockers with an 80-in.-radius trammel between the front end and the middle of the rear leg.

PHOTO C: Band-saw just outside your layout line, then refine the rocker arc with a sander to ensure smooth movement.

PHOTO D: Use a stick of scrap wood and a spring-clamp stop to mark the rockers' top arcs 2 in. from the bottom arcs.

elevated rocker posts. This makes it easier to create the groove on the bottom of each leg. The grooves are ½ in. wide and ⅝ in. deep to accept the rocker tongues.

After rounding over the long edges of the rails, cut the ends at angles just like the legs (3° for the fronts and 15° for the backs). To assemble the four pieces of each side assembly, lay all four pieces for one side on your bench, and clamp them together in their proper orientation. Then use a 1-in. Forstner bit to counterbore for the heads of the lag screws you'll use to connect everything together. The counterbores in the rockers are 2 in. deep, and the ones at the rail joints are 1 in. deep. The lag screws are ⁵⁄₁₆ × 6 in., with ⁵⁄₁₆-in. washers. Use an ¹¹⁄₃₂-in. bit to bore through the counterbored pieces, and create a ¼-in.-dia. pilot hole deep into the mating pieces. Be sure they are deeper than the screws to avoid splitting the wood. If you choose white oak rather than pine, you may need to drill ⁹⁄₃₂-in. pilot holes instead to avoid splitting. To be safe, test-drive a screw on a piece of scrap. If you use treated lumber, clean the surfaces with a rag dampened with mineral spirits and allow them to dry before gluing. Then apply a liberal coat of water-resistant exterior glue, and tighten all the lag screws. Glue 1-in. plugs into the counterbores and sand them flush after the glue dries.

THE SEAT ASSEMBLY

This assembly consists of three seat braces, three back braces, three stretchers and two bridges. The braces provide screwing surfaces for the cedar slats, and the stretchers offer lateral strength. Begin by cutting all six braces according to the scaled drawing, then rip the stretchers and assemble the back and seat braces with half-lap joints, 1¼-in. screws and glue. Then attach the three stretchers.

Clamp a piece of scrap wood across the inside of each leg assembly, and rest the seat assembly on the scraps. Then, clamp all three assemblies together to lock them in position while you drill holes for the carriage bolts. Drill through the side frame and the seat braces with a ½-in. bit, and secure everything with ½ × 3½-in. carriage bolts, keeping the nuts and washers to the inside.

The legs are braced diagonally to prevent them from wobbling. Cut all four diagonal braces. Install the bridges first using glue and 3-in.-long galvanized screws. Screw and glue the front braces in place, then trim the back braces to length and install them. No two benches will be identical, so I allowed just a little

PHOTO E: Install slats and arms with stainless-steel, roundhead screws. Use ⅜-in. spacers to aid alignment, and predrill holes.

PHOTO F: Four diagonal braces with mitered ends are installed with screws and glue to prevent the rocker from wobbling. This added support will guarantee fluid rocking action.

extra length on these braces.

The cedar slats are milled from western red cedar that's ⅞ in. thick with a smooth and a rough side. Cut each slat to size and round over the edges on the smooth side on a router table. Next, make the cedar arms. Note that the sides and fronts are mitered and secured with glue and screws.

FINISHING YOUR ROCKER

It is better to finish the rocker frame and the individual cedar slats and arms separately so you can seal each piece fully. Then you won't have to worry about slopping solid stain on the surfaces that will be left natural.

I finished the treated-pine frame with a solid-color acrylic stain after cleaning the surfaces with mineral spirits to remove the excess treatment chemicals. According to research done by the Forest Products Laboratory in Madison, Wisconsin, acrylic stains actually bond better to treated wood than oil stains. Check with your local paint supplier for a quality exterior varnish with ultraviolet ray absorbers for the cedar slats and arms.

INSTALLING THE SEAT SLATS

The cedar slats are attached with #8 × 1½-in. stainless-steel, roundhead screws (**See Photo E**).

Unlike brass, they won't stain the cedar. And the round head will shed water. If you plan to leave the rocker in direct sunlight, you might want to countersink the screws slightly so no one gets a hot seat. *TIP: Use the waste pieces from the rockers as forms to keep the frame from rocking while installing the slats.*

You'll need to predrill the cedar using a ⅛-in. pilot bit, and then predrill the treated lumber with a ¹⁄₁₆-in. bit to avoid any splitting. Don't glue the slats down—they need to move a little as the frame expands and contracts. Use one screw on each end and another in the middle.

Install the slat that goes at the back of the seat first, then work your way to the front. Use two pieces of ⅜-in.-thick scrap as spacers. Drive a finish nail halfway through each piece so it doesn't fall through the slats while you work. When all the seat slats are in place, work your way up the back. You will need to trim the last slat on both the seat and the back to fit.

Now, attach the arms using stainless-steel screws, and you're ready to enjoy warm spring evenings and cool iced tea.

Kitchen Nook

Why settle for a table and chairs in your kitchen if you're the kind of person who would choose a booth at your favorite restaurant? Booths offer all the benefits in homes that they do in restaurants. They're cozy and they create a sheltered space with separation from cluttered counters and noisy neighbors. They encourage you to linger and talk, especially when you corral youngsters on the inside. They also make efficient use of space and simplify cleaning because you don't have to move chairs to sit down or sweep up. In fact, every square inch of table and benches is put to use with the opposing-seat design shown here.

Kitchen Nook

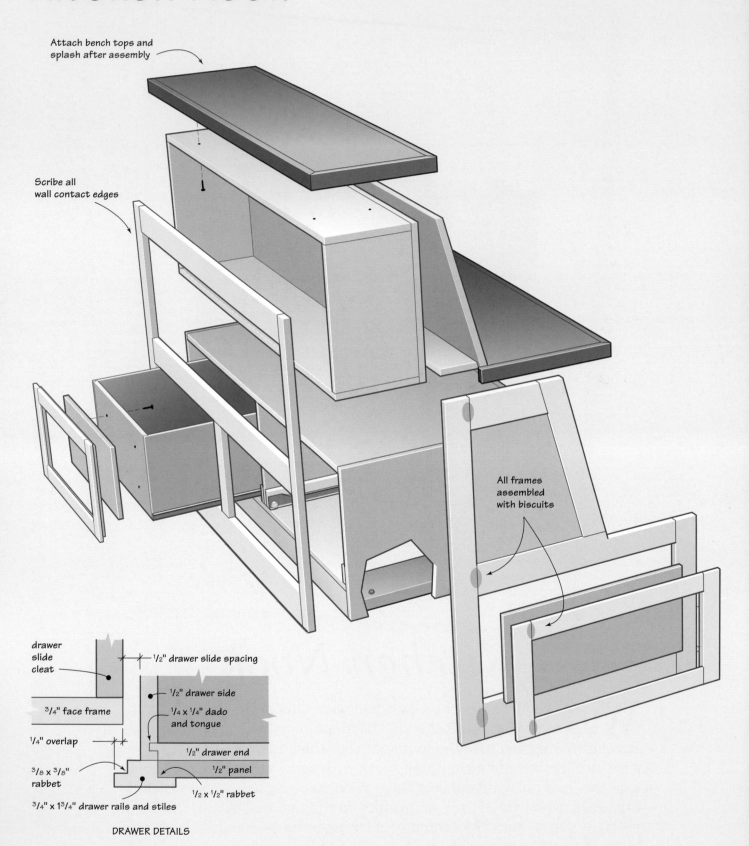

Attach bench tops and splash after assembly

Scribe all wall contact edges

All frames assembled with biscuits

drawer slide cleat

1/2" drawer slide spacing

1/2" drawer side

3/4" face frame

1/4 x 1/4" dado and tongue

1/4" overlap

1/2" drawer end

1/2" panel

3/8 x 3/8" rabbet

1/2 x 1/2" rabbet

3/4" x 1 3/4" drawer rails and stiles

DRAWER DETAILS

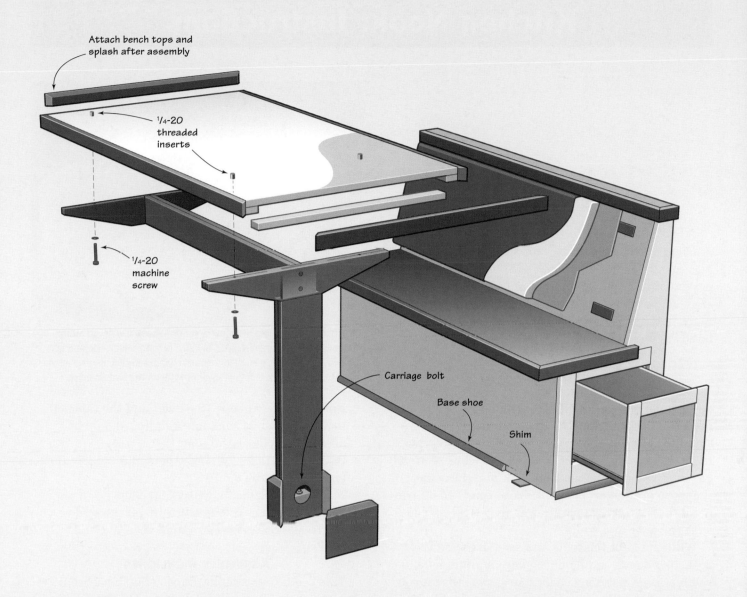

Attach bench tops and splash after assembly

¹/₄-20 threaded inserts

¹/₄-20 machine screw

Carriage bolt

Base shoe

Shim

NOTE:
Part dimensions for the kitchen nook are not listed because optimum sizes will vary according to the available space in your home. Minimum clearances for comfort are indicated here (See *Front Elevation,* right) and on page 40.

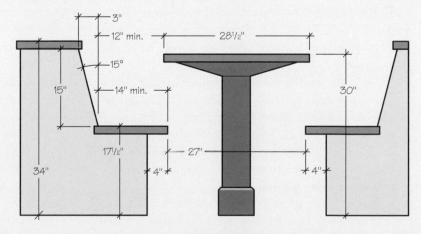

3"
12" min.
15°
15"
14" min.
34"
17¹/₂"
4"
28¹/₂"
30"
27"
4"

FRONT ELEVATION

39

A booth makes perfect sense in a kitchen because it opens huge opportunities for additional storage and surface areas. Our booth's three deep drawers provide a generous amount of concealed storage, the shelf keeps as many as 40 cookbooks within arm's reach of the stove and the bench top doubles as a handy serving station.

WILL IT FIT?

When we asked Club member Richard Steven to design this project, the biggest challenge was to create a comfortable, functional booth that would fit a small (4 × 5½-ft.) space without overpowering the room. His solution was to keep the benches relatively low and include an open bookshelf to reduce mass in the more prominent bench. He also specified off-white paint for the vertical surfaces so they would blend with the floor and walls.

While he kept the table and seat sizes and the bookshelf depth and height to bare minimums, the booth still provides space for four people (five if you add a chair on the end). Stout phone books fit in the end drawer, and 10-in. cookbooks stand on the shelf.

Determining these minimum dimensions was, without doubt, the most demanding aspect of this project. Whether you replicate our design or modify it to fit your space, follow these guidelines:

- To be comfortable for four people, the tabletop should be at least 28½ in. wide and 48 in. long. Larger is better if you have room.
- Make the seats at least 14 (and no more than 19) in. deep and 48 in. long. Cantilever them over the base at least 4 in. to provide space to pull your feet back when seated.
- Allow at least 12 in. between the back of the seat and the edge of the table (14 in. is better). The distance between the edge of the table and the angled seat back at table height is irrelevant because people sit up straight when eating.

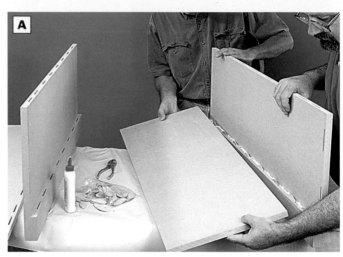

PHOTO A: With the help of an extra set of hands, attach the bottom to the front with glue and biscuits. The size of the project, coupled with the heavy material it's made of, means that assistance may be necessary at times. Note the double layer of MDF on the bottom edge.

- Build the seats about 18 in. tall and the table 30 in. The bottom of the table banding should be about 12 in. above the seat.
- Position the table leg so the person seated on the end can straddle it.
- Make the bookshelf about 11 in. deep.
- Hold the back cushions 1 to 2 in. off the seats.
- Angle seat backs no more than 15°.

ASSEMBLY HIGHLIGHTS

This booth uses simple shapes and joinery that require only a few power tools to create. A table saw and a drill are essential; we also recommend a plate joiner and a router. Plate-joining biscuits not only aid alignment but also eliminate the need to plug counterbored screws.

Building benches with angled backrests and cantilevered seats is easy with our modular approach. First, fabricate the top and bottom subassemblies with biscuits, screws and glue (**See Photos A-C**). Then, join the sections and install the seat backs and face frames (**See Photos D-G**).

Build and finish the bench tops, seats and tabletop separately, checking their fit as you go (**See Photo H**). Don't attach them, however, until you've installed the booth. You'll retain access to secure the benches to wall studs and have fewer edges to scribe and fit at each step. Then the seats and tops will hide the screws when you are finished.

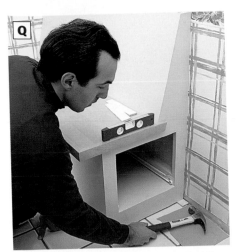

PHOTO Q: Slide the corner bench against the walls and temporarily level it front-to-back and side-to-side with shims.

PHOTO R: After scribing and shaping the edges that abut the walls, relevel the bench and screw it to the wall studs.

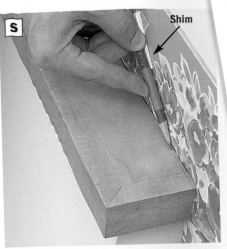

PHOTO S: Scribe the bench top as you did the bench, using a shim to space the pencil lead along the widest part of the gap. Keep the pencil plumb.

PHOTO T: Outline the bench footprint with tape. Fasten a nailing cleat into the floor joist, ⅛ in. inside the end frame, using a lag screw.

PHOTO U: Position and level the table support and mark the wall cleat and the floor for drilling into the framing.

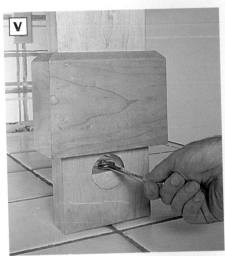

PHOTO V: Bolt the table leg through the floor and screw the cleat to the wall. Then mount the tabletop and backsplash.

place, scribe **(See Photo S)** and install the top with finishing nails.

Scribe and screw the other bench to the wall in much the same way, but anchor the free end to the floor. The best way is to secure a nailing cleat through the floor and into the joists with lag screws **(See Photo T).** Hold the cleat back ⅛ in. from the end so the bench is drawn toward the wall when you screw it to the cleat. *TIP: Chamfer the cleat's top edges in order to make it easier to position the bench around it.*

The tabletop rests on a support structure you screw to the wall studs and bolt through the floor. Temporarily position the framework and mark the wall cleat and the floor for drilling **(See Photo U).** Secure the tabletop to the framework using threaded

inserts, machine screws and construction adhesive before you install it. The inserts' coarse threads hold better in MDF than most screws.

Set the table in position and crawl under it to screw the cleat to the wall. Make sure to get at least two screws solidly into the wall framing. Finally, slip a carriage bolt up from below the leg and tighten the nut **(See Photo V).**

PHOTO B: Join the back to the front and bottom. Also install the end to help keep everything aligned.

PHOTO C: Clamp the end between the front and the back; then install and clamp the seat underlayment as shown.

PHOTO D: To prevent it from twisting, lay the seat-back frame flat on the workbench while screwing it together.

PHOTO E: Fasten the seat-back frame flush to the back of the seat case with glue and several screws.

Scribing is only possible if, during construction, you let the edges that will touch the wall extend about ½ in. beyond the flat surfaces. Take these overhangs into consideration when sizing and assembling the pieces. To achieve the offset when slotting the stock for biscuits, mark both edges of the inset joint; then, pivot the inset panel down on the inner line and use it as a fence to position the plate joiner.

The table frame is screwed to the wall and has only one leg. To prevent the tabletop from twisting if someone bears down on an outside corner, it must be secured well to the frame and anchored to the floor. We used machine screws, threaded inserts and construction adhesive to mount the medium-density fiberboard substrate to the frame. A top-tightened carriage bolt secures the leg through the tile floor at a grout line.

We chose materials according to their suitability for specific applications. For instance, we chose a brand of laminate for the counter because it does not show dark resin if scratched or chipped. The painted and hidden surfaces are a combination of MDF and poplar because they take paint well and form strong glue joints. The natural finished pieces are maple plywood with solid maple edge-banding. We chose this material based on the look of the cabinets that are in the home where we installed the booth.

Because MDF is a dense material, you must predrill for screws to avoid splitting it. You also should fill the edges with a paste wood filler and sand them before priming.

MDF is rigid on edge, but it can sag in horizontal applications, such as the tabletop substrate, if not adequately supported. For an even stronger table, glue the MDF substrate to a same-size sheet of ¾-in. plywood rather than building up the edges with narrow strips of MDF.

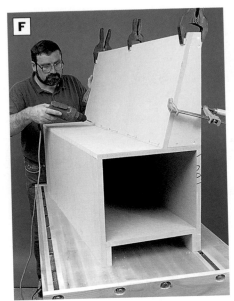

PHOTO F: Glue and clamp the seat back to its frame. Screw the back only along the bottom edge.

PHOTO G: Attach the poplar face frame to the case with glue and nails, leaving scribes at the case back.

PHOTO H: Check the fit of the seat, but don't attach it to the seat case permanently until after you install the booth.

NO-SEW CUSHIONS

Cushioned backs can make a kitchen booth more comfortable and a lot more attractive by adding color and texture to the wooden benches. You don't need to know anything about sewing to achieve sensational results from upholstering. However, to guarantee a trouble-free project, it certainly pays to know professional techniques.

We wanted these cushions to touch the banded bench tops, nearly span the width of the seat backs and stop about an inch shy of the seats themselves. Since we planned to let the padding spill over the edges and wrap the fabric to the back, we subtracted ¼ in. from the finished dimensions when sizing the hardboard backs.

Each cushion consists of fabric stretched over 1 in. of fiberfill batting, ½-in. high-density foam and ¼-in. hardboard. Cut the foam about 1 in. larger than the hardboard on all sides. Lightly coat the hardboard and the foam with spray adhesive and press them together **(See Photo I).** Trim the foam about ⅜ in. larger than the hardboard so it will curl over the edges when you stretch the fabric **(See Photo J).** Cut a piece of fiberfill the same size as the foam and glue it to the foam using spray adhesive. To taper the perimeter, grasp the outer 2 in. of fiberfill and pull it away, parallel with the top, in small handfuls **(See Photo K).**

The fabric should be about 6 in. larger than the hardboard so you can wrap it over the edges and secure it from the back **(See Photo L).** Use a pneumatic stapler loaded with ¼-in.-long chisel-point staples. The easiest way to get the fabric pattern even is

to place a temporary staple in the center of each side. Then work your way to the corners, adjusting the fabric as you go **(See Photo M).** If you goof, don't be afraid to pull the staples and try again. Fold the corners as you would fold hospital bedsheets **(See Photos N & O).**

Attach the cushions with hook-and-loop strips. Reinforce the strips with staples **(See Photo P).**

Home centers carry hardboard and spray adhesive; fabric stores carry everything else you'll need, including fabric, foam, fiberfill and hook-and-loop.

INSTALLATION TIPS

Before installing the bench, mark the locations of the wall studs. Fit the corner bench first so you have room to work. With the top off, slide it tight against both walls and temporarily level it side-to-side and front-to-back using tapered shims **(See Photo Q).** Then scribe the edges that touch the walls and remove the excess stock using a belt sander or a block plane.

Some people use a compass to mark scribes. We prefer to shim a pencil so the point naturally matches the widest area of the gap. This enables us to slide the vertical pencil along the wall while the point marks the cut line on the surface.

When you relevel, use enough shims to spread the load and avoid rocking. Screw through the back and into the wall studs at the top and bottom **(See Photo R).** We made the bench backs of MDF, so we secured them with washer-head cabinet screws to avoid tear-through. With the bench in *(Continued on page 44)*

PHOTO I: Attach the foam to the ¼-in. hardboard with spray adhesive. A light coating on each surface works best.

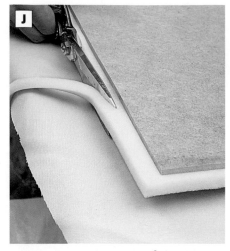

PHOTO J: Trim the foam so it's ⅜ in. wider than the hardboard. The extra width will fold over with the fabric.

PHOTO K: Attach the fiberfill to the foam with spray adhesive. Then tear along the sides to form the tapered edge.

PHOTO L: Stretch and align fabric over the cushion. Use the material's pattern as your guide. Staple it every 2 in.

PHOTO M: Begin each corner by stapling the fabric tight, but do not overstretch. Set one staple back slightly from the edge.

PHOTO N: Make a small pleat and secure it with three staples.

PHOTO O: Fold the remaining edge at 90°, pull it over the other pleat and secure with staples. Cut off excess fabric.

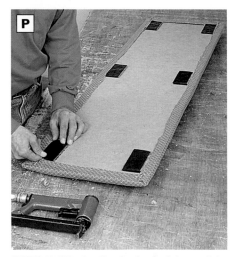

PHOTO P: Attach adhesive-backed, heavy-duty hook-and-loop strips to the hardboard. Staple the bottom sections at each corner.

PHOTO B: Join the back to the front and bottom. Also install the end to help keep everything aligned.

PHOTO C: Clamp the end between the front and the back; then install and clamp the seat underlayment as shown.

PHOTO D: To prevent it from twisting, lay the seat-back frame flat on the workbench while screwing it together.

PHOTO E: Fasten the seat-back frame flush to the back of the seat case with glue and several screws.

Scribing is only possible if, during construction, you let the edges that will touch the wall extend about ½ in. beyond the flat surfaces. Take these overhangs into consideration when sizing and assembling the pieces. To achieve the offset when slotting the stock for biscuits, mark both edges of the inset joint; then, pivot the inset panel down on the inner line and use it as a fence to position the plate joiner.

The table frame is screwed to the wall and has only one leg. To prevent the tabletop from twisting if someone bears down on an outside corner, it must be secured well to the frame and anchored to the floor. We used machine screws, threaded inserts and construction adhesive to mount the medium-density fiberboard substrate to the frame. A top-tightened carriage bolt secures the leg through the tile floor at a grout line.

We chose materials according to their suitability for specific applications. For instance, we chose a brand of laminate for the counter because it does not show dark resin if scratched or chipped. The painted and hidden surfaces are a combination of MDF and poplar because they take paint well and form strong glue joints. The natural finished pieces are maple plywood with solid maple edge-banding. We chose this material based on the look of the cabinets that are in the home where we installed the booth.

Because MDF is a dense material, you must predrill for screws to avoid splitting it. You also should fill the edges with a paste wood filler and sand them before priming.

MDF is rigid on edge, but it can sag in horizontal applications, such as the tabletop substrate, if not adequately supported. For an even stronger table, glue the MDF substrate to a same-size sheet of ¾-in. plywood rather than building up the edges with narrow strips of MDF.

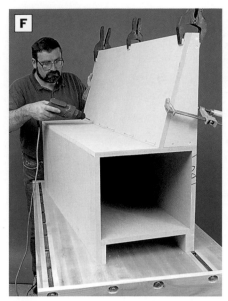

PHOTO F: Glue and clamp the seat back to its frame. Screw the back only along the bottom edge.

PHOTO G: Attach the poplar face frame to the case with glue and nails, leaving scribes at the case back.

PHOTO H: Check the fit of the seat, but don't attach it to the seat case permanently until after you install the booth.

NO-SEW CUSHIONS

Cushioned backs can make a kitchen booth more comfortable and a lot more attractive by adding color and texture to the wooden benches. You don't need to know anything about sewing to achieve sensational results from upholstering. However, to guarantee a trouble-free project, it certainly pays to know professional techniques.

We wanted these cushions to touch the banded bench tops, nearly span the width of the seat backs and stop about an inch shy of the seats themselves. Since we planned to let the padding spill over the edges and wrap the fabric to the back, we subtracted ¼ in. from the finished dimensions when sizing the hardboard backs.

Each cushion consists of fabric stretched over 1 in. of fiberfill batting, ½-in. high-density foam and ¼-in. hardboard. Cut the foam about 1 in. larger than the hardboard on all sides. Lightly coat the hardboard and the foam with spray adhesive and press them together (See Photo I). Trim the foam about ⅜ in. larger than the hardboard so it will curl over the edges when you stretch the fabric (See Photo J). Cut a piece of fiberfill the same size as the foam and glue it to the foam using spray adhesive. To taper the perimeter, grasp the outer 2 in. of fiberfill and pull it away, parallel with the top, in small handfuls (See Photo K).

The fabric should be about 6 in. larger than the hardboard so you can wrap it over the edges and secure it from the back (See Photo L). Use a pneumatic stapler loaded with ¼-in.-long chisel-point staples. The easiest way to get the fabric pattern even is

to place a temporary staple in the center of each side. Then work your way to the corners, adjusting the fabric as you go (See Photo M). If you goof, don't be afraid to pull the staples and try again. Fold the corners as you would fold hospital bedsheets (See Photos N & O).

Attach the cushions with hook-and-loop strips. Reinforce the strips with staples (See Photo P).

Home centers carry hardboard and spray adhesive; fabric stores carry everything else you'll need, including fabric, foam, fiberfill and hook-and-loop.

INSTALLATION TIPS

Before installing the bench, mark the locations of the wall studs. Fit the corner bench first so you have room to work. With the top off, slide it tight against both walls and temporarily level it side-to-side and front-to-back using tapered shims (See Photo Q). Then scribe the edges that touch the walls and remove the excess stock using a belt sander or a block plane.

Some people use a compass to mark scribes. We prefer to shim a pencil so the point naturally matches the widest area of the gap. This enables us to slide the vertical pencil along the wall while the point marks the cut line on the surface.

When you relevel, use enough shims to spread the load and avoid rocking. Screw through the back and into the wall studs at the top and bottom (See Photo R). We made the bench backs of MDF, so we secured them with washer-head cabinet screws to avoid tear-through. With the bench in (Continued on page 44)

PHOTO I: Attach the foam to the ¼-in. hardboard with spray adhesive. A light coating on each surface works best.

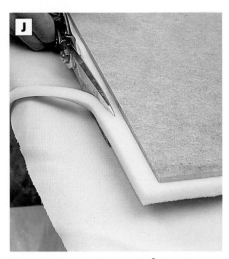

PHOTO J: Trim the foam so it's ⅜ in. wider than the hardboard. The extra width will fold over with the fabric.

PHOTO K: Attach the fiberfill to the foam with spray adhesive. Then tear along the sides to form the tapered edge.

PHOTO L: Stretch and align fabric over the cushion. Use the material's pattern as your guide. Staple it every 2 in.

PHOTO M: Begin each corner by stapling the fabric tight, but do not overstretch. Set one staple back slightly from the edge.

PHOTO N: Make a small pleat and secure it with three staples.

PHOTO O: Fold the remaining edge at 90°, pull it over the other pleat and secure with staples. Cut off excess fabric.

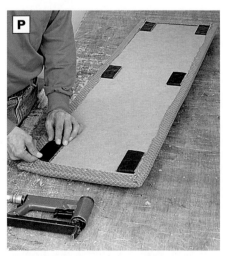

PHOTO P: Attach adhesive-backed, heavy-duty hook-and-loop strips to the hardboard. Staple the bottom sections at each corner.

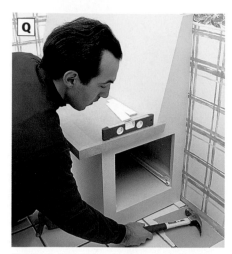

PHOTO Q: Slide the corner bench against the walls and temporarily level it front-to-back and side-to-side with shims.

PHOTO R: After scribing and shaping the edges that abut the walls, relevel the bench and screw it to the wall studs.

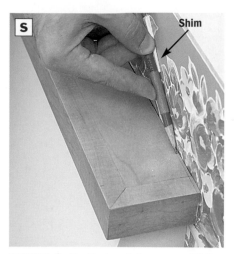

PHOTO S: Scribe the bench top as you did the bench, using a shim to space the pencil lead along the widest part of the gap. Keep the pencil plumb.

PHOTO T: Outline the bench footprint with tape. Fasten a nailing cleat into the floor joist, ⅛ in. inside the end frame, using a lag screw.

PHOTO U: Position and level the table support and mark the wall cleat and the floor for drilling into the framing.

PHOTO V: Bolt the table leg through the floor and screw the cleat to the wall. Then mount the tabletop and backsplash.

place, scribe **(See Photo S)** and install the top with finishing nails.

Scribe and screw the other bench to the wall in much the same way, but anchor the free end to the floor. The best way is to secure a nailing cleat through the floor and into the joists with lag screws **(See Photo T).** Hold the cleat back ⅛ in. from the end so the bench is drawn toward the wall when you screw it to the cleat. *TIP: Chamfer the cleat's top edges in order to make it easier to position the bench around it.*

The tabletop rests on a support structure you screw to the wall studs and bolt through the floor. Temporarily position the framework and mark the wall cleat and the floor for drilling **(See Photo U).** Secure the tabletop to the framework using threaded inserts, machine screws and construction adhesive before you install it. The inserts' coarse threads hold better in MDF than most screws.

Set the table in position and crawl under it to screw the cleat to the wall. Make sure to get at least two screws solidly into the wall framing. Finally, slip a carriage bolt up from below the leg and tighten the nut **(See Photo V).**

Beverage Bar

Because we know how awkward it can be to serve refreshments when entertaining outdoors, we've come up with this conveniently mobile beverage bar that's guaranteed to bring special cheer to your next backyard barbecue.

The design features a hinged top that flips up to provide a sheltered cubby for glasses and pivots into the frame to form a large, flat top for plates and trays. The shelf holds bottles, napkins and utensils, while the bottom is open to allow access to a cooler, a waste can and a recycling container from either side.

Beverage Bar

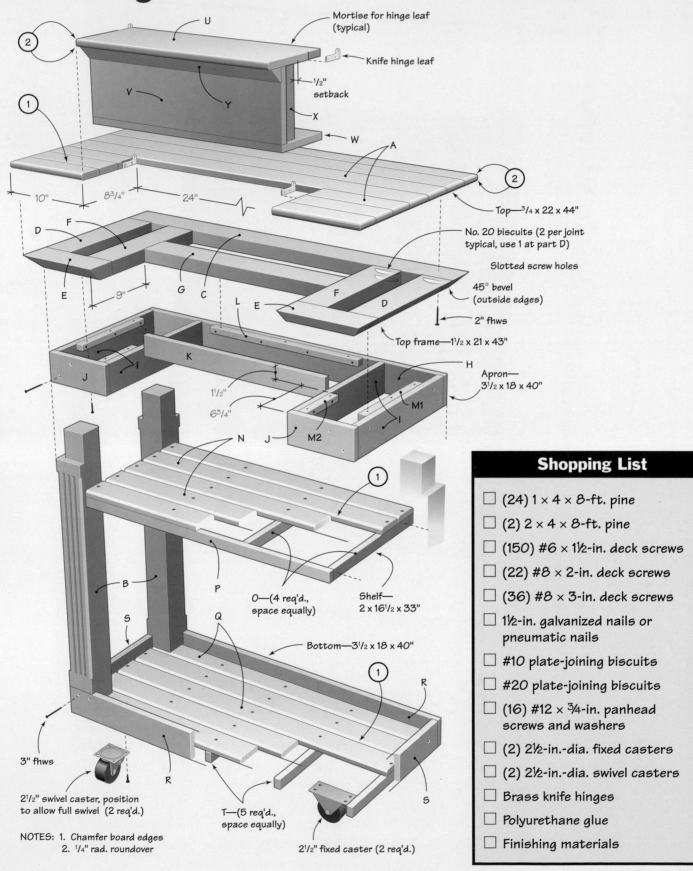

Mortise for hinge leaf (typical)

Knife hinge leaf

1/2" setback

U

V

Y

X

W

A

10"

8³/₄"

24"

Top—³/₄ x 22 x 44"

No. 20 biscuits (2 per joint typical, use 1 at part D)

Slotted screw holes

D F

E

9"

G C

L E

F

D

45° bevel (outside edges)

2" fhws

Top frame—1¹/₂ x 21 x 43"

J I

K

H

Apron— 3¹/₂ x 18 x 40"

1¹/₂"

6³/₄"

M1

I

J M2

N

B

P

S

Q

O—(4 req'd., space equally)

Shelf— 2 x 16¹/₂ x 33"

Bottom—3¹/₂ x 18 x 40"

R

3" fhws

R

2¹/₂" swivel caster, position to allow full swivel (2 req'd.)

T—(5 req'd., space equally)

2¹/₂" fixed caster (2 req'd.)

S

NOTES: 1. Chamfer board edges
2. ¹/₄" rad. roundover

Shopping List

- ☐ (24) 1 × 4 × 8-ft. pine
- ☐ (2) 2 × 4 × 8-ft. pine
- ☐ (150) #6 × 1¹/₂-in. deck screws
- ☐ (22) #8 × 2-in. deck screws
- ☐ (36) #8 × 3-in. deck screws
- ☐ 1¹/₂-in. galvanized nails or pneumatic nails
- ☐ #10 plate-joining biscuits
- ☐ #20 plate-joining biscuits
- ☐ (16) #12 × ³/₄-in. panhead screws and washers
- ☐ (2) 2¹/₂-in.-dia. fixed casters
- ☐ (2) 2¹/₂-in.-dia. swivel casters
- ☐ Brass knife hinges
- ☐ Polyurethane glue
- ☐ Finishing materials

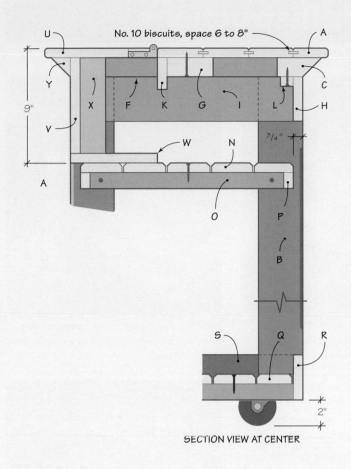

No. 10 biscuits, space 6 to 8"

9"

3/4"

2"

SECTION VIEW AT CENTER

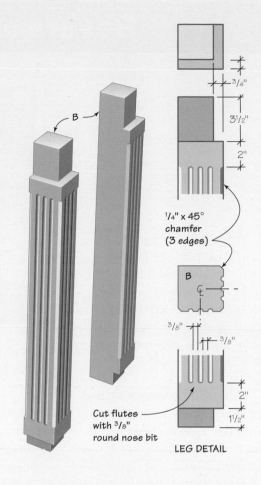

1/4" x 45° chamfer (3 edges)

Cut flutes with 3/8" round nose bit

3/4"

3 1/2"

2"

3/8"

3/8"

2"

1 1/2"

LEG DETAIL

Bench Cutting List

Part/Description	No.	Size	Material
A Top	1	3/4 × 22 × 44 in.*	Pine
B Legs	2	3 1/2 × 3 1/2 × 33 3/4 in.	Cedar

Top Frame Cutting List

C Front	1	1 1/2 × 3 1/2 × 43 in.**	Pine
D Sides	4	1 1/2 × 3 1/2 × 14 in.**	"
E Ends	2	1 1/2 × 3 1/2 × 9 1/2 in.**	"
F Side stretchers	2	1 1/2 × 3 1/2 × 14 in.	"
G Inside stretcher	1	1 1/2 × 3 1/2 × 24 in.	"

Apron Cutting List

H Front	1	3/4 × 3 1/2 × 40 in.	Pine
I Sides/stretchers	4	3/4 × 3 1/2 × 16 1/2 in.	"
J Ends	2	3/4 × 3 1/2 × 8 in.	"
K Inside stretcher	1	3/4 × 2 1/2 × 24 in.	"
L Front cleat	1	3/4 × 1 × 20 in.	"
M1 Side cleats	2	3/4 × 1 × 13 in.	"
M2 Side cleats	2	3/4 × 1 × 8 in.	"

Shelf Cutting List

N Decking	5	3/4 × 3 1/2 × 33 in.***	Pine
O Sides/rails	4	3/4 × 1 1/4 × 15 in.	"
P Front/back	2	3/4 × 1 1/4 × 33 in.	"

Bottom Cutting List

Q Decking	5	3/4 × 3 1/2 × 38 1/2 in.***	Pine
R Front/back	2	3/4 × 3 1/2 × 40 in.	"
S Sides	2	3/4 × 3 1/2 × 16 1/2 in.	"
T Rails	3	3/4 × 1 1/4 × 16 1/2 in.	"

Hinged Box Cutting List

U Top	1	3/4 × 8 3/4 × 23 3/4 in.	Pine
V Front	1	3/4 × 7 1/2 × 23 3/4 in.	"
W Bottom	1	3/4 × 6 3/4 × 23 3/4 in.	"
X Sides	2	3/4 × 2 × 7 1/2 in.	"
Y Molding	1	1 1/2 × 1 1/2 × 23 3/4 in.	"

*Glue together with 1 × 4s
**Bevel top edges; see drawing
***Cut width of pieces to fit

Since the beverage bar is a natural gathering place on any patio, we included architectural touches and rich colors that enhance its attractiveness. The fluted faces of the legs, the beveled frame and the two-tone paint job all highlight the detailing.

CLIMATE CONSIDERATIONS

Nothing lasts forever, but by using the right materials and construction techniques, you can extend the life of your project.

This structure rides on casters, resides on a deck and is fully primed and painted, so I used standard dimensional lumber to keep the cost down. Building the cart entirely out of cedar would have been better because of its superior rot resistance and dimensional stability, but cedar was more than three times the price of pine. I did choose 4 × 4 cedar for the legs because they needed to be smooth and straight for fluting and chamfering.

To avoid trapping moisture and promoting wood rot, I built the cart using simple butt joints that shed water better than complex joints. I also used waterproof polyurethane glue and a combination of simple fasteners (biscuits and galvanized nails and screws).

I prefer polyurethane glue to epoxy for projects like this because it requires no mixing, it's less

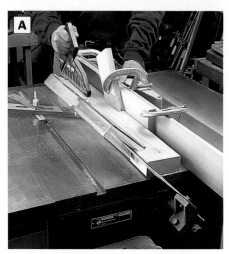

PHOTO A: Use a short fence and feather-boards on the side and top of the stock to ensure accurate bevel cuts in the top frame.

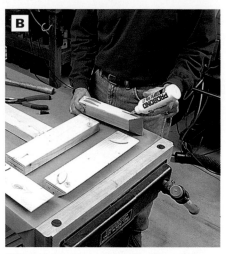

PHOTO B: Join the top frame's center section with poly glue and biscuits; then assemble the rest of the parts.

expensive and it has a long open time. Polyurethane is not a structural gap filler like epoxy and contains no water like wood glue, so the biscuits must fit snugly into the slots in the top. Glue the faces of the joints as well as the biscuit slots. If necessary, spritz loose biscuits with water before assembly to swell them. You also could fabricate the top from tongue-and-groove flooring.

If you build your bar cart entirely out of cedar or redwood and give it a natural finish, use stainless steel screws rather than galvanized, which can discolor untreated wood.

STOCK SELECTION

When picking your stock, keep these things in mind: Wet lumber will warp, twist and check even after it's finished. Construction-grade dimensional lumber may have a kiln-dried stamp on it, but if it has been outdoors and rained upon, the stamp is only decorative. The boards may feel dry, but if they feel cooler than the sur-

PHOTO C: Clamp the frame together—but not too tightly—to prevent the poly glue from forcing the pieces apart as it expands.

rounding air, the wood probably has a high moisture content.

You should also avoid wood with too many defects such as knots and checks. Because dimensional lumber is meant for construction and not furniture making, you'll probably have to do a lot of digging through the pile. Above all, look for boards with straight edges. A crooked board will need to be jointed and that

PHOTO D: Attach the top frame to the top with screws driven through slotted holes. Allow a ½-in. margin around the edge.

PHOTO E: Position the apron on the frame so the apron's inside stretcher is flush against the frame's inside stretcher.

PHOTO F: Attach the apron to the frame by driving screws through the front and side cleats and the inside stretcher.

will change its dimension.

The pieces that you use for the top must be especially straight because you glue and join them together like a tabletop. This creates a surface that will stay fairly flat. If the board edges don't butt tightly, use a hand plane or a jointer to finesse the fit. Chamfer the top edges of the boards with a block plane to form narrow channels in the assembled top. This detail is not just for looks; it will save you the job of leveling the joint lines after glue-up. Use polyurethane glue and plate-joining biscuits spaced about 8 in. apart to align and reinforce the joints **(See Photo B).**

Clamp polyurethane glue joints securely overnight—the glue expands as it cures **(See Photo C).**

In hindsight, I probably over-built the top frame and would do it differently next time. Instead of building a 2 × 4 frame with beveled edges, I would construct a 1 × 6 frame and apply a mitered molding around the top of the apron.

If you build it as I did, bevel the pieces C, D and E on your table

saw **(See Photo A).** Kickback and burning are enough of a problem when beveling straight, square stock, but when you're doing this to a 2 × 4 it's worth the extra time to set up your saw properly. Use a short fence, featherboards and a guard/splitter. It's also particularly important to bore slotted screw holes into the frame assembly for the screws that hold the top to the beveled frame **(See Photo D).** These two assemblies will expand at different rates, so without the slots, the tabletop

joints would pull apart.

The apron sits on the frame assembly with its inside stretcher flush against the frame's inside stretcher **(See Photo E).** The apron is secured with screws driven through the front and side cleats, and the inside stretcher **(See Photo F).**

Although cedar is better than pine for the legs, I still needed to joint and plane the stock. The stock must fit squarely into the top and bottom assemblies, and it's also easier to rout the flutes

PHOTO G: Cut the shoulders of the notches on the leg ends on the table saw; cut the cheeks using a fence on the band saw.

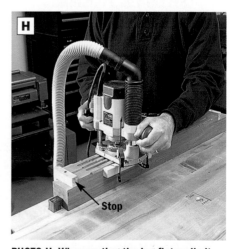

PHOTO H: When routing the leg flutes, limit the router's travel by screwing stops at the end of the notches.

and chamfers if the stock is square. I removed as little stock as possible so the final leg dimension would be close to 3½ in. sq. The ends of the legs must be notched to create an attractive, secure fit with the top and bottom **(See Photo G).**

A plunge router works better than a fixed-base router for cutting the flutes because it's easier to start the stopped cuts. Use a ⅜-in. core box or round-nose bit and set the depth to achieve a half-circle profile. You can set up stops as I did **(See Photo H),** although you may need to modify the setup to work with your router. Use the same setup to chamfer the leg edges so the ends of the chamfers align with the flutes.

The legs are attached first to the bottom with glue and 3-in. deck screws through the front of the aprons **(See Photo I).** Follow a similar procedure with the top, making sure that the assembly sits squarely before driving the screws **(See Photo J).** The shelf location is most easily determined by turning the cart on its side, marking its position and then attaching with two screws at each corner **(See Photo K).**

FITTING & FINISHING

It's best to fit and then remove the hardware before you finish the cart. I used heavy-duty brass furniture-grade knife hinges to mount the hinged box. They're relatively small, easy to mount and should hold up outdoors. Use a back saw to mortise the box and a chisel to mortise the top to accept the hinges. The mortise dimensions should correspond to the length and thickness of the hinges. Mount the hinges in the top mortises with steel screws in predrilled holes so you don't risk snapping the softer brass screws

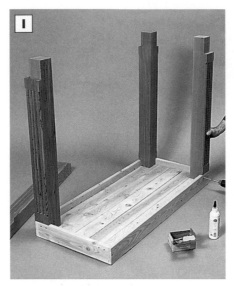

PHOTO I: Prebore holes in the apron, then attach the legs with 3-in. deck screws.

PHOTO J: Apply glue to the leg tops; then place the top assembly squarely on the legs and drive screws through the apron.

that come with the hinges.

Place the hinged box on the top in its open position; then slide it back so the extended hinges fit in their mortises. Attach the hinges with steel screws here as well. The box should now swing freely into its closed position. (Note that the drawing of the box is slightly different from what's shown in the photos. The box sides in the drawing are inset slightly to prevent them from binding against the cart's apron.) You may need to shim the hinges slightly to make them work, but wait until you reinstall them after finishing so you can allow for paint buildup. I used standard 2½-in. rubber-wheel casters—two with fixed wheels and two with pivoting wheels. The fixed-wheel set can be mounted fairly close to the edge, but the pivoting set requires enough clearance to rotate 360°. Use #12 × ¾-in. panhead screws to mount the casters to the bottom decking.

Before you paint, remove all of the hardware and the shelf. Painting the shelf and box separately allows better access to the bottom of the top assembly. Prime

PHOTO K: Turn the cart on its side, mark the shelf position, then screw the shelf to the legs with two screws in each corner.

all surfaces with oil-based exterior primer. Cover countersunk screw heads with polyester wood filler and caulk joints between the top, the beveled frame and the apron. We applied two coats of semigloss acrylic house trim paint.

Portable Desk

Those who take a relaxed approach to paperwork or just like to snack with their feet up will appreciate this lap desk. It features a flat top and a combination of raised sides and recesses to corral beverages, pencils and a cordless phone. And there's plenty more storage space beneath the piano-hinged top. It's ideal for someone who wants to take a little pain out of bill paying. It also works well for bedridden family members, TV diners and kids who insist they can do homework while watching their favorite program.

Portable Desk

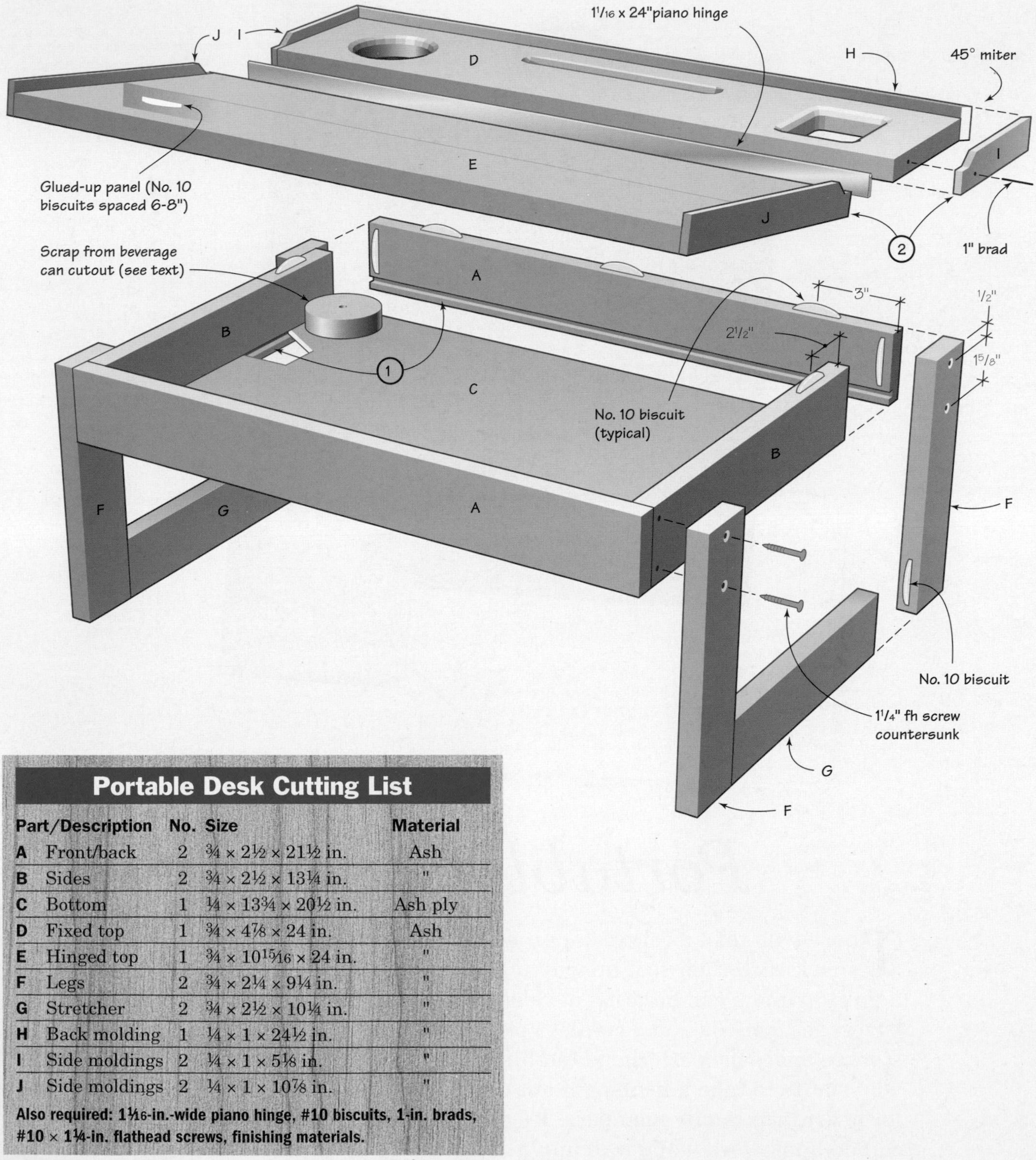

J
I
1$^1/_{16}$ x 24" piano hinge
D
H
45° miter
E
I
Glued-up panel (No. 10 biscuits spaced 6-8")
J
2
1" brad
Scrap from beverage can cutout (see text)
A
3"
1/2"
B
2$^1/_2$"
1$^5/_8$"
1
C
No. 10 biscuit (typical)
B
F
G
A
F
No. 10 biscuit
1$^1/_4$" fh screw countersunk
G
F

Portable Desk Cutting List

Part/Description		No.	Size	Material
A	Front/back	2	¾ × 2½ × 21½ in.	Ash
B	Sides	2	¾ × 2½ × 13¼ in.	"
C	Bottom	1	¼ × 13¾ × 20½ in.	Ash ply
D	Fixed top	1	¾ × 4⅞ × 24 in.	Ash
E	Hinged top	1	¾ × 10$^{15}/_{16}$ × 24 in.	"
F	Legs	2	¾ × 2¼ × 9¼ in.	"
G	Stretcher	2	¾ × 2½ × 10¼ in.	"
H	Back molding	1	¼ × 1 × 24½ in.	"
I	Side moldings	2	¼ × 1 × 5⅛ in.	"
J	Side moldings	2	¼ × 1 × 10⅞ in.	"

Also required: 1$^1/_{16}$-in.-wide piano hinge, #10 biscuits, 1-in. brads, #10 × 1¼-in. flathead screws, finishing materials.

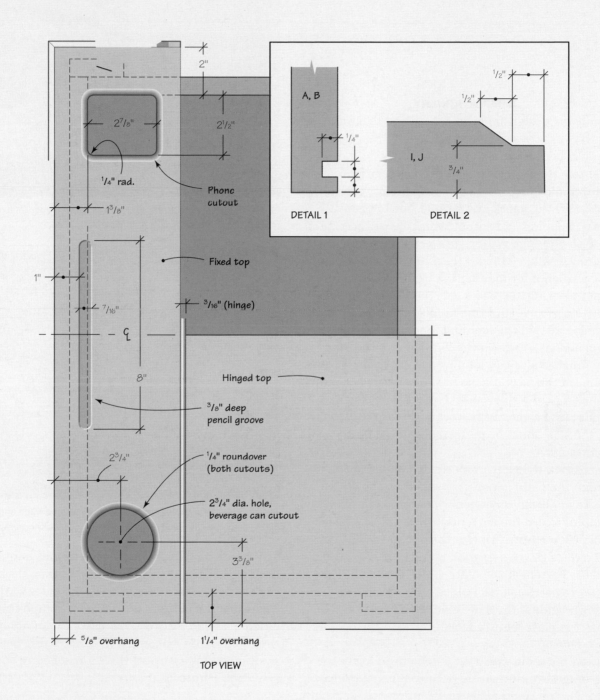

2"

$2^7/_8$"

$2^1/_2$"

$^1/_4$" rad.

Phone
cutout

$1^3/_8$"

Fixed top

1"

$^3/_{16}$" (hinge)

$^7/_{16}$"

C_L

8"

Hinged top

$^3/_8$" deep
pencil groove

$^1/_4$" roundover
(both cutouts)

$2^3/_4$"

$2^3/_4$" dia. hole,
beverage can cutout

$3^3/_8$"

$^5/_8$" overhang

$1^1/_4$" overhang

TOP VIEW

A, B

$^1/_4$"

DETAIL 1

$^1/_2$"

$^1/_2$"

I, J

$^3/_4$"

DETAIL 2

PHOTO A: Hold the front and back pieces against your table saw rip fence to make the face slots with your plate joiner.

SIMPLE JOINERY

I built the desk from solid ash planed to a uniform ¾-in. thickness. Ash is a good choice for this particular project because it is a hard, yet fairly light, wood. The bottom panel is ¼-in. ash plywood, but hardboard would do just fine. I relied on a plate (biscuit) joiner for all the joints and a table saw to make all the cuts. Shaping and cutouts were easy to accomplish with a plunge router, an electric drill, a jig saw and a router table (which I used to make molding).

The sequence for making the lap desk is really very simple: Cut the pieces, cut the biscuit slots and the bottom groove, mill the details in the fixed top, assemble and add the molding. Begin the project by ripping and crosscutting the four sides of the desk box to finished sizes on a table saw. Next, lay out the locations of the biscuit slots at the ends of each piece. The slots for the #10 biscuits typically are 2¼ in. wide. Because some of the workpieces are only 2½ in. wide, the slots must be perfectly centered or they will show through.

To position the slots properly, it's important that you align the plate joiner precisely with the workpiece. To maintain consistency and proper alignment, it's helpful to use the rip fence of your table saw for support (See Photo A). Use the outside surface of each piece as the registration plane to make the cut. I used the bottom of the plate joiner against the saw table for registration, so I placed the outside surface face down against the saw table (See Photo B). If you use the plate joiner's fence, cut with the outside surface face up.

I fitted my table saw with a dado head to cut the ¼ × ¼-in. grooves for the desk bottom panel (See Photo C). You could also use a router with a straight bit or make two passes with a normal (⅛-in.-kerf) table saw blade. Don't worry about the ends of the grooves showing; these will be covered by the legs. Cut the desk bottom and sand it before assembly.

PHOTO B: Use your table saw top as a worksurface when aligning the plate joiner and the side pieces for slotting. Brace the workpiece.

When assembling the various biscuit joints of the desk box, apply glue to the joining faces, the slots and the biscuits themselves. Attach the sides to the front, then slide the bottom in dry before completing the assembly (See Photo D). Square the assembly by first measuring diagonals, then adjusting both the position and pressure of the clamps before the glue sets (See Photo E).

DESKTOP DETAILS

Cut the pieces for the desktop to size, again using biscuits for alignment. Glue up two or three narrow pieces to form the hinged section.

PHOTO C: Cut the ¼ × ¼-in. grooves for the bottom panel on a table saw or with a router table and straight bit.

PHOTO D: Join the sides and front with glue and biscuits. Insert the bottom dry, then attach the back with glue and biscuits.

PHOTO E: Clamp the corner joints tight as the glue sets. Uniform diagonal distances will ensure the assembly is square.

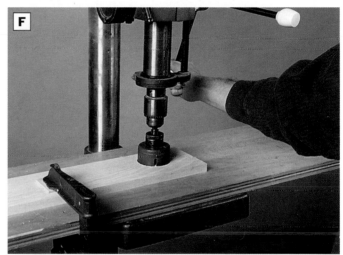

PHOTO F: Clamp the piece and make the beverage cutout with a 2¾-in. hole saw. Back off often so you don't burn the wood.

A 2¾-in.-dia. circle cutter makes quick work of boring the beverage cutout **(See Photo F).** Withdraw the blade frequently to remove the buildup of sawdust; otherwise, you might burn the sides of the hole. If you prefer your beverage to stand a little taller in the cutout, you can glue the scrap to the desk bottom.

Check the dimensions of your phone and modify the size of the square cutout as necessary. Bore the ½-in. holes for the ¼-in. radiused corners before you cut out the opening with a jig saw. Sand or file the sides of both cutouts in order to remove the saw marks; then ease the edges with a router and a ¼-in. roundover bit.

It's easier to hinge the two parts of the desktop before attaching the fixed portion to the desk box. To do this, position the hinge so the top of the knuckle is flush with the top of the desk surface **(See Photo G).** Mark the screw hole locations. To avoid splitting the

wood when installing the hinge, bore ¹⁄₁₆-in.-dia. pilot holes. Lubricating the screws with soap will also make installation easier.

Mark the locations of biscuits to attach the desktop to the box and cut the slots in both parts **(See Photo H).** Remove the piano hinge before assembling, then join the fixed portion of the desktop to the box with glue and biscuits. Clamp them together securely until the glue sets.

Next, use a router, edge guide and ⁷⁄₁₆-in. core box bit to cut the pencil slot in the desktop **(See Photo I).** Before you start, clamp the desk to the workbench and mark the locations for the ends of the slot. With the plunge router running, slowly lower the bit into the workpiece and make the cut (you may want to rout the groove before gluing the top to the desk box—it makes no difference in the outcome).

Cut the parts for the desk legs to size, then lay out

PHOTO G: Join the desktop pieces with a piano hinge before installing, but remove the hardware for finishing.

PHOTO H: Clamp a straightedge to the fixed top before cutting the biscuit slots. Then make matching slots in the table box.

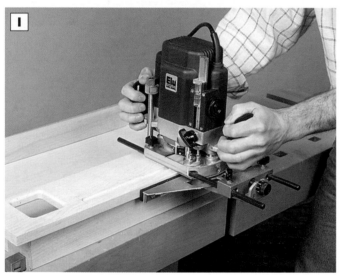

PHOTO I: Use a 7/16-in. core box bit and an edge guide to mill the pencil slot in the fixed portion of the top.

PHOTO J: Secure the leg assemblies with spring clamps and join with countersunk, #10 × 1¼-in. flathead screws.

the corner joint biscuit slots. Cut the slots and assemble the legs, clamping each assembly to pull the joints tight while the glue dries. Drill and countersink pilot holes for #10 × 1¼-in. flathead screws in each leg. Then attach the legs to the box (See Photo J).

FINISHING TOUCHES

I applied molding around three sides of the desktop to keep papers, checkbooks and other items from sliding off. To make the molding, rip ¼ × 1⅛-in. ash strips on the table saw. Then, cut a radius on the top edge of each strip with a bead cutter on a router table. You could also use a block plane to shape the edges, or simply sand them to a desired contour.

Use a miter box or table saw to cut the molding strips to length, then attach them along the edges

of the top panels with glue and 1-in. brads. For the desktop to pivot properly, you will have to taper the ends of the molding on both sides of the hinge. Use a dovetail saw and chisel to make the cuts.

Sand the entire desk, ease all sharp edges and remove the dust before finishing. It's a good idea to apply multiple topcoats to a frequently-used surface such as a desktop. I applied three even coats of satin polyurethane varnish for increased durability. For best results, be sure to recoat in the time specified by the manufacturer.

Wainscot

Wood wainscoting used to be common in homebuilding because it looked good and provided a durable surface where walls got the most abuse. A Midwest farmhouse kitchen might feature beaded fir boards painted bright white, while the dining room in an old New England estate might be finished with polished mahogany raised panels. Although not as common as it once was, custom wainscot makes a stylish addition to any home.

Wainscot

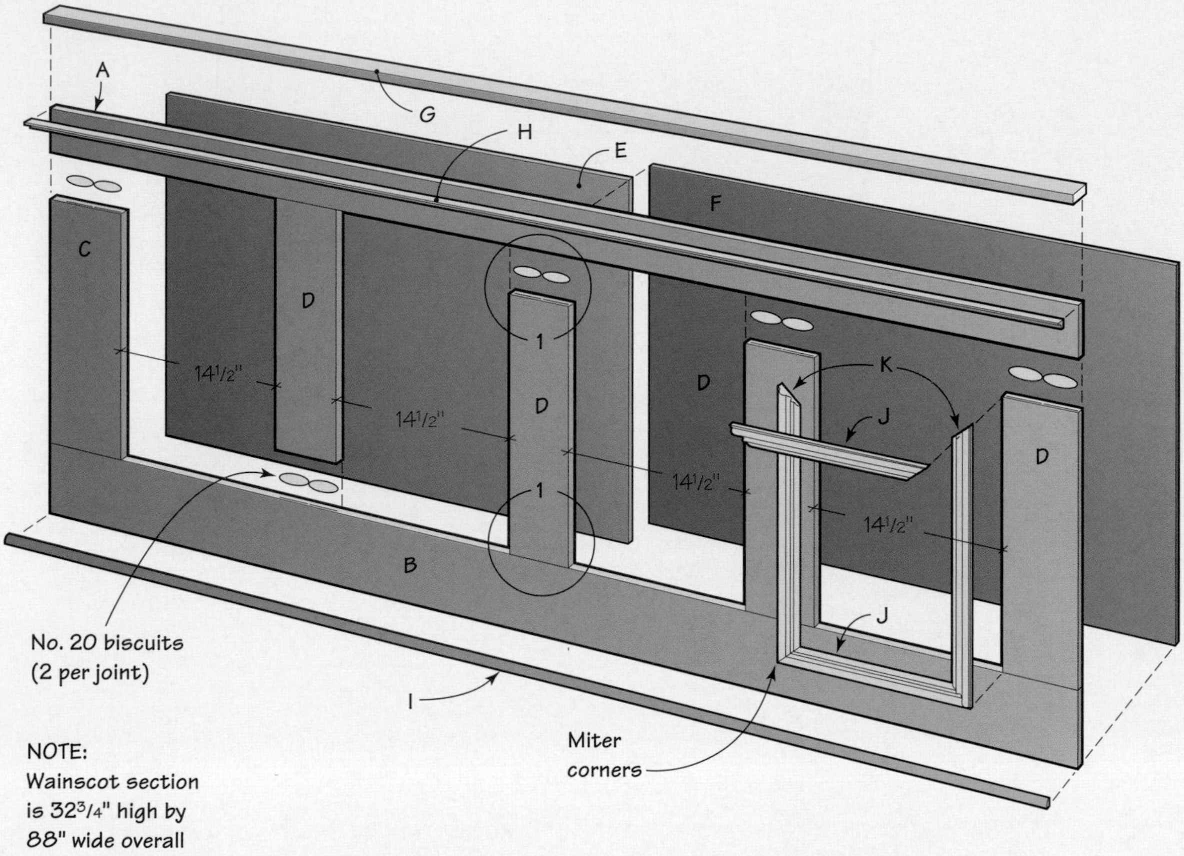

A
G
H
E
F
C
D
D
D
D
1
1
K
J
J
B
I
$14^1/_2$"
$14^1/_2$"
$14^1/_2$"
$14^1/_2$"
No. 20 biscuits
(2 per joint)
Miter
corners
NOTE:
Wainscot section
is $32^3/_4$" high by
88" wide overall

Wainscot Cutting List

	Part/Description	No.	Size	Material
A	Top rail	1	¾ × 4½ × 86¾ in.	Pine
B	Bottom rail	1	¾ × 7 × 86¾ in.	"
C	Stile (left)*	1	¾ × 6¾ × 20½ in.	"
D	Stile (others)	4	¾ × 5½ × 20½ in.	"
E	Panel (left)	2	½ × 32 × 44 in.	Birch ply
F	Panel (right)	2	½ × 32 × 42¾ in.	"
G	Cap	1	¾ × 2½ × 86¾ in.	Pine
H	Cove molding	1	¾ × ¾ × 86¾ in.	Stock
I	Shoe molding	1	½ × 1⅙ × 86¾ in.	"
J	Panel molding (rails)	8	11⁄16 × 19⁄16 × 14½ in.	"
K	Panel molding (stiles)	8	11⁄16 × 19⁄16 × 20½ in.	"

Also required: Wood glue, 1-in. flathead screws, 1-in. brads, 4d and 8d finish nails, #20 biscuits.
***Wider because partially hidden by frame on adjacent wall.**

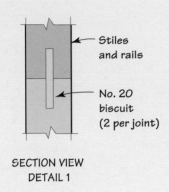

Stiles and rails

No. 20 biscuit (2 per joint)

SECTION VIEW
DETAIL 1

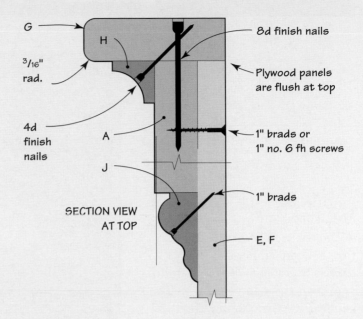

G

H

3/16" rad.

4d finish nails

A

J

8d finish nails

Plywood panels are flush at top

1" brads or 1" no. 6 fh screws

1" brads

E, F

SECTION VIEW
AT TOP

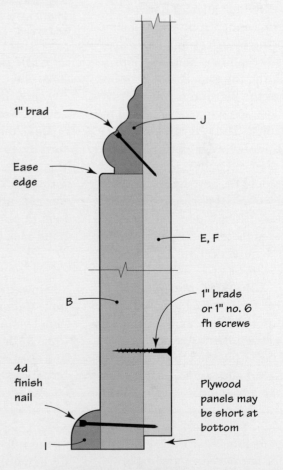

1" brad

J

Ease edge

E, F

B

1" brads or 1" no. 6 fh screws

4d finish nail

I

Plywood panels may be short at bottom

SECTION VIEW AT BOTTOM

With labor rates and material costs what they are today, authentic wood wainscoting is rare in modern homes. But there's no reason you can't build your own right in your shop. The general construction method shown here is eminently adaptable to any room's situation. The section I built happens to be scaled for a small bathroom.

The beauty of this approach is that the wainscoting panels are mostly made in the workshop. Building the panels off-site minimizes the disruption and mess at the location where they are to be installed. The rails and stiles are butt jointed with biscuits. Then the plywood panels are secured from behind. For simplicity, you could shape the frame's interior edges with a router, but we added mitered molding for a more traditional panel design.

CHOOSING MATERIALS

Our wainscoting is based on a traditional frame and panel design that is detailed with molding. Because I planned to paint the surface, I chose materials with economy in mind: 1× select pine for the rails and stiles, ½-in. birch plywood for the recessed panels and stock moldings for the trim. If you prefer hardwoods and a natural finish for your project, you will have more to consider up front.

PHOTO A: For tight joints, assemble the rails and stiles with pairs of #20 biscuits installed end to end.

While lumberyards commonly stock pine and oak trim, they rarely keep cherry, walnut or maple trim on hand. If you can't find matching plywood, boards and molding at the yard, try a local millwork shop or custom woodworker.

Remember that you will need wood with uniform color and grain pattern if you plan to use a natural or semitransparent finish. Achieving this can be both difficult and expensive. The best way to obtain a uniform look is to specify sequence-matched plywood panels. In this method, all panels are made from the same veneer log, with the veneers kept in sequence from one panel to the next. Short of this option, try to hand-pick panels from a supplier's stock.

PLANNING & LAYOUT

Since the objective is to achieve uniform-sized panels and few rooms have uniform dimensions, layout is the most challenging aspect of any panel wainscoting project. I prefer to construct wainscoting in long sections in the shop, then install the sections on-site and add the cap, cove and shoe moldings there. This requires careful measurement and layout, but allows for precision joinery and a minimum of visible fasteners and on-site inconvenience.

Wainscoting is generally installed at a height of 30 to 48 in. My design is 32¾ in. tall. Consider function, material yield and existing visual references (such as the heights of windowsills or furniture) when developing your layout.

Begin by measuring the length of the walls and creating a scale drawing. Note the location of any openings, such as outlets, switches, heat reg-

PHOTO B: Secure large plywood panels to the back of the frame with screws or brads, concealing joints behind stiles.

PHOTO C: To speed finishing and prevent damage, sand the plywood and frame before installing the panel molding.

isters, windows and doors. Also check the corners of the room for plumb, using a level to see if any shimming or scribing will be needed to achieve a tight fit.

Determine a rough size for your panels by making a scale drawing of a sample wall. Experiment with several options before choosing the right one.

I started by determining the widths of the rails and stiles, so the only real variable was the panel width. I chose a 7-in. bottom rail, 4½-in. top rail and 5½-in. stiles. These dimensions made good use of the 1× lumber (the top rail and cap were ripped from a single 1 × 8). The sizes also worked well visually with the more substantial rail at the base.

After deciding on a rough size for the panels, finalize the layout. Plan the order in which the walls will be covered. Once a wall is covered, the next wall becomes shorter by the thickness of the previous paneling. To keep the stile width uniform, the first wall treatment will require a wider stile in the corner.

Determining the precise dimensions for the panels requires some simple math. To calculate the width of your panels (before moldings), add the width of all stiles and subtract the total from the wall length. Divide the sum by the number of panels to yield the panel width.

Uniformity of panel sizes around the room is an admirable goal, but in practice this is not always possible. You can work toward this goal by making minor modifications in the width of panels and stiles on different walls. A slight difference in the width of stiles (up to ¼ in.) and even greater variation in the width of panels is rarely noticeable from wall to wall. These incremental differences add up over the length of a wall, providing substantial flexibility.

When the wainscoting abuts a door or window casing, you must accommodate the difference in thickness between the wainscoting and the casing. I turn the cap molding down to run vertically along the casing. Miter the joint at the point where the top cap meets the casing. If you use this detail, be sure to allow for this ¾-in. thickness when laying out panels.

Openings for outlets and heat registers can occur either in the frame or panel area but should not bridge both. There's no best way to handle these situations. Sometimes it is better to modify your layout to accommodate these features. Other times, it is easier to move a receptacle an inch.

CONSTRUCTION

Once you are confident with your plan and you've got your materials in hand, begin construction. Rip and crosscut the frame parts to finished dimensions. If you have a corner that is out of plumb in your room, include a scribe of ¼ to ⅜ in. in addition to your layout dimension. Plane it as needed.

Lay out and cut the joining plate slots in the rails and stiles with the face sides against the bench to ensure uniform registration. Apply glue to the slots and plates and assemble the frame using bar clamps until the glue sets (See Photo A).

Cut the plywood to size so that each section will span as many panel openings as possible while centering end joints behind stiles. Be sure to orient the grain vertically. Even with paint-grade wood, the grain will tend to telegraph through the finish, and a vertical grain pattern is considered standard. Lay the frame face down on a padded worksurface to avoid marring the assembly and secure the plywood panel stock to the back using either 1-in. flathead screws or 1-in. brads **(See Photo B).**

Locate the seams in the plywood behind the stiles. If the plywood is a bit shorter than the frame height, keep it flush to the top edge of the frame to help support the cap molding. It's a good idea to sand the plywood and frame before you attach the panel molding **(See Photo C).** Miter the panel molding to length using a miter box, miter saw or table saw **(See Photo D).** Then install the pieces around each panel with 1-in. brads. If you are wainscoting a large room, consider buying or renting a pneumatic brad nailer to install the molding **(See Photo E).** These convenient tools drive and set the brads without predrilling, splitting or hammer dings. The joints will be tighter and you will save time.

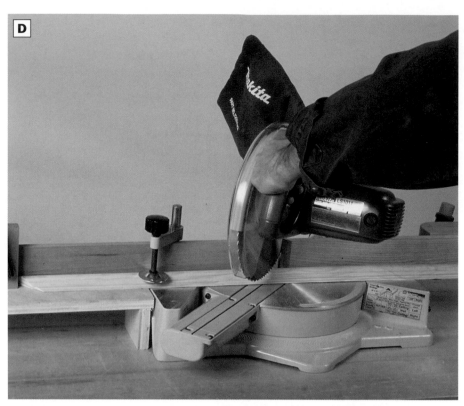

PHOTO D: Clamp a stopblock to your miter saw to ensure uniform sizes when completing mitering of panel moldings.

INSTALLATION

At this point, the wainscoting is ready for installation. The best results will come from fabricating the wainscoting for each wall in a single section. If a seam must be made, locate it at the center of a stile. Simply omit the joining plates in one of the adjoining rail ends and slide the parts together face down on the floor in front of their intended position. Join sections by driving screws or nails through the back of the panel into the common stile.

Bring a section of wainscoting to your site, in the predetermined order, and use 8d or 10d finish nails to fasten it through the wall and into the studs. Nail through the top and bottom rails. Scribe the ends of each wall section as needed in order to achieve tight corner joints. When all sections have been installed, install the cap (the back may have to be scribed to fit an irregular wall surface). Use a block plane to remove the excess stock, then use 8d finish nails to attach the cap.

Next, cut and install the cove molding under the cap. For best results, cope the inside corner joints and secure the sections with 4d finish nails. Finally, cut and install the base shoe molding along the floor. Be sure to set all nailheads before priming the wood, then fill the holes and apply the topcoat.

PHOTO E: Secure mitered moldings around each recessed panel with 1-in. brads. A pneumatic nailer speeds the work.

Quilt Rack

When the editors of *Handy* asked me to build a wooden display system that would enable quilters to display some of their creations as interchangeable wall hangings, there were several factors to consider. The design had to accommodate decorative quilts of different thicknesses. It needed to work without modifying or damaging the quilts. And it had to reflect the architectural detailing of the home (*Continued on page 66*).

Quilt Rack

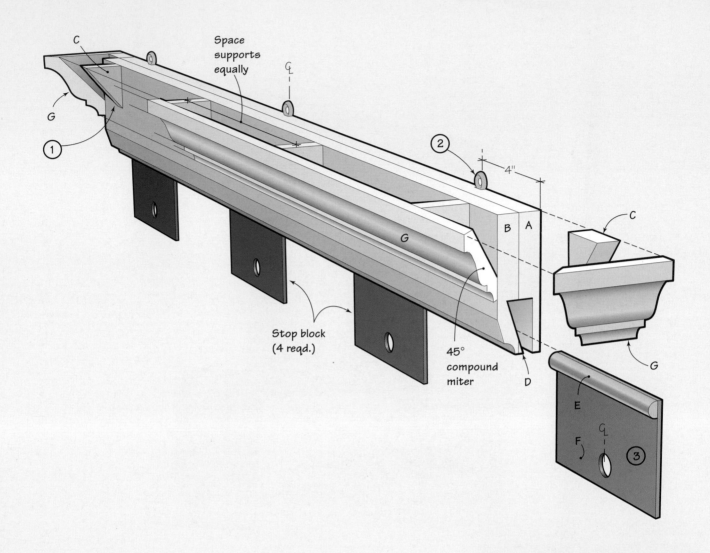

Space supports equally

Stop block (4 reqd.)

45° compound miter

Quilt Rack Cutting List				
Part/Description	**No.**	**Size**		**Material**
A	Hanger back	1	¾ × 4½ × 42 in.	Oak
B	Hanger front	1	¾ × 4½ × 42 in.	"
C	Crown support	5	¾ × 1¹¹⁄₁₆ × 2 in.	"
D	Hanger middle	1	¼ × ¾ × 42 in.	"
E	Stop stock	1	½ × 2 × 26 in.	"
F	Pull stock	1	⅛ × 3½ × 26 in.	Hardboard
G	Crown stock	1	¹¹⁄₁₆ × 3⁷⁄₁₆ × 72 in.	Oak

Shopping List

- ☐ 96-in. 1 × 6 red oak
- ☐ 72-in. ¹¹⁄₁₆ × 3⁷⁄₁₆-in. red oak crown molding
- ☐ ⅛ × 3½ × 26-in. tempered hardboard
- ☐ (3) Figure-8 fasteners
- ☐ Pneumatic brads
- ☐ Wood glue
- ☐ Color-matched wood putty
- ☐ Finishing materials

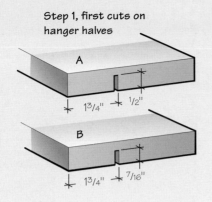

Step 1, first cuts on
hanger halves

A

1¾" ½"

B

1¾" 7/16"

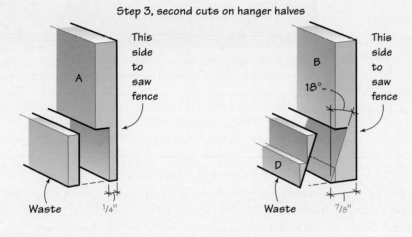

Step 2, glue D to B

B

D

Step 3, second cuts on hanger halves

A

This
side
to
saw
fence

Waste ¼"

B

18°

D

This
side
to
saw
fence

Waste 7/8"

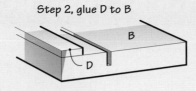

Top
1¹¹/₁₆"

50°

C

40°

2"

DETAIL 1

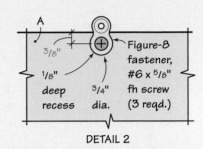

A

3/8"

1/8"
deep
recess

¾"
dia.

Figure-8
fastener,
#6 x 5/8"
fh screw
(3 reqd.)

DETAIL 2

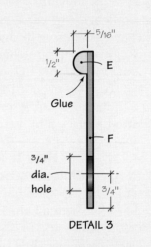

5/16"

½"

E

Glue

F

¾"
dia.
hole

¾"

DETAIL 3

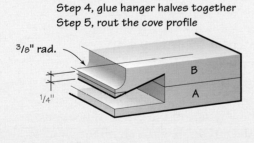

Step 4, glue hanger halves together
Step 5, rout the cove profile

3/8" rad.

¼"

B

A

Step 6, cut bevel on front
edge of B, then trim to
finished length of 41"

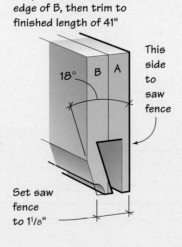

18°

B A

This
side
to
saw
fence

Set saw
fence
to 1⅛"

HANGER ASSEMBLY SEQUENCE

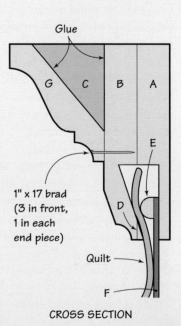

Glue

G C B A

E

1" x 17 brad
(3 in front,
1 in each
end piece)

D

Quilt

F

CROSS SECTION

Quilt Rack: Instructions

After some trial (and a little error), I came up with the slot-and-wedge design you see here and incorporated crown molding that mirrors the trim on nearby kitchen cabinets. The result is classic woodwork that complements any quilt without overpowering it.

As I quickly learned, there are no standard widths or thicknesses for homemade quilts. Since a quilting friend of mine has made several 39-in. creations, I made this hanger 41 in. long to support quilts of that size even if they stretch a bit. If you build a hanger for a different-sized quilt, just make the slotted portion 2 in. longer than the fabric.

How it works

With the stopblocks resting in the tapered slot, it takes only one person to hang a quilt. But honestly, it's a lot easier with a helper. Starting from an end, one person pushes the first stopblock to the top of the slot. Then the helper slips the fabric up into the slot in front of the block as high as it will go. When the first person pulls down on the block, the bullnosed profile pinches the fabric against the slot's tapered face (sometimes you have to wiggle the wedge to get it past the hem). Repeat the process with the other wedges. Then, once the quilt is secured, go back and adjust the fit to get it taut and level. The wedges should be spaced approximately 12 in. on-center.

Cutting sequence

With some woodworking projects, the sequence of cutting and fabrication doesn't matter much. This isn't one of them. There is more to this tapered-slot design than immediately meets the eye. For instance, the hanger is a glue-up of three (not just two) pieces of oak. And the bullnosed stops on the pulls are slightly wider than semicircles.

Because of these details, you need to cut and glue the pieces in the order shown in the technical art and

PHOTO A: After gluing the hanger middle to the hanger front, rip the 18° bevel in the built-up face with the blade tilted toward the fence.

photos or the tapered holding mechanism won't work properly. These features will make the difference between your quilts serving as attractive wall art or as forgotten throw rugs.

Although the finished hanger is 41 in. long, you'll notice that pieces A, B and D measure 42 in. in the cutting list. With the multi-step cutting, gluing and shaping that are required to make the hanger, I prefer to trim the ends after assembly. This method ensures that all the pieces will be flush. More importantly, if a little tearout results from sawing or routing it will get cut off in the end, maintaining a refined appearance in the finished project.

Cut the hanger slot and assemble the hanger front and back by following steps 1 through 3 in the technical drawing **(See Photos A & B).**

Note that you rip the angled face of part B with the fence mounted in the direction the blade tilts. If your blade only tilts to the left, the fence should be mounted to the left side of the blade. If your saw cannot perform the cut as shown, you might want to clamp a tall L-shaped fence to your saw table. If you do, make sure it is extremely stable and perfectly parallel to the blade. You also could consider a different cutting and fabrication scheme. Exercise extreme caution if you deviate from my plan.

Once the hanger assembly is fabricated, shaped and trimmed to length, bore ⅛-in.-deep, ¾-in.-dia. holes in the back to accept the figure-8 (desktop) fasteners **(See Photo C).**

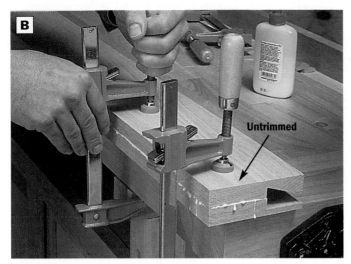

PHOTO B: Glue and clamp the hanger front and back together before you trim the ends.

PHOTO C: Counterbore the back and trim each recess with a chisel for the figure-8 fasteners.

MAKING THE STOPS

I experimented with a few stop designs before settling on the simple solution you see here. The most important principle that guided me was the need for a narrow pinch point to hold the heavy fabric. It would have been easier to maneuver fabric past a continuous, wedge-shaped stop than this somewhat finicky bullnosed rib, but the quilt would have slipped out of the slot with the least encouragement if the pressure were distributed over a broader area.

Since the block doesn't show once the quilt is installed, I used hardboard for the pulls. You might be tempted to simply rip a dowel for the half-round stops, but this is not advisable. Instead of attempting this unstable and potentially dangerous operation, I routed a ¼-in. radius on a piece of ½-in.-thick stock **(See Photo G)** and ripped the ⁵⁄₁₆-in. strip from the board **(See Photo H).** Set the wide part of the board between the fence and the blade so the narrow strip falls away from the blade when you complete the cut. The substantial width of the board allows you to push it through cleanly with a push stick rather than dangerously forcing through a narrow dowel rod. *TIP: It's faster and easier to fabricate one long stopblock and crosscut it into 6-in.-long sections than it is to cut the parts and assemble them individually.* To avoid tearout when boring the ¾-in.-dia. finger holes in the hardboard, complete the cuts from the back side.

CROWN MOLDING CAUTIONS

Lay out the shapes of the crown molding supports (See *Detail 1,* page 65) on a workpiece that's ¾ × 2 × 16 in., then cut them with a band saw or a jig saw **(See Photo D).** The waste pieces and the keepers look similar, so it's a good idea to mark the cutoffs

with X's so you don't mix them up. (If you cut them on a table saw, be careful. The small pieces can get thrown by the blade when you complete the cuts.)

Glue the supports to the hanger, temporarily securing them with strips of masking tape. Remember, the triangular supports are not symmetrical. There are two wrong orientations and only one right one.

Because the crown molding is the quilt hanger's most prominent feature, the joints should fit tightly and the profiles should align perfectly. You can measure all of the pieces and cut them precisely, but it actually is easier and more accurate to start with a compound miter cut on one end of a piece of molding stock and mark the cut for the other end using the hanger itself as a guide. You'll save material if you cut the returns (end pieces) first, followed by the middle piece. That way, you'll also avoid the dangerous task of recutting short pieces.

Photo E shows one way to make a compound

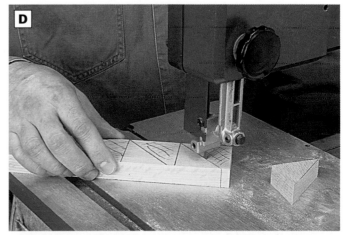

PHOTO D: Color in the waste areas to avoid confusion when cutting the crown supports.

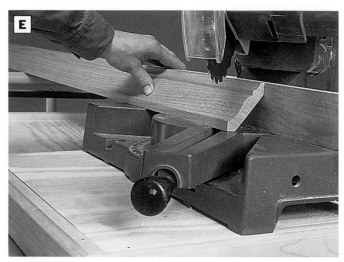

PHOTO E: Position the stock upside down and set the blade at 45° when cutting the crown molding on a power miter saw.

PHOTO F: Install the crown with brads and draw the joints together with tape before the glue dries.

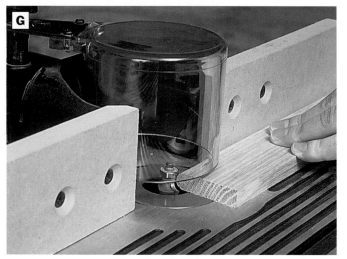

PHOTO G: Cut a bullnose profile in one edge of a piece of ½-in.-thick stock for the stopblock.

PHOTO H: Rip a 5⁄16-in. strip from the bullnosed edge and glue the trim pipe to the pull stock.

miter cut on a power miter saw (the same cut can be made using a manual miter box). The table saw provides another option for cutting miters. You can make the necessary cuts by cranking the saw's bevel gauge to 33° and pivoting its miter gauge to 63°. If you use the table saw technique, be sure to double-check your angles with a protractor and a T-bevel, as the saw's gauges can become skewed from repeated use. It's also a good idea to experiment with a piece of scrap before committing the good molding.

To make their joints as discreet as possible, the crown pieces are secured with glue and brads. It can be awkward fastening angled pieces with a traditional hammer and nails. A pneumatic brad nailer makes this task a lot easier. The best technique is to rest the hanger on its back. Apply a bead of glue along the base of the molding and the faces of the triangular crown supports and position the molding.

Predrill through the molding and into the hanger. This will reduce the risk of splitting the narrow molding and make sure that it's securely fastened to the hanger (even a powerful tool like the pneumatic nailer has a difficult time driving through hardwoods such as oak). Then install the brads, countersinking them with a nailset. Tape the tops of the crown joints together to keep them tight while the glue dries. Cross-nailing isn't necessary.

After sanding the piece, I finished the outside surfaces with oil stain and polyurethane.

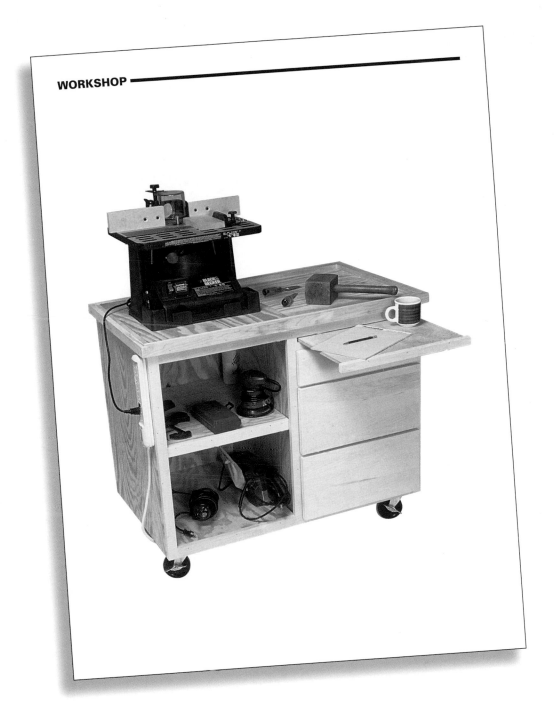

Tool Cart

With more and more woodworking tools competing for space in garage and basement workshops, versatility and mobility have become more important than ever. If your shop space is limited and you have several benchtop tools, this cart is the perfect accessory. Store it out of the way and wheel it to the center of the space as a tool stand, an assembly table or a workbench. The drawer stack is great for storing the small hand tools, wrenches and bits you use most. And the open shelves are just right for portable sanders, jigs and routers (*Continued on page 72*).

Tool Cart

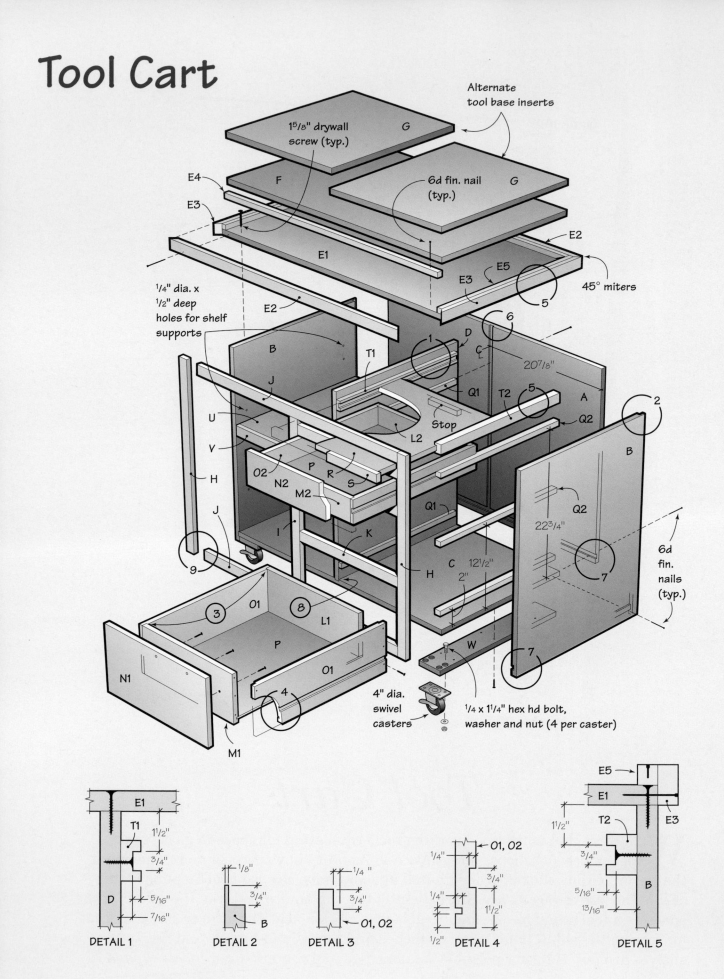

Alternate tool base inserts

1⁵/₈" drywall screw (typ.)

6d fin. nail (typ.)

45° miters

¼" dia. x ½" deep holes for shelf supports

20⁷/₈"

Stop

22³/₄"

6d fin. nails (typ.)

12½"

2"

4" dia. swivel casters

¼ x 1¼" hex hd bolt, washer and nut (4 per caster)

DETAIL 1

E1
T1
1½"
3/4"
D
5/16"
7/16"

DETAIL 2

1/8"
3/4"
B

DETAIL 3

1/4"
3/4"
O1, O2

DETAIL 4

O1, O2
1/4"
3/4"
1/4"
1½"
1/2"

DETAIL 5

E5
E1
T2
E3
1½"
3/4"
5/16"
13/16"
B

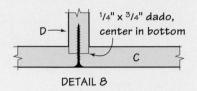

1/4" $\mathcal{C}$ A

3/4"

DETAIL 6

A, B

3/4" 1/4"

3/4"

DETAIL 7

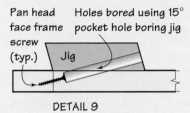

D → 1/4" x 3/4" dado, center in bottom

C

DETAIL 8

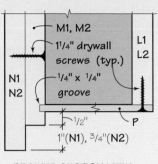

M1, M2

1 1/4" drywall screws (typ.)

L1
L2

1/4" x 1/4" groove

N1
N2

1/2"

1"(N1), 3/4"(N2)

P

DRAWER SECTION VIEW

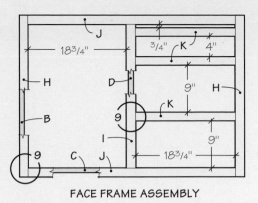

J

18 3/4"

3/4" K 4"

H

D

9" H

K

B

9

9"

9

I

C J

18 3/4"

FACE FRAME ASSEMBLY

Pan head face frame screw (typ.)

Holes bored using 15° pocket hole boring jig

Jig

DETAIL 9

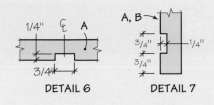

Shopping List

- ☐ (4) 4-in. locking casters
- ☐ (3) 8-ft. 1 × 8 clear aspen
- ☐ (8) 8-ft. 1 × 2 clear aspen
- ☐ (1) 6-ft. 1 × 12 clear aspen
- ☐ (3) 3/4-in. 4 × 8 BC plywood
- ☐ (1) 1/4-in. 4 × 8 lauan plywood
- ☐ (1) 5/8-in. 2 × 2 birch fibercore
- ☐ (16) 1/4 × 1 1/4-in. hex bolts
- ☐ (16) 1/4-in. hex nuts
- ☐ (16) 1/4-in. flat washers
- ☐ (4) Shelf pins
- ☐ (1) Power strip

Tool Cart Cutting List

Part	Description	No.	Size	Material
A	Back	1	3/4 × 30 1/4 × 41 3/4 in.	Plywood
B	Side	2	3/4 × 23 7/8 × 30 1/4 in.	"
C	Bottom	1	3/4 × 23 3/8 × 41 in.	"
D	Divider	1	3/4 × 23 3/8 × 29 in.	"
E1	Top	1	3/4 × 24 5/8 × 42 in.	"
E2	Top edge (long)	2	3/4 × 1 1/2 × 43 1/2 in.	Aspen
E3	Top edge (short)	2	3/4 × 1 1/2 × 26 1/8 in.	"
E4	Top cleat (long)	2	3/4 × 3/4 × 40 1/2 in.	"
E5	Top cleat (short)	2	3/4 × 3/4 × 25 5/8 in.	"
F	Top insert	1	3/4 × 23 3/4 × 41 1/8 in.	Plywood
G	Tool base	*	3/4 × 20 1/2 × 23 3/4 in.	"
H	Stile (left/right)	2	3/4 × 1 1/2 × 30 1/4 in.	Aspen
I	Stile (center)	1	3/4 × 1 1/2 × 27 1/4 in.	"
J	Rail (top/bottom)	2	3/4 × 1 1/2 × 39 in.	"
K	Rail (middle)	3	3/4 × 1 1/2 × 18 3/4 in.	"
L1	Drawer back (large)	2	3/4 × 6 1/2 × 17 1/2 in.	"
L2	Drawer back (small)	1	3/4 × 2 3/4 × 17 1/2 in.	"
M1	Drawer front (large)	2	3/4 × 7 1/4 × 17 1/2 in.	"
M2	Drawer front (small)	1	3/4 × 3 1/2 × 17 1/2 in.	"
N1	Drawer face (large)	2	3/4 × 10 × 19 3/4 in.	"
N2	Drawer face (small)	1	3/4 × 5 × 19 3/4 in.	"
O1	Drawer side (large)	4	3/4 × 7 1/4 × 23 in.	"
O2	Drawer side (small)	2	3/4 × 3 1/2 × 23 in.	"
P	Drawer bottom	3	1/4 × 17 1/2 × 22 1/2 in.	Lauan
Q1	Drawer slide (left)	3	3/4 × 9/16 × 23 in.	Aspen
Q2	Drawer slide (right)	3	3/4 × 15/16 × 23 in.	"
R	Pullout	1	5/8 × 18 5/8 × 22 1/2 in.	Birch
S	Pullout face	1	3/4 × 1 1/8 × 19 3/4 in.	Aspen
T1	Pullout slide (left)	1	3/4 × 1 1/2 × 23 in.	"
T2	Pullout slide (right)	1	1 1/8 × 1 1/2 × 23 in.	"
U	Shelf	1	3/4 × 19 3/4 × 22 in.	Plywood
V	Shelf face	1	3/4 × 1 1/2 × 19 3/4 in.	Aspen
W	Caster plate	2	3/4 × 4 × 23 1/8 in.	Plywood

*One plus one blank per benchtop tool.

I bolted all of my benchtop power tools to ¾-in. plywood panels that slip into the recessed top of the cart. They stack in a simple slotted rack when they're not in use and drop into position as needed. I also fitted the cart with the best locking swivel casters I could find so I could move it around effortlessly. The power strip contains two outlets that are always on and five more that are activated by a switch. That's very useful because I like to connect my band saw, shaper and miter saw to a utility vac to control dust. With the switched and unswitched outlets handy, it's easy to turn the vac on or off as needed.

This is an ordinary tool cart, but building it will give you a chance to practice some key cabinetmaking techniques, such as producing invisible butt joints in plywood, assembling a face frame with hidden screws and building overlay drawers with hardwood slides.

I made the panels out of ¾-in. BC plywood, the drawer bottoms out of ¼-in. lauan, and the pullout out of ⅝-in. fibercore plywood. The face frame, drawers, slides and top trim are solid aspen. Aspen is a lot cheaper than other hardwoods and a joy to work with because of its fine, straight grain. I designed this cart to stand just over 3 ft. tall because I'm 6 ft. 2 in. If you are considerably shorter, you may want to trim the vertical dimensions and simply eliminate one of the drawers.

SAW FIRST, THEN DADO

Begin by cutting all your parts to size. That includes both the plywood panels and the solid wood components. Then, install a dado head in your table saw. I'd tell you to set your dado head to ¾ in. wide, but my lumberyard's ¾-in. BC plywood was ¹⁄₁₆ in. skinnier, so check your stock and set your blade accordingly. All of the dadoes are ¼ in. deep unless otherwise specified. The first dado runs vertically up the center of the back panel. Plough it out on the side that faces the inside of the cabinet so it will receive

PHOTO A: For invisible butt joints, set the dado cutter height so it cuts one ply or ⅛ in. shy of the side panel's thickness.

the vertical divider. Recess the next dado ¾ in. from the bottom edge to accept the bottom panel. While your fence is set for the proper recess, dado the bottoms of the side panels too. Finally, dado the middle of the bottom panel for the center divider.

Before you remove the dado head from your saw, use it to create invisible butt joints where the side panels will meet the back **(See Photo A).** Set the height of the dado blade so it is ⅛ in. shy of the panel thickness. Then, set the fence so that the width of the cut is the same as your stock's thickness.

Run both side panels through the saw with the back edges against the fence and the finished side of the plywood facing up. This will remove all but the outside ply. When you assemble the carcase, this remaining ply will cover the edges of the back panel.

ASSEMBLY

To assemble the carcase, begin by joining the sides to the bottom with glue and 6d finish nails. Next, lay the assembly face down and attach the back the same way. Nail through the back into the side and bottom panels, then return the cabinet to an upright position. Clamp the thin side plies to the back panel

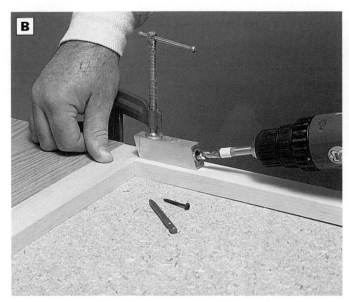

PHOTO B: A jig and special pocket screw bit ensure perfect pocket hole alignment for assembling the face frame with concealed screws.

PHOTO C: Use scrap blocks to position drawer slides for gluing and screwing. Finish with the bottom slides.

edges to ensure a tight fit. Next, glue and secure the divider, using 1⅝-in. drywall screws in the bottom and 6d finish nails in the back.

While the glue sets, begin to assemble the face frame rails and stiles **(See Photo B).** You could join the sections with biscuits or dowels but, like most cabinet shops, I used hidden pocket screws. Pocket screws are screws that are driven into the workpieces at a 15° angle from the back sides. This is easy with the aid of a simple metal alignment jig. It guides a unique stepped bit that both counterbores and creates a pilot hole for the screw. To use this method, lay all the face frame elements in their correct positions but facing down on your bench. Drill the holes, apply the glue, screw everything together and sand the joints flush. Then attach the face frame with glue and nails.

ALL-WOOD DRAWERS

With the drawer parts cut to size, mill ¾-in.-wide grooves in the aspen side pieces 1½ in. up from the bottom to accept the drawer slides you attach to the carcase. Then reset your dado head to ¼ in. wide and run the channels for the drawer bottoms ½ in. up from the bottom on the sides and the fronts. If you don't plan to install drawer pulls, rout finger holes into the bottoms of the drawer faces before screwing them to the drawer fronts. Use glue and screws to attach the sides to the ends. But slide the drawer bottoms into their grooves before the glue dries and check each drawer for squareness by measuring across its diagonals.

The aspen drawer slides should be almost ⅛ in.

smaller than the grooves in the drawer sides to allow for expansion and contraction. For safety, cut them from larger stock rather than attempting to trim smaller pieces.

I used scraps of wood cut to the right height (2 in. for the bottom drawer, 12½ in. for the middle one, and 22¾ in. for the top drawer) to align the drawer slides. Then I predrilled, glued and screwed them in place **(See Photo C).** Before you install the drawers, glue and screw the pullout shelf guides into the carcase, then slide it into the slots. Screw a piece of ¾-in. scrap to the bottom of the board so that it won't pop out. You might want to install a second stop a few inches from the end so the surface doesn't sag when fully extended. Wax the drawers and slides with ordinary paraffin wax so they slide smoothly. Once the pullout shelf and its stop are installed, you can install the top with screws and glue.

To make the shelf, merely trim the sides of a plywood panel with strips of aspen. It rests on adjustable shelf pins installed in holes drilled in the cabinet walls. All four sets of holes must be aligned horizontally or the shelf will rock when installed. This is accomplished with an indexed template made from scrap plywood **(See Photo D).** Hold the guide snug to the back and then the face frame. Be sure to use a stop on your drill bit to avoid drilling through the sides of the cabinet.

Complete construction by trimming the top with reinforced aspen edging. Begin by installing ¾ × ¾-in. cleats around the top. Then install 1½-in. aspen edge banding around the plywood and the cleats. Miter the edges so all end grain is concealed. The double-

PHOTO D: This homemade jig ensures uniform drilling for the adjustable shelf pins. Use a depth stop to make sure you don't drill through the sides of the cabinet.

PHOTO E: Bolt the casters to plywood plates and then glue and screw the plates to the recessed cart bottom.

wide lip will be useful for clamping if you use the cart as an assembly table.

I chose four large (4-in.) locking swivel casters so they would roll easily over the garage floor and I would have room to slip my foot under the cart to engage them. I bolted them to ¾-in. plywood plates, with counterbores for the bolt heads, and then screwed the plates to the recess in the cart bottom (**See Photo E**).

I love the convenience of the interchangeable half-width plywood tool bases. Sometimes I drop two tools into the cart top. Other times, I inset just one and a blank. When using the cart as an assembly table, I use the recessed top and raised rim for clamping. The standard-sized bases not only ensure that each tool is stable when in use; they also enable me to stack them on a simple cleated "power tower" rack for compact storage. In this shop, compact is always good.

Computer Desk

There's no shortage of affordable, ready-to-assemble workstations for home computers and printers. But finding one that will survive seasonal trips to school or daily abuse within a home office is a different matter. Heavy but weak particleboard composition, flimsy hardware and small dowels are the norm. Once assembled, they don't come apart easily, unless, of course, you try to move them. Here's a design that fits the bill; combining structural soundness and easy portability in one spacious unit.

Computer Desk

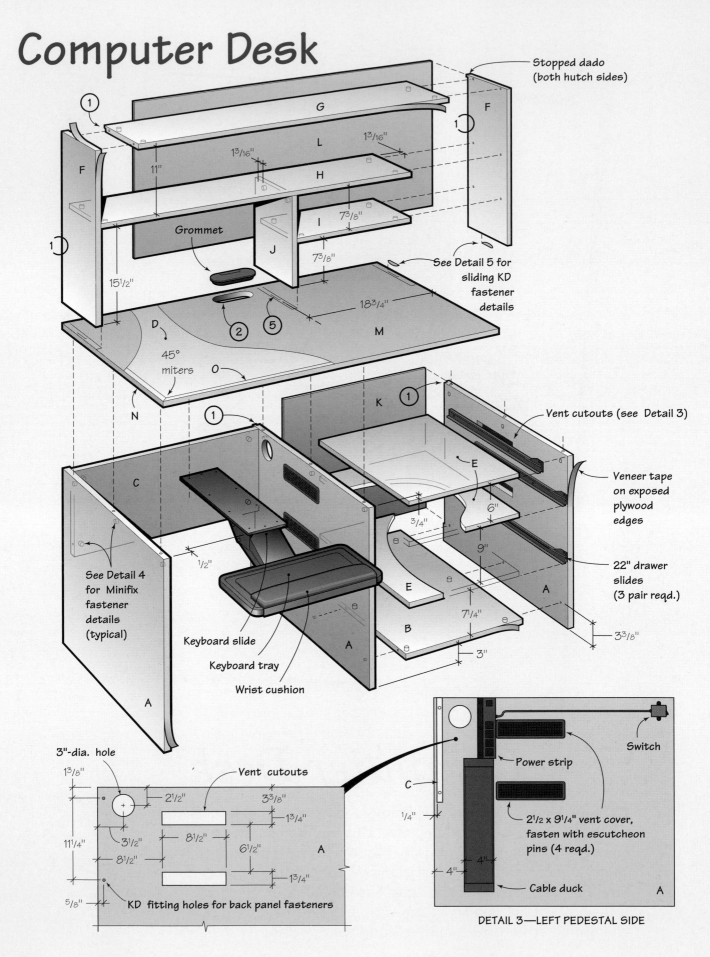

Stopped dado (both hutch sides)

G

F

F

1

1

L

$1^3/16$"

$1^3/16$"

H

11"

I

$7^3/8$"

Grommet

J

$7^3/8$"

See Detail 5 for sliding KD fastener details

$15^1/2$"

2

5

$18^3/4$"

M

D

45° miters

O

N

K

1

Vent cutouts (see Detail 3)

C

E

Veneer tape on exposed plywood edges

See Detail 4 for Minifix fastener details (typical)

$1/2$"

$3/4$"

6"

9"

22" drawer slides (3 pair reqd.)

Keyboard slide

Keyboard tray

Wrist cushion

E

A

B

$7^1/4$"

3"

A

$3^3/8$"

A

3"-dia. hole

$1^3/8$"

Vent cutouts

$2^1/2$"

$3^3/8$"

$1^3/4$"

$3^1/2$"

$8^1/2$"

$6^1/2$"

$11^1/4$"

$8^1/2$"

A

$1^3/4$"

$5/8$"

KD fitting holes for back panel fasteners

C

$1/4$"

Switch

Power strip

$2^1/2$ x $9^1/4$" vent cover, fasten with escutcheon pins (4 reqd.)

4"

4"

Cable duck

A

DETAIL 3—LEFT PEDESTAL SIDE

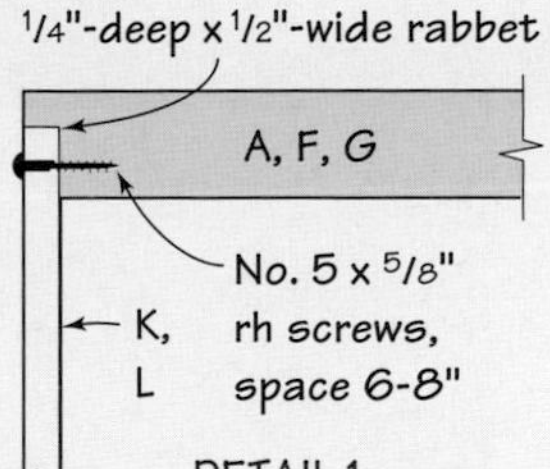
1/4"-deep x 1/2"-wide rabbet
A, F, G
No. 5 x 5/8"
rh screws,
space 6-8"
K,
L
DETAIL 1

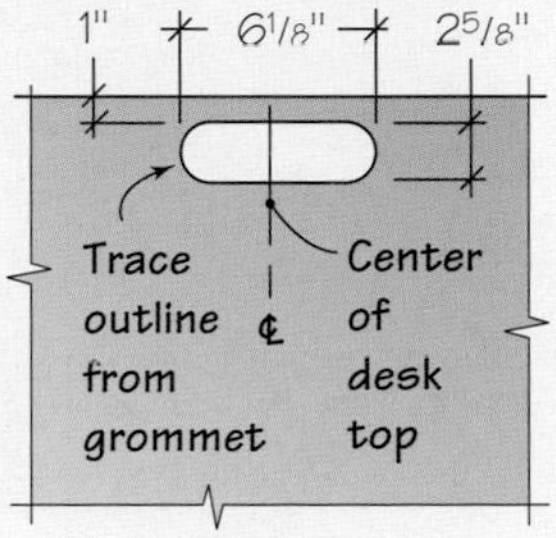
1"
6 1/8"
2 5/8"
Trace
outline
from
grommet
℄
Center
of
desk
top
DETAIL 2

Computer Desk Cutting List				
Part/Description		**No.**	**Size**	**Material**
A	Desk side	3	¾ × 28¼ × 30-in.	Oak ply
B	Desk bottom	1	¾ × 18 × 29¾-in.	"
C	Desk back	1	¾ × 14 × 27-⅞-in.	"
D	Desktop	1	¾ × 29¼ × 46½-in.	Birch ply
E	Desk shelf	3	¾ × 17 × 22-in.	Oak ply
F	Hutch sides	2	¾ × 10½ × 28-in.	"
G	Hutch top	1	¾ × 10½ × 46½-in.	"
H	Hutch shelf (long)	1	¾ × 10¼ × 46½-in.	"
I	Hutch shelf (short)	1	¾ × 10¼ × 18-in.	"
J	Hutch divider	1	¾ × 10¼ × 15½-in.	"
K	Rack back	1	¼ × 17½ × 25¼-in.	"
L	Hutch back	1	¼ × 27¾ × 47½-in.	"
M	Laminate (rough)	1	31½ × 49½-in.	
N	Edge-band (side)	2	¾ × ¾ × 30-in.	Red oak
O	Edge-band (front)	1	¾ × ¾ × 48-in.	"

Also required: (3) Slide-fitting biscuit connectors, (33) Minifix fittings, (4) vents, 13⁄16-in. red oak edge tape, grommet, (3 pairs) drawer slides, keyboard slide, keyboard tray, wrist rest, power strip, cable duck, #5 ⅝-in. roundhead wood screws, water-based contact cement, finishing materials.

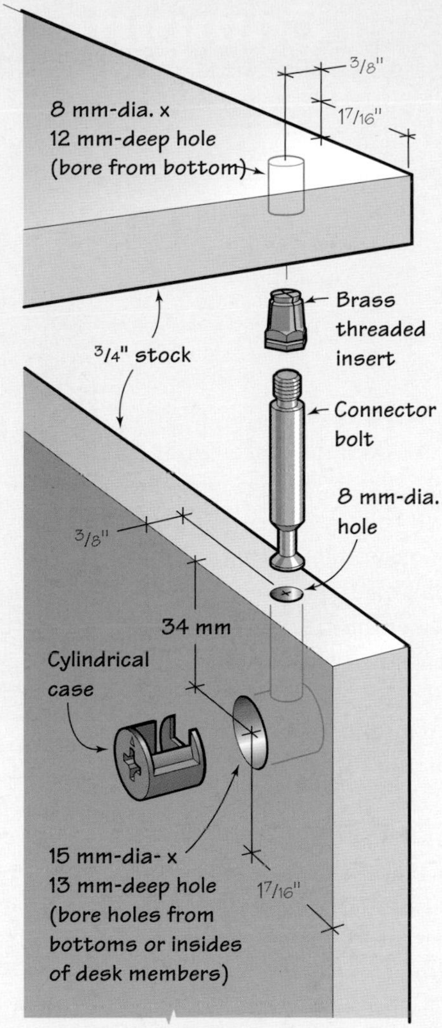
3/8"
17/16"
8 mm-dia. x
12 mm-deep hole
(bore from bottom)
Brass
threaded
insert
3/4" stock
Connector
bolt
8 mm-dia.
hole
3/8"
34 mm
Cylindrical
case
15 mm-dia- x
13 mm-deep hole
(bore holes from
bottoms or insides
of desk members)
17/16"
DETAIL 4—MINIFIX FASTENERS

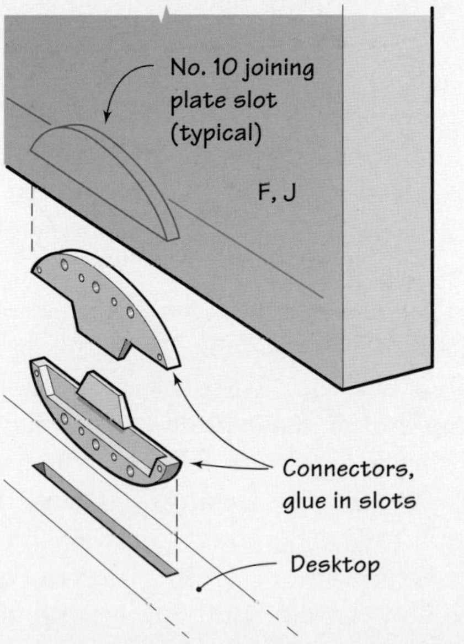
No. 10 joining
plate slot
(typical)
F, J
Connectors,
glue in slots
Desktop
DETAIL 5—SLIDING KD FASTENERS

The Club asked me to design a computer workstation that would overcome all the typical problems of ready-to-assemble workstations. It had to be able to survive repeated assembly and disassembly so it could be transported easily. It also had to be functional and durable while in use. Fortunately, you don't have to be a master woodworker to build an attractive, strong computer desk that really works. Just use quality materials and verify that your equipment will fit the openings before you install the shelves.

I specified lumber core red oak plywood, rather than veneer core plywood or particleboard, for its warp resistance and strength. I also finished the top with plastic laminate to provide a scratch-resistant, easy-to-clean surface that would survive sweaty drink glasses and hard-bearing ballpoint pens. I selected two types of knock-down fasteners to join the components. The hutch unit is secured to the base with interlocking slide fittings that resemble joining plates (biscuits). The desktop, sides and hutch, meanwhile, use Minifix-brand fasteners. They rely on threaded inserts, locking bolts and cam-type disks that resemble cross dowels.

The base unit contains pull-out shelves that support a sideboard, a CPU and a printer. The key-

PHOTO A: Trim the edge-banding tape with a sharp chisel and diagonal strokes. Change direction if the tape begins to tear.

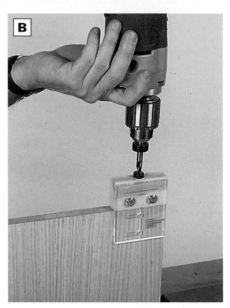

PHOTO B: The Minifix jig clamps to the work-piece as a guide for precisely aligned holes for knock-down fasteners.

board retracts under the desktop on a separate tray. A power strip provides convenient, surge-protected electrical receptacles, as well as a jack for a telephone or a modem. And a cable manager keeps the various cords and wires neat and secure.

PANEL CUTTING TIPS

Begin by cutting the various panels. First, cut the 4 × 8 plywood sheets into manageable pieces using a circular saw and a straightedge. Then make the finished cuts on a table saw. For the best results, use a combination blade and keep the finished sides of the pieces facing up.

To finish the exposed edges of the panels, cut strips of veneer edge tape about 1 in. longer than each edge. Clamp each panel in a vise, center the tape over the edge and use a household iron (set to high temperature/no steam) to melt the adhesive. While the tape

is still hot, press it down firmly with a veneer roller or a softwood block. Then, use a sharp chisel to trim the overhanging tape flush with the panel faces and the ends **(See Photo A).**

INSTALLING KD FASTENERS

The desk and hutch joints are made with Minifix knock-down (KD) fasteners. They consist of a cylindrical case that rotates to accept a connecting bolt attached to the mating piece. The special Minifix jig speeds marking.

To begin, mark centerlines for the fasteners on the workpieces and clamp the jig in place. Mark the locations for the 15mm holes with a center punch, then bore an 8mm hole in the panel edge using the jig as a guide **(See Photo B).** Repeat this process for each fastener location, then bore the 15mm holes, preferably on a drill press, aligning the centerline with a matching index line on the fence of

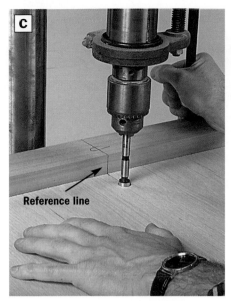

PHOTO C: A reference line on the drill press fence makes it easy to bore accurate 15mm holes for the Minifix cylinders.

PHOTO D: Drive the inserts flush with the panel surface, then thread a connector bolt into each insert.

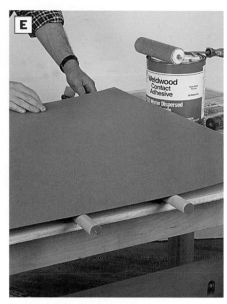

PHOTO E: Position the laminate over the base surface and remove the dowels one at a time to ensure proper alignment.

the drill press **(See Photo C).** Use a depth stop on your bit and be careful to bore perpendicular to the surface where you can't use the jig.

Install the brass inserts in the 8mm holes with a hammer **(See Photo D),** then lock them in place with a connector bolt. Temporarily remove the bolts.

Use a router and an edge guide to cut ¼ × ½-in. rabbets to accept the backs of the base unit and the hutch. Note that the rabbets in the hutch sides end ¼ in. short of the top edge. So stop your router at the ¼-in. mark and square the ends with a sharp chisel.

MAKING THE DESKTOP

For durability, the desktop is edged in solid oak and covered with plastic laminate. To fabricate the substrate, cut the less costly birch plywood to size. Glue and clamp the mitered ¾-in.-thick edges to the panel so they are flush with the top.

Cut the plastic laminate sheet so that it overhangs the desktop by ¾ in. on all sides. Cut the laminate with a jig saw, supporting the sheet on both sides of the cut

to avoid cracking.

Remove all dust from the laminate and desktop and apply contact cement to both surfaces. Let the cement dry until it no longer "pulls" when you touch it. As the name implies, contact cement bonds on contact, so you only get one chance to position the laminate. I place dowels on the surface about 10 in. apart and lay the laminate over them so it overlaps the edges uniformly **(See Photo E).** Then remove one dowel at a time, beginning at an end. Seat the laminate using a 3-in. "J" roller or a rolling pin. Trim the laminate flush with the edges using a router fitted with a flush-trimming bit. Then ease the sharp edges with a mill file, working from the top down to avoid chipping the surface.

INSTALLING THE HARDWARE

Place the desktop upside down on a padded surface to mark and drill the holes for connector bolts on the bottom side. First install the inserts, then remove the connector bolts.

While the top is inverted, drill

pilot holes for the keyboard slides. Mount the track, but leave the keyboard carriage off. Then, turn the top over and cut the opening for the cable grommet with a jig saw **(See Photo F).**

Computer equipment needs ventilation to avoid overheating. I installed a pair of vents in the sides of the equipment tower **(See Photo G).** You will need to cut an access hole in the tower's inner side for cables to pass through. Determine the optimum spacing between the shelves in the equipment tower for your components.

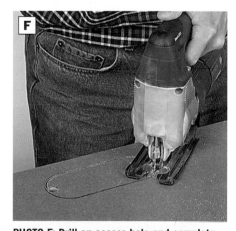

PHOTO F: Drill an access hole and complete the cutout for the grommet using a jig saw with tape on the bottom of the shoe.

PHOTO G: Attach the vents to the side panels (or to the back) using the decorative brass escutcheon pins.

PHOTO H: Install the cable manager with screws rather than adhesive so it can be removed.

PHOTO I: Use the special alignment tool to orient the slide-fitting biscuit connector before the glue dries.

PHOTO J: Fasten the backs to all shelves and uprights at 4- to 6-in. intervals to stiffen the assemblies.

Drill pilot holes and install the shelf tracks. Then, attach the guide rollers to the edge-banded shelving. Fasten the surge protector strip and cable manager to the left of the tower **(See Photo H)**. The hutch unit is held to the desktop with slide-fitting biscuit connectors that fit into joining plate slots. Lay out the slot locations in both the desktop and bottom of the hutch using the special alignment tool **(See Photo I)**. Cut the slots with a plate (biscuit) joiner and install the fasteners with carpenter's wood glue.

ASSEMBLY SEQUENCE

To begin assembly, replace the connector bolts and press the Minifix cylinders into their 15mm holes. Join the equipment tower bottom to the two sides by inserting the connector bolts into the holes until the casing can engage by turning the Phillips head cam. Join the desktop to the equipment tower and the left

side, then assemble the hutch components. Place the hutch assembly on the desktop and engage the slide fasteners. If the fit is snug, use a mallet and a block to better align the parts.

Next cut the ¼-in. plywood to size for the back panels and predrill it for the ¾-in. mounting screws that will fasten to the fixed shelves and uprights **(See Photo J).** Position the pull-out shelves in the equipment tower. Mount the keyboard tray on the carriage using the pilot holes on the underside of the tray. Slide the carriage onto the track and install the stop bumper and wrist support. Once you determine that the pieces fit, disassemble them and finish each one separately.

Mantel

Just because a fireplace is made of metal and burns natural gas doesn't mean it can't make great use of wood. Nothing gives a modern home a more traditional look than a custom wood mantel. This sleek design handsomely frames any fire, while its moderately wide top provides ample space to display a few of your household treasures.

Mantel

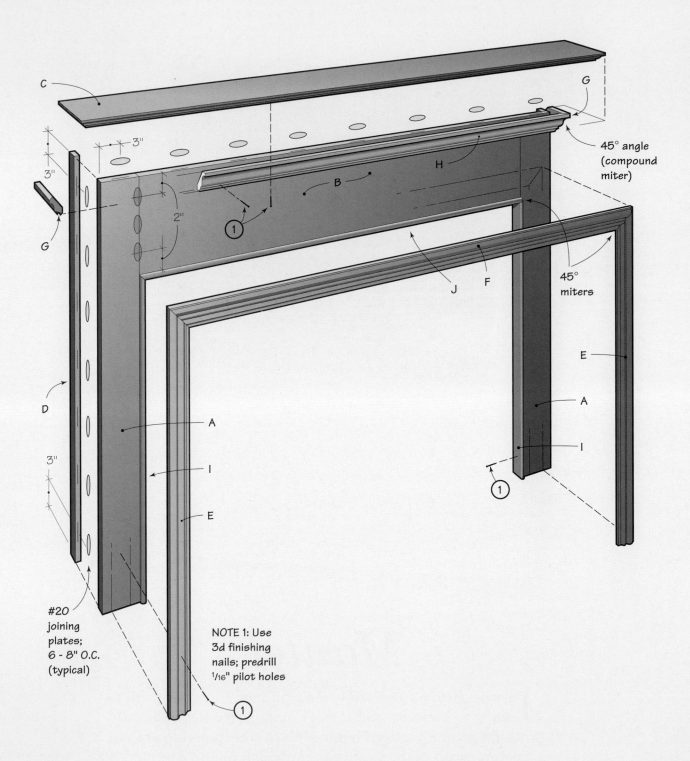

C

G

3"

3"

G

2"

1

B

H

45° angle
(compound
miter)

J

F

45°
miters

E

D

A

A

3"

I

E

I

E

#20
joining
plates;
6 - 8" O.C.
(typical)

NOTE 1: Use
3d finishing
nails; predrill
¹/₁₆" pilot holes

1

1

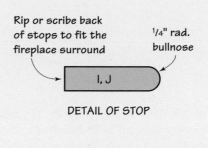

Rip or scribe back
of stops to fit the
fireplace surround

¹/₄" rad.
bullnose

I, J

DETAIL OF STOP

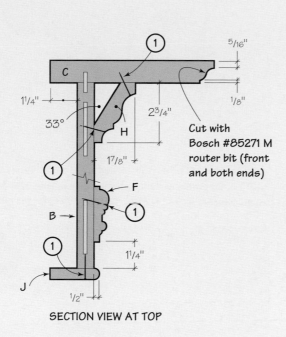

5/16"

C

1

1/8"

1¹/₄"

2³/₄"

33°

H

Cut with
Bosch #85271 M
router bit (front
and both ends)

1

1⁷/₈"

F

B →

1

1

1¹/₄"

J →

1/2"

SECTION VIEW AT TOP

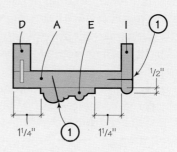

D   A   E   I   1

1/2"

1¹/₄"   1   1¹/₄"

SECTION VIEW AT SIDE

Mantel Cutting List

Part/Description	No.	Size	Material
A Upright	2	¾ × 5 × 52¼ in.	Red oak
B Top rail		¾ × 11¾ × 61 in.	"
C Mantel top		1 × 7½ × 69 in.	"
D Side return	2	¾ × 1¼ × 52¼ in.	"
E Face molding (upright)	2	1¹/₁₆ × 2½ × 44¼ in.	"
F Face molding (top)		1¹/₁₆ × 2½ × 58½ in.	"
G Crown molding (return)	2	2¾ × 3¼ × 12 in.	"
H Crown molding (face)		2¾ × 3¼ × to fit	"
I Stop (upright)	2	½ × 2 × 50 in.	"
J Stop (top rail)		½ × 2 × 40½ in.	"

Also required: 3d finish nails, glue, #20 biscuits, finishing materials.

PHOTO A: Clamp the workpiece to your bench, good side down, and use a plate joiner to make the football-shaped slots for the biscuits.

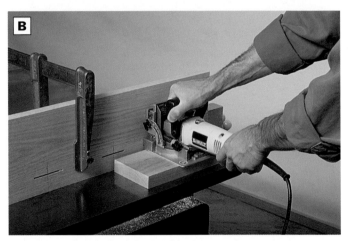

PHOTO B: A 1¼-in. spacer block ensures the proper offset when cutting the plate slots along the bottom side of the mantel top.

Since this is intended to be a custom project, the size of the interior space and the height of the projecting mantel are easily modified to meet your needs. Check your local building department and the installation instructions that came with your fireplace unit to ensure you provide sufficient clearance to combustibles. The area between the firebox and the wood should be surfaced with a material that won't burn, such as brass, marble, stone, brick or tile. Most manufactured fireplaces can be ordered with three-piece brass or marble surrounds to further simplify installation.

I built my fireplace surround from solid red oak boards and moldings. I was fortunate to have a board wide enough to make the broad top rail from a single piece of lumber. If you can only find narrow stock, it is a simple matter to glue up two or more boards to make up the required width. You also could substitute a piece of ¾-in. plywood.

CUT & SHAPE THE PARTS

Start by ripping and then crosscutting the stock for the uprights and top rail to finished size. Also, rip a board to approximately 5 in. wide and crosscut it to the same length as the uprights. Later, you will rip this piece again to form the two side returns.

Lay out the locations of the joining (biscuit) plate slots where the top rail and the two uprights will be butted. Clamp each piece to the work bench to cut the slots **(See Photo A).** Be sure to hold the plate joiner firmly and keep it tight to the bench top when plunging the tool. This will ensure the faces will be flush when they are assembled.

Next, mark the locations of the plate slots on the backs of the uprights and on both edges of the 5-in.-wide piece you prepared for the side returns. It is safer to cut the slots in the broader piece and then rip it to form the two narrow returns than it would be to slot two narrow pieces separately. Taking the

more cautious approach, mark each edge of the return blank with the slot locations, cut the slots and then rip the 1¼-in.-wide returns from the blank.

Before cutting the slots in the back side of an upright, clamp the piece to a vertical support, such as a table saw rip fence, and hold the plate joiner tight to the table. Apply glue to the plate slots and plates that join the uprights and top rail. Insert the plates and assemble the three pieces. Clamp the pieces together until the glue sets.

Rip and crosscut the mantel top to finished size. Mark the locations of the plates that join the mantel to the top edge of the rail-upright assembly. Note that the mantel extends 1¼ in. past the back side of the top rail, so the slots must be offset by that dimension. To aid in locating the slots on the broad piece,

PHOTO C: When joining pieces, apply glue to slots and plates, install the plates and clamp the assembly until the glue sets.

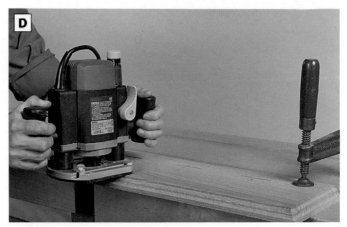

PHOTO D: Use an ogee-profile router bit with a ball-bearing pilot to shape the lower edges of the mantel sides and front.

simply place a 1¼-in.-thick scrap block beneath the plate joiner when cutting the slots **(See Photo B).**

Cut the slots in the top edge of the rail-upright assembly. Clamp the rail-upright assembly to the bench and cut the plate joiner slots in the top edges according to the technical drawing.

Join the returns to the back side of the uprights with biscuits and glue **(See Photo C).** Apply glue to both the slots and the biscuits, position the pieces and clamp them together until the glue sets.

To shape the front and side profiles of the mantel, use a piloted ogee router bit **(See Photo D).** A piloted bit has a ball-bearing guide that ensures the bit runs smoothly along the edge of the workpiece. This technique results in consistent contours along the entire length of the workpiece. Prevent mistakes by using a scrap block to test the depth of the cut. Make any necessary adjustments before proceeding to expensive stock.

Clamp the 1-in.-thick mantel to the workbench, upside down. Make the cuts on the ends of the board first, working counterclockwise. But before you cut, glue scrap blocks to the leading and trailing edges flush with the end of the board. They will prevent you from rounding over the corners (especially at the edges that will butt against the wall). They also will prevent tearout or splintering as the spinning router bit exits the workpiece.

NOTE: Because of the grain configuration, my piece of oak began to tear out when I started to rout the front edge using the standard counterclockwise approach, so I switched to a climb (clockwise) cut. Climb cutting is inherently more dangerous because the bit is pulled into the stock and can kick back. As a professional woodworker, I sometimes use this technique to save an expensive piece of wood from the scrap box. However, I would not recommend it for

woodworkers with limited experience. You should be extremely confident in your skills before attempting to climb cut with a router.

Once the mantel's edges are shaped, join it to the bottom assembly with biscuits, glue and clamps.

MOLDING DETAILS

I used stock moldings—chair rail and crown—to detail the piece. Cut the chair rail molding to the specified lengths. Attach the chair rail to the first upright and then to the top rail using 1¼-in. brads or 3d finish nails **(See Photo E).** Drill ¹⁄₁₆-in.-dia. pilot holes through the molding to prevent splitting. Also, be sure to slide a scrap of 1¼-in.-thick stock under the surround wherever you nail so you don't stress the glue joints. Apply a bit of glue to the mitered ends of the molding to help keep the joints tight. Set the nailheads below the wood surface.

The crown molding used under the mantel is a standard 3¼-in. crown with a combination cove and ogee profile. It sits at an angle of 33° to the face of

PHOTO E: Secure the face molding with 3d finish nails. Predrill with a ¹⁄₁₆-in. bit to prevent splitting and countersink the heads.

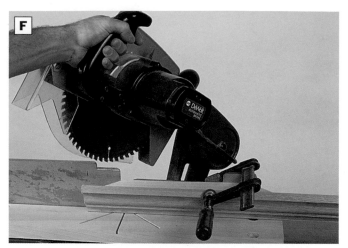

PHOTO F: The crown molding is held in its installed orientation for mitering with the aid of an angled support block and a clamp.

PHOTO G: To be safe, miter longer sections of crown molding for the returns. Then mark the ends for the square cuts.

the surround. If you use a different molding, check the proper angle of application so that your miters will come together properly.

In cutting the corner joints for this type of molding, a compound angle cut is necessary. The standard approach to cutting compound miters for crowns is to flip the molding upside down so the narrow top edge rests flat on the base of the miter table and the narrow back edge rests on the back fence. Then you set the saw angle to 45° and make the cut. With the upside-down approach, some woodworkers have trouble visualizing how the cut should go. And the fence may not offer a tall enough bearing surface for the molding's back edge to contact. Another approach is to fabricate a support block for the miter saw to help hold the molding in the proper (upright) position **(See Photo F).** First, measure your molding's relative angle to the face of the surround. Then rip a support block at that angle from some scrap lumber. Use double-faced tape to secure the block to the miter box fence. Position the crown molding against the support block and use a clamp to hold it in place. Check that the clamp is clear of the blade path and cut the miter.

Cut and apply the crown to the face of the surround, again predrilling for the 3d finish nails. Then fasten it to both the surround and the mantel bottom.

Because the side returns are short, cutting their miters could be a dangerous process. Instead, miter the ends of longer sections (at least 12 in. long). Then mark the ends to make the easier (and safer) square cuts to size **(See Photo G).**

The inside edges of the surround are finished off with stops, which can be ripped or scribed to accommodate the noncombustible material that borders the firebox. Rip stock to a dimension of ½ × 2 in. to form

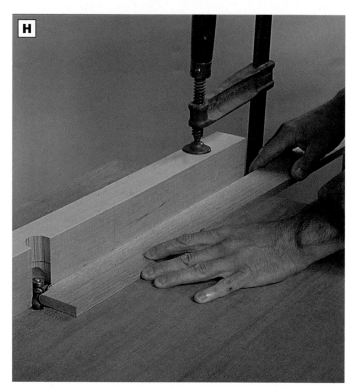

PHOTO H: Rout a bullnose profile on the front edges of the stop material. For safety, use a push stick to complete the cut.

the stops. Then, rout the front edges using a ½-in. round-profile bit **(See Photo H).** Cut the stops to length with mitered cuts at the joints, but do not install them at this time. Be sure to apply finish to the assembly and the stops separately before you attach the stops.

Flower Bed

We at the Handyman Club of America can't decide whether this flower bed project is deeply symbolic or just plain corny. But as avid do-it-yourselfers, we all agree that it is fun to build and that it puts a smile on the face of everyone who sees it. What's more, creating a garden showpiece for spring can be a great way to beat the winter doldrums.

Flower Bed

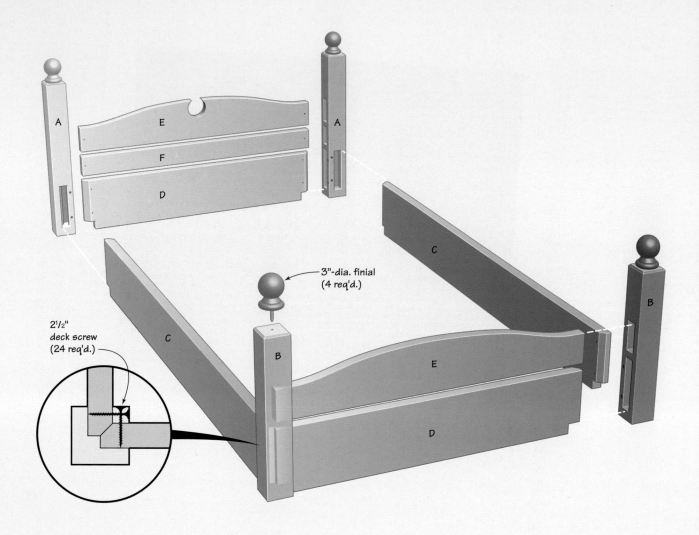

3"-dia. finial
(4 req'd.)

2¹/₂"
deck screw
(24 req'd.)

Flower Bed Cutting List

Part/Description	No.	Size	Material
A Headboard posts	2	3½ × 3½ × 27 in.	Cedar
B Footboard posts	2	3½ × 3½ × 22½ in.	"
C Side rails	2	1½ × 9¼ × 75 in.	"
D Bottom rails	2	1½ × 9¼ × 44½ in.	"
E Top rails	2	1½ × 7¼ × 44½ in.	"
F Mid-rail	1	1½ × 3½ × 44½ in.	"

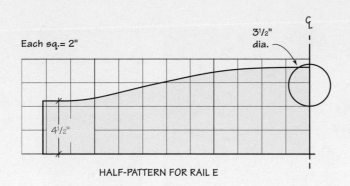

Each sq.= 2"

3½" dia.

4½"

HALF-PATTERN FOR RAIL E

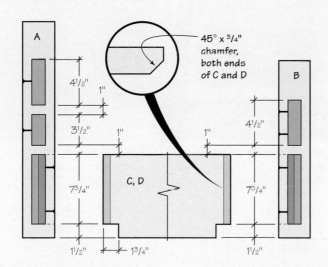

A

B

45° x ¾" chamfer, both ends of C and D

4½" 1"

3½" 1"

1"

4½"

7¾"   C, D

7¾"

1½"   1¾"

1½"

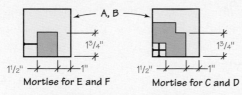

A, B

1¾"

1½"   1"

Mortise for E and F

1¾"

1½"   1"

Mortise for C and D

MORTISE-AND-TENON DETAILS

Shopping List

- ☐ (1) 4 × 4 × 120-in. cedar
- ☐ (3) 2 × 10 × 96-in. cedar
- ☐ (1) 2 × 8 × 96-in. cedar
- ☐ (1) 2 × 4 × 96-in. cedar
- ☐ (4) 3-in.-dia. ball finials
- ☐ (24) 2½-in. deck screws
- ☐ Finishing materials

Portability is generally not a term associated with flower beds, but because this clever design is constructed like a traditional bed, with a separate headboard and footboard, you can leave it disassembled until the planting season arrives. This modular concept can be a real advantage if you're short on space and need to store it over the winter.

MATERIALS MATTER

I used cedar to make the flower bed because it has good rot resistance, it's affordable and it's easy to cut. Redwood also is a good choice, but it's more expensive and has become hard to find in some parts of the country. Of course, you can use pressure-treated lumber, but it should be kiln-dried after treatment (the boards are stamped KDAT) to reduce its tendency to split and twist. There are other wood species such as white oak, teak and mahogany that hold up well outdoors, but these exotic choices will undoubtedly be more expensive and not as readily available as cedar.

All the flower bed parts are made from commonly available dimensional lumber. You may not be able to buy finials that are identical to the ones I used, but this is a good opportunity to express yourself by buying some

PHOTO A: Draw a 2-in. grid on half of the top rail to lay out the curve. The headboard and footboard curves are identical.

PHOTO B: Cut just outside the curve line with a band saw. Be sure to support the stock on the outfeed side.

that suit your taste or by getting creative and making your own. For that matter, you might want to change the entire design of the bed to a style that better suits your tastes. Perhaps you're looking to dress up the backyard of your old Victorian or stucco bungalow. A few modifications and an appropriate paint job will produce a handsome outdoor complement in the style of your home.

To get started, cut all the parts to length for the subsequent steps.

CUTTING CURVES

When marking and cutting the curve on the top rails, keep in mind that it's more important that the curve be smooth than it is to exactly duplicate my pattern. By first cutting half of the curve on one rail and then making a cardboard pattern from the curve to

mark the opposite side and the other rail, you'll get smooth, consistent results. To help you visualize how the completed rail will look, try cutting one side of the pattern out of a piece of paper folded in half. When you unfold the paper, you'll have the shape of the completed rail.

First, mark a centerline on the top rail. (You can do this on either the headboard or the footboard rail. Also mark the position of the circular cutout on the headboard top rail with a compass.) Using a straightedge and pencil, draw a 2-in. grid on one half of the rail. Refer to the half-pattern in the drawing and, using a pencil, transfer the curve to the grid freehand (See Photo A). Note that the curve ends where the tenon begins—about 2 in. before either end of the board. Refine the curve by sight and with a pencil and eraser.

Once you've refined the curve to your satisfaction, cut it with a jig saw or a band saw **(See Photo B).** A band saw is a better choice because it will generally produce a smoother, straighter cut than a jig saw. These advantages result because a band saw blade moves in only one direction and the workpiece is supported on two sides.

Now you need to remove the saw marks and refine the curve. Start with a half-round file or a rasp to remove any high spots **(See Photo C);** then use a sanding block and 100-grit paper to sand the edge smooth.

When the curve is smooth, trace it onto cardboard (thin card stock is best) to make a half-pattern. Cut out the pattern with a sharp utility knife. Tape the pattern to the opposite side of the rail, against the centerline, and trace the pattern **(See Photo D).** Cut, file and sand as you did before; then give the same treatment to the second rail.

To bore the decorative hole in the top of the headboard top rail, use a heavy-duty drill and a 3½-in.-dia. hole saw **(See Photo E).** Be sure to put a backup board under the rail to avoid damaging your worksurface. Use a clamp to secure both workpiece and the scrap to your workbench. Ensure

PHOTO C: Refine the cut edge with a half-round file or rasp; then sand the curve smooth with 100-grit paper.

PHOTO D: Trace the curve onto a piece of cardboard to make a half-pattern; then transfer the curve to the other side.

a straight cut by keeping a firm grip on the drill, and using the side grip if it has one. Don't force the hole saw into the board; rock it back and forth gently and let the saw teeth do the work.

To prevent chipping or tearout, turn the rail over before you finish boring the hole and complete it from the other side. You may need to clean up the hole with a file or sandpaper to ease sharp edges.

STURDY JOINTS

I used simple mortise-and-tenon joints to join the posts with the headboard rails, footboard rails and side rails. Most of the work is in making the mortises. The tenons, on the other hand, are straight, with the exception of the side rails and bottom rails, which are notched and chamfered. The actual width of the rails may vary according to your personal modifications. Just be sure to size the mortises to fit each rail. Remember that each post is unique; orient the mortises correctly for the

PHOTO E: Clamp the top headboard rail securely, then use a 3½-in. hole saw to make the decorative cutout in the top of the rail.

left and right headboard, footboard and rail tenons.

It's best to remove most of the waste from the mortises with a drill press and a 1¼-in.-dia.

PHOTO F: Hog out most of the waste from the mortises with a 1¼-in. Forstner bit mounted in a drill press.

PHOTO G: Complete the mortises with a router and ½-in. straight bit. Use an edge guide to control the router.

PHOTO H: A pull stroke keeps the waste from flying when cutting the rail chamfers with a slide compound miter saw.

Forstner bit or spade bit with a short center point, so the bit does not penetrate the opposite side of the workpiece (you may need to file down the center point of an existing bit). If you're careful, you also can bore the holes with a hand-held drill. Bore a series of holes along the center of each mortise, staying within the layout marks **(See Photo F).**

Next, clean out the mortises with a plunge router and a ½-in. straight bit. Use your router's edge guide to pilot the cut. To prevent accidentally gouging the work, be sure that the guide rides on the side of the post farthest from the edge you're routing **(See Photo G).** Make multiple passes at increasing depths with the router to prevent it from stalling under heavy load. When you're done routing, square the mortise corners with a sharp chisel.

Cut the notches in the ends of the side rails and the bottom rails with a jig saw. Then, cut the 45°

chamfers (for joint clearance) on the rail ends with a compound miter saw or a hand saw. If you use a miter saw, cut slowly to help prevent the waste piece from shattering or being thrown by the saw blade **(See Photo H).** Bore holes in the top of the posts for the finials, then screw them in place and you're ready to assemble the rest of the bed.

Assembly & finishing

You don't need to use glue to assemble the flower bed—only 2½-in. deck screws (once the bed is filled with soil, you won't have to worry about it racking). Assemble the headboard and then the footboard. Drive screws through the posts into the rails. Use two screws at each corner for the bottom, side and footboard top rails; the other rails receive one screw per corner.

To keep the bed from deteriorating outside, you'll need to apply a finish. Use a semitransparent

stain with UV blockers, an acrylic paint or a solid-color stain. Consider using an epoxy consolidant on the post bottoms to prevent the wood from wicking moisture. To further protect the wood, line the bed with landscape fabric.

When you've finished the project, find a suitable place in your yard, fill the bed with soil and plant flowers. We used different species to make it look like a quilt and pillow shams were on the bed. White alyssum outlines the shams, and ageratum and marigolds were used for the pattern. Choose flowers that get no more than 3 to 4 in. tall. A word of warning: The variety of marigolds we used eventually grew too tall for our bed.

Sink Board

We think the best handyman woodworking projects are those that make homes more convenient, comfortable and attractive. They're also not readily available in stores. A good project teaches clever shop techniques that have broad applications. This handy sink board measures up beautifully on all counts.

Sink Board

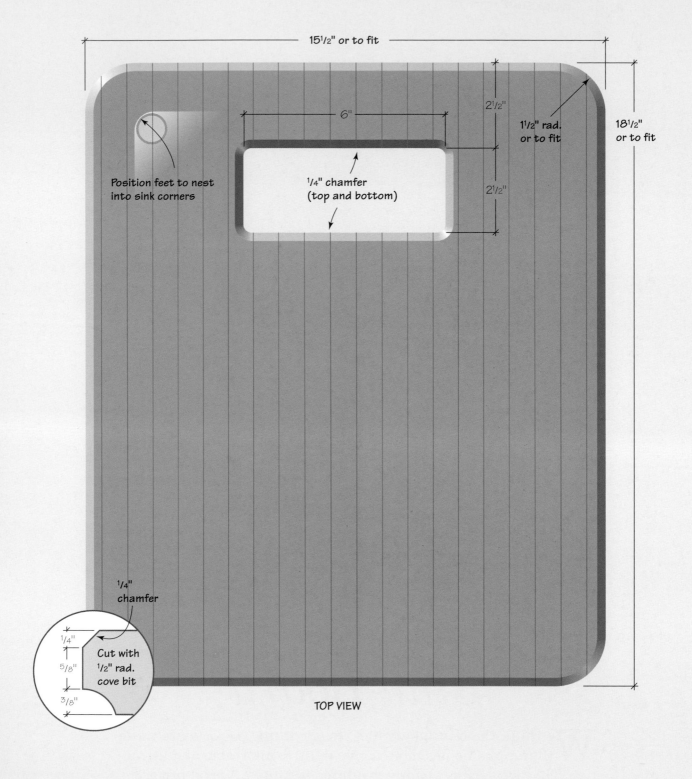

15¹/₂" or to fit

Position feet to nest
into sink corners

6"

2¹/₂"

1¹/₂" rad.
or to fit

18¹/₂"
or to fit

¹/₄" chamfer
(top and bottom)

2¹/₂"

¹/₄"
chamfer

¹/₄"

5/8"

3/8"

Cut with
¹/₂" rad.
cove bit

TOP VIEW

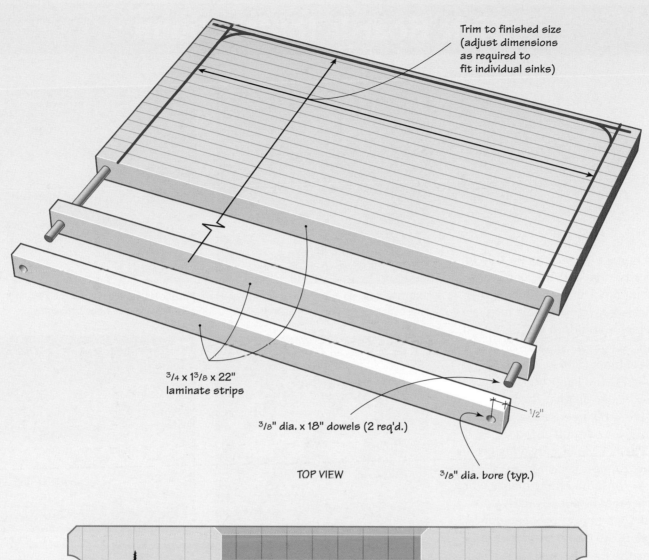

Trim to finished size
(adjust dimensions
as required to
fit individual sinks)

³/₄ x 1³/₈ x 22"
laminate strips

³/₈" dia. x 18" dowels (2 req'd.)

TOP VIEW

1/2"

³/₈" dia. bore (typ.)

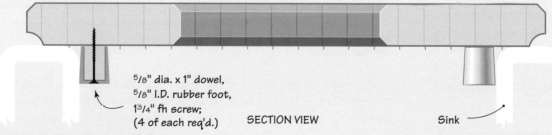

⁵/₈" dia. x 1" dowel,
⁵/₈" I.D. rubber foot,
1³/₄" fh screw;
(4 of each req'd.)

SECTION VIEW

Sink

Shopping List*

- ☐ (1) 1 × 10 × 8-ft maple
- ☐ (4) 1-in.-dia. × 1⅛-in. rubber feet
- ☐ (4) #8 × 1¾-in. wood screws
- ☐ (1) ⅜-in.-dia. × 36-in. dowel
- ☐ (1) ⅝-in.-dia. × 5-in. dowel
- ☐ Polyurethane glue
- ☐ Finishing materials

*Makes a 1¼ × 15½ × 8½-in. board.

Sink Board: Instructions

PHOTO A: A simple drill press jig ensures uniform boring for the alignment dowels.

PHOTO B: Coat the top of each strip with polyurethane glue while laminating.

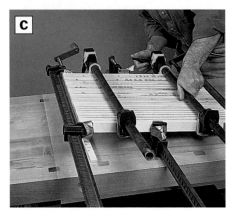

PHOTO C: Apply even pressure to the stack and prevent cupping by alternating clamps top and bottom.

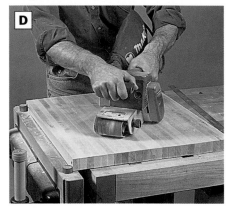

PHOTO D: Remove the glue and level the surface of the board with a belt sander and 100-grit abrasives.

If you buy a large, high-end kitchen sink, you may be able to get a custom cutting board that fits on top. But if you have an older sink, you probably have settled for a standard cutting board that sits on the counter or stores in a cabinet. The key to this design is the long rubber feet—they wedge against the sink's inside walls to stabilize the board while you are cutting.

The board not only adds precious counter space, I hear it's also great for hiding dirty dishes when unexpected company arrives. Although many store-bought models are designed to be used over the garbage disposer, you might find my board more functional over the other basin. Either way, you can enjoy a large sink and your countertop too.

CONSTRUCTION SECRETS

If you've never built a laminated butcher block top, you may be wondering, What's the big deal about building a board? This project features a special alignment technique that prevents the small pieces from sliding around as you glue them up.

I built my board using a band saw, a jig saw, a drill press, a plunge router, a belt sander and a hand plane. You also could substitute a table saw and hand plane for the band saw and sander. To

save the time and effort of milling rough stock, I bought an 8-ft.-long maple 1 × 10 (about 6½ bf) at my local home center. That was plenty for the cutting board plus a little extra. Avoid open-pore hardwoods such as oak and softwoods such as pine or cedar. Open-pore woods are not suitable for food preparation surfaces because they can trap food particles.

Because the S4S (surfaced four sides) boards were milled to a thickness of ¾ in., they only needed to be ripped into 1⅜-in.-wide strips and glued face to face. This method produces a thicker board that is considerably more

warp-resistant. What's more, the surface of the board is more durable because the cut edges are typically quartersawn faces.

Be aware that wide dimensional hardwood sold at home centers often is made from strips that are glued together. It won't hurt if you cut and use a strip with a joint, provided it's not too close to the surface of the board. However, you may want to cut around the joints if you don't want them to show on the finished board.

Polyurethane glue is best for this project. It has a long open time, and it's waterproof and nontoxic once it cures. While the

PHOTO E: Bore starter holes in the corners of the cutout using a Forstner bit. Use a jig saw to complete the cutout.

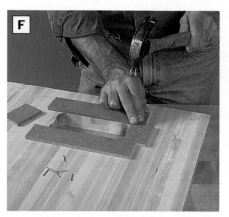

PHOTO F: To make a simple router template, fasten hardboard strips around the cutout with brads.

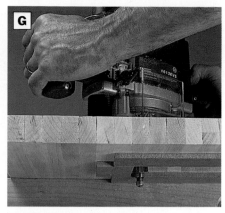

PHOTO G: Clean up the sides of the cutout with a ½-in.-dia. flush-trim bit. Rout clockwise around the hole.

directions say you can accelerate drying by lightly misting the mating surfaces with water, it may not be a good idea with this project. You'll need all the open time you can get for stacking, gluing and clamping. It's critical to clamp workpieces securely when using this type of glue because it expands as it dries.

CAUTION: Avoid getting polyurethane glue on your hands. It will cause stains that won't come clean for days.

To keep the 20-plus strips in the stack from sliding apart when I glued up the blank, I bored a hole near both ends of each strip to accept ⅜-in.-dia. dowels. The dowels register the strips accurately so there's no need for a special clamping fixture, and they also help to prevent the glue-up from bowing and twisting when you apply clamping pressure. The dowels enable you to stack the strips so you can apply the glue to a level surface. This minimizes the glue mess. It doesn't matter what wood the dowels are made from; they get cut off when you trim the blank to size.

MAKING THE BLANK

Sinks vary, so you'll need to measure yours in order to determine the correct size for the board.

Consider the position of the faucet and the radius of the outside corners. The edge of the board should be slightly recessed from the outer rim. This will keep the feet close to the corners for maximum stability on the counter.

Begin by crosscutting your stock 2 in. longer than the finished board to leave room to trim off the doweled ends. It's very important that the board sections you cut are exactly the same length for the dowel registration system to work. That's why I crosscut before I rip the narrow strips. Before you rip the stock into strips, figure the maximum number of strips that you can get out of the board. You should be able to get at least six strips from each section of 1 × 10, cutting with a band saw or a table saw. If the stock seems slick or burnished from planing, sand the faces to roughen them for gluing.

Rip the stock into 1⅜-in.-wide strips using a table saw or a band saw. A band saw wastes less stock because of its narrow blade kerf. Sometimes wood may bow when you cut it. You may want to joint the edges of the board (that ride against the saw fence) after each cut with a hand plane or a jointer. This will ensure that the pieces remain fairly straight.

Lay out the strips and arrange

them to create a random color and grain pattern. Clamp the strips together squarely; then clearly mark the top and one side so that you can reassemble them correctly with glue.

Build a simple jig to align the ends of the strips in the drill press for uniform boring. The jig consists of wood strips nailed to a backup board that is clamped to the table (**See Photo A**). Make sure the table is level. Mark the hole position on one strip; then slip it into the jig and clamp the jig so the mark is centered under a ⅜-in. brad-point wood-boring bit.

Slip each strip down over the alignment dowels and coat the top with glue before installing the next piece (**See Photo B**). If necessary, tap down the strips with a mallet as you build the stack. With polyurethane glue, you need only coat one side of each strip. Spread the glue with a brush or a stick for even coverage.

When you've completed the assembly, clamp the pieces together with at least three heavy-duty bar clamps or pipe clamps (**See Photo C**). (Light-duty clamps can't provide enough even pressure to draw so many pieces together.) Alternate the clamps top and bottom to prevent cupping and apply even pressure, but don't

PHOTO H: Trim the board to size with a band saw. Use a ¼-in.-wide blade for the radiused corners.

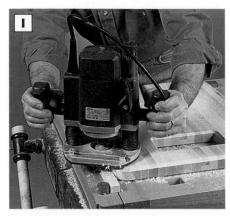

PHOTO I: Finish the top edge of the board with a piloted chamfer bit and the bottom edge with a cove bit.

PHOTO J: Tape a cardboard pattern of the board to the sink rim to determine the position of the feet.

overtighten. Sight down the edge of the board to be sure the blank is flat and adjust the clamps accordingly if it isn't. Leave the clamps on for 24 hours; then use a hand plane or belt sander to surface the faces **(See Photo D).**

MILLING & DETAILING

Lay out the perimeter of the board and the opening for the (waste) hole in the back of the cutting board. Bore starter holes in the corners of the waste cutout with a Forstner bit mounted in a drill press **(See Photo E).** Use a jig saw to cut out the rough opening of the waste hole. Be sure to support the waste piece to prevent it from falling out and jamming the saw blade. Next, smooth the edges of the hole with a router. Nail hardboard strips to the bottom of the board to create a template for a ½-in. flush-trim router bit **(See Photo F).** Use the sides of the starter holes to align the edges of the hardboard guides.

When routing, go slowly, particularly if you're using a light-duty router. Make several passes until the pilot bearing rides smoothly on the hardboard strips **(See Photo G).** The router bit forms the ¼-in. radius in the corners. Remove the template strips; then rout a chamfer on the top and

bottom edges of the hole. Don't change the router setup with the chamfer bit; you'll use it again on the top outside edge.

Cut the board to size on the band saw. First, rip the board to width; then cut the radiused corners and the ends **(See Photo H).** Use a hand plane or a belt sander to smooth the straight edges and either a block sander or an oscillating spindle sander to smooth the corners.

Rout the chamfer around the top edge of the board; then use a ½-in.-radius cove bit to create a finger hold along the bottom **(See Photo I).** Sand the top and the bottom smooth with a random-orbit sander or pad sander and 150-grit paper.

FINISHING & CARE

The rubber feet are the kind that are used on the legs of folding metal chairs. You can buy them at any home center. I inserted ⅝-in. hardwood dowels in the leg holes to fill the space and then bored holes through the dowels and used 1¾-in. flathead wood screws to attach the feet to the board.

It's easier to position the feet on the bottom of the board if you make a cardboard pattern of the finished board. Trace the outside of the board onto stiff cardboard;

then cut out the pattern with a utility knife. Cut out the center of the pattern leaving a 4-in.-wide border. Tape the pattern to the sink. Then reach under the pattern with an assembled foot **(See Photo J).** Locate each corner of the sink with the foot; then push up on the foot so the screw punctures the bottom of the pattern. Place the pattern on the bottom of the board and transfer the marks.

Before finishing the board, wipe the surface with a damp cloth to raise the grain. After the wood dries, sand it with 150-grit paper. Coat the board with vegetable oil or butcher block oil.

Because this board has so many laminated pieces, it must be treated carefully. To prevent it from warping or delaminating, it's important that you not submerge it in water or let water stand on it for more than a few minutes. When you clean the board, wipe off the excess water promptly. If you need a board that can take repeated soakings, make one with fewer laminations.

Radiator Cover

T̲he good thing about some old-fashioned dining room radiators
is that they provide even heat without kicking up a dust storm.
The bad thing is that they tend to be industrial-quality ugly and a
waste of space. Now, any unsightly radiator can be hidden behind
an attractive hardwood facade offering ample display space.

Radiator Cover

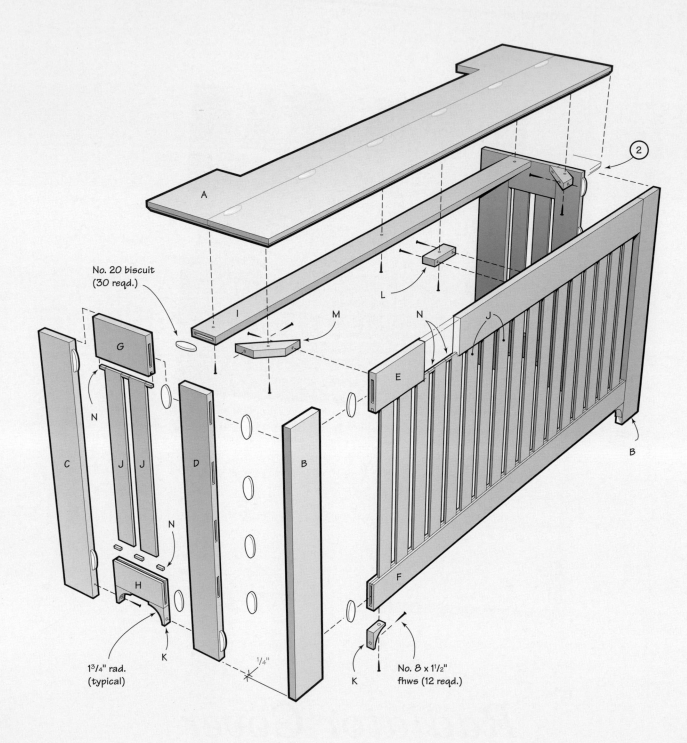

No. 20 biscuit
(30 reqd.)

A

G

I

L

M

N

E

N

J

C

J   J

D

B

J

N

F

B

H

K

2

1³/₄" rad.
(typical)

¹/₄"

K

K

No. 8 x 1¹/₂"
fhws (12 reqd.)

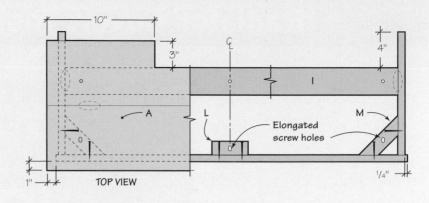

10"

3"

4"

Elongated
screw holes

1"

1/4"

TOP VIEW

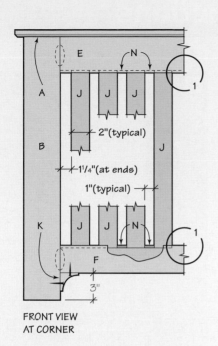

E

N

A

J J J

2" (typical)

B

1 1/4" (at ends)

1" (typical)

J

K

N

F

3"

1

1

FRONT VIEW
AT CORNER

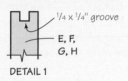

1/4 x 1/4" groove

E, F,
G, H

DETAIL 1

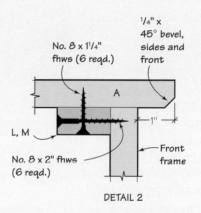

No. 8 x 1 1/4"
fhws (6 reqd.)

1/4" x
45° bevel,
sides and
front

A

L, M

1"

No. 8 x 2" fhws
(6 reqd.)

Front
frame

DETAIL 2

Shopping List

- ☐ (6) ¼ × 2 × 96-in. oak
- ☐ (2) 12-ft. 1 × 4 oak
- ☐ (1) 11-ft. 1 × 8 oak
- ☐ (1) 9-ft. 1 × 10 oak
- ☐ (30) #20 plate-joining biscuits
- ☐ (6) #8 × 2-in. flathead wood screws
- ☐ (12) #8 × 1½-in. flathead wood screws
- ☐ (6) #8 × 1¼-in. flathead wood screws

Radiator Cover Cutting List

Part	Description	No.	Size	Material
A	Top	1	¾ × 14½ × 62½ in.*	Red oak
B	Front legs	2	¾ × 4 × 29¼ in.	"
C	Side legs (back)	2	¾ × 4 × 29¼ in.	"
D	Side legs (forward)	2	¾ × 3¼ × 29¼ in.	"
E	Front rail (top)	1	¾ × 4 × 52½ in.	"
F	Front rail (bottom)	1	¾ × 3 × 52½ in.	"
G	Side rails (top)	2	¾ × 4 × 6½ in.	"
H	Side rails (bottom)	2	¾ × 3 × 6½ in.	"
I	Stretcher	1	¾ × 3 × 58½ in.	"
J	Slats	21	¼ × 2 × 19¾ in.	"
K	Corner brackets	6	¾ × 2 × 2 in.	"
L	Top cleat	1	¾ × 1½ × 4 in.	"
M	Corner braces	2	¾ × 1½ × 6¼ in.	"
N	Fillets	48	¼ × ¼ × 1 in.**	"

*Width of top may vary depending on
installation requirements; see text.
**Nominal measurement, cut to fit.

By investing a couple of days in the workshop and a weekend at the finishing table, we created the ultimate radiator cover-up. It's functional and attractive, while it incorporates many of the home's architectural details. Most importantly, we turned what was a major eyesore into a piece that's both handsome and practical.

One word of caution: The heating system in our radiator uses hot water—not steam. Steam radiators get much hotter than water-filled radiators and could damage a wooden cover. They're better candidates for metal covers.

DESIGN SENSE

We made this radiator cover entirely from red oak to match the existing woodwork. The project really is more like finish carpentry than furniture building. The joinery consists of simple butt joints that are assembled with either plate-joining biscuits or screws. If you don't have a plate joiner, you can substitute dowels or screws. You might even want to strengthen the cover with half-lap joints where the legs meet the rails if you plan to use it as a seat.

The slats fit into grooves cut in the rail edges and are held in place by tiny fillets (spacers). The fillets are glued in place, but the slats float in the grooves. This allows the slats to expand and contract.

PHOTO A: With the workpiece clamped securely, rout the chamfer on the bottom edge of the top with a chamfer bit.

The cover fits our installation perfectly, but since radiators differ greatly in size, yours probably will need to be a different width, height or length. Adjust the dimensions accordingly. Also note that because the top fits against the window apron, we made it narrower than if it fit against the wall. The back legs fit against the wall. Your situation might vary.

MATERIAL ISSUES

Milling stock for this project from rough lumber can take almost as long as making it, so I opted to buy oak that already had been milled to size. This approach allowed me to build the cover with relatively few tools: a table saw, router, drill, plate joiner, random orbit sander and a few hand tools. You'll find that many lumberyards and home centers sell oak and

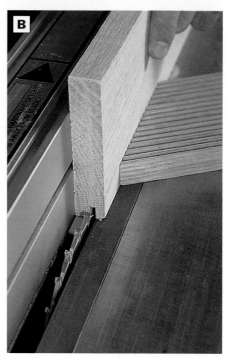

PHOTO B: Groove the rails on a table saw with a ⅛-in. blade. Flip the stock end-for-end to make the second pass.

other species milled to dimensional lumber sizes for finish carpentry applications.

Be sure to select square, straight boards, because you won't be able to correct problems with stock that's already been milled. If you can't find ¼-in.-thick oak for the slats, you may need to resaw thicker pieces on your band saw or table saw. Resawing can be tricky, particularly on a table saw. Always use a featherboard to keep the workpiece pressed firmly against the fence, use the saw's splitter and don't force stock through the blade.

One of the most important aspects of building this project is that you cut workpieces accurately. The pieces won't fit together properly if they aren't square. Before you begin cutting, check your saw to be sure the

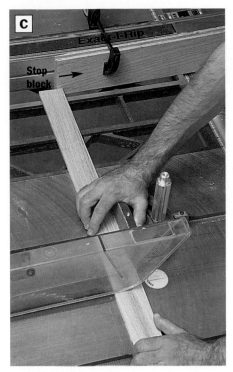

PHOTO C: Clamp a stopblock on the saw fence to cut the slats. Attaching sandpaper to the face of the miter gauge reduces slippage.

PHOTO D: Lay out the parts before gluing to ensure that they fit. Mark the biscuit locations with a square.

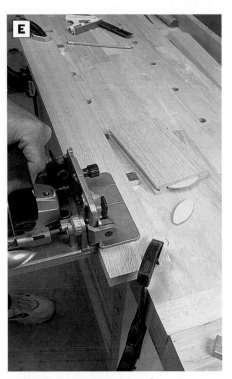

PHOTO E: Use the plate-joiner fence to register the slot positions. Always work off the front face of the stock.

blade is perpendicular to the table and the miter gauge. After you make cuts, use a try square to confirm that the edges are square.

MAKING THE TOP

It's likely that you'll have to glue up two or more pieces to make the top, so it's best to make the top first to give the glue time to dry. Be sure to use oversize pieces to allow for trimming later, and try to match the grain and color of the pieces so they'll blend together once assembled.

A perfect seam between the pieces is essential if you want the joint to disappear and, more importantly, for the finished top to hold together (most glues used for woodworking have no strength across a gap). You can make fine adjustments to the joint edge with a well-tuned hand plane and some patience. Add biscuits to the joint for strength and alignment.

To assemble the top, first coat both edges of the joint with glue;

then apply even clamping pressure with bar clamps starting from the center and working your way to the sides. Alternate the clamps, top and bottom to equalize the pressure, and don't over-tighten them. The easiest way to deal with squeeze-out is to wait until the glue becomes gummy, then use a cabinet scraper to remove it. Sand the top smooth after the glue dries.

Trim the top to its finished size by cutting the ends first; then rip it to width on the table saw. Mark the position of the ventilation notch on the back edge and use a band saw or jig saw to cut it out. Finally, rout the chamfer on the bottom edge of the front and sides **(See Photo A).**

ASSEMBLE THE FRONT & SIDES

Before you cut the rails to length, you'll need to cut ¼ × ¼-in. grooves in them for the slats. You can use a router fitted with an edge guide, a router table or a

table saw equipped with a dado blade. We simply made two passes on the table saw with a ⅛-in.-kerf combination blade **(See Photo B).** Once you've cut the grooves, cut the rails to length.

Next, cut the slats to length **(See Photo C).** Now you can lay out the parts and mark biscuit positions in the legs and rails **(See Photo D),** and then cut the biscuit slots **(See Photo E).** Remember that there's a left and right side, so be sure to label the workpieces accordingly.

Assemble the front rails and slats on a smooth, flat surface. Using scrap pieces to space the slats apart **(See Photo F),** fit the slats in the rail grooves all at once. Repeat the same operation when assembling the side rails and slats. Glue and clamp the legs to the rails.

Now cut lengths of ¼ × ¼-in. stock for the spacers. Position the slats evenly and determine the length of the spacers. They should

103

fit loosely against the slats to give the slats room to expand. Because the spacers are tiny, it's best to cut them with a Japanese pull saw **(See Photo G).** Glue the spacers in place.

Next, cut the mating biscuit slots between the front and the sides **(See Photo H)** and the slots for the stretcher. Note that the sides are inset ¼ in. from the edges of the front legs.

Before final assembly you need to make and install the corner brackets **(See Photo I)** and also make the corner braces and top screw cleat. We cut them on a band saw. Bore elongated screw holes in the braces and cleat for attaching the top. Glue and clamp the sides to the front; then install the braces and the cleat.

INSTALLATION & FINISHING

Every installation will be a little different, but here are a few things to keep in mind.

It is easier to cut the baseboard and fit the cover against the wall than to cope the sides to fit around the baseboard. We made the outside cut in place using a hand saw and removed the baseboard behind the radiator so we could trim it back and refit it. The opposite was true for the window apron because it was straight. In that case, we coped the sides and left the apron intact. And because the walls weren't straight, we scribed the back legs to the wall and contoured them with a block plane.

Another option: You also may want to install screw cleats on the walls to prevent the radiator cover from tipping forward or sliding side to side.

We finished the piece with two coats of custom-mixed oil stain and satin finish polyurethane to match the surrounding woodwork.

PHOTO F: To assemble the front, clamp stops on the ends of a worktable and draw the assembly together by driving wedges.

PHOTO G: Convert a rail cutoff into a mini-miter box to cut the fillets. A pull saw produces a fine cut.

PHOTO H: Clamp the sides to the front and index off the plate-joiner base to recess the biscuit slots for the sides.

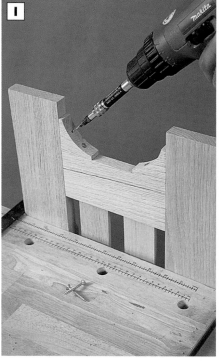

PHOTO I: After drilling screw holes, glue and screw the corner brackets to the legs and bottom rails.

Oval Frame

Oval frames make unique gifts because their construction seems to defy logic: How do you get those curved pieces to join snugly and how do you clamp them? However, by using the methods outlined here, you'll find that these frames are not only easy to make, but also can be produced in great numbers. The layout methods I use are precise, flexible and repeatable. The clamping method is very effective because you don't cut the outside curve until after assembly.

Oval Frame

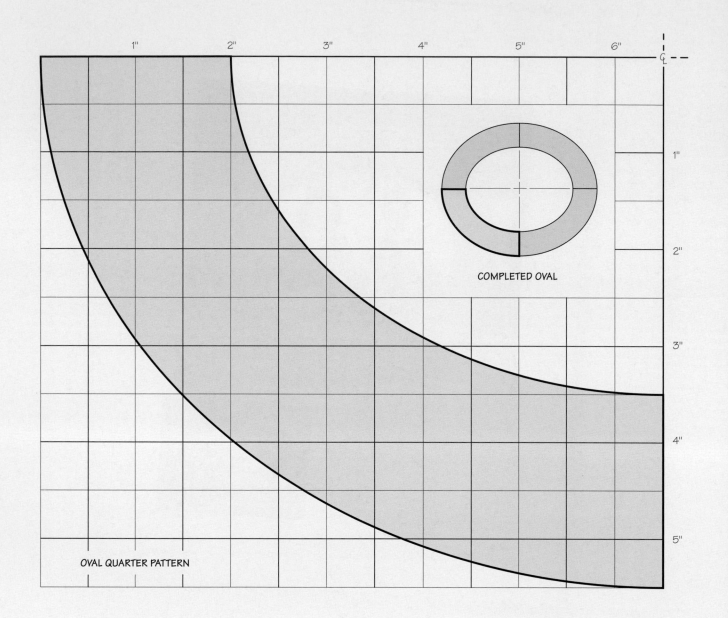

1"   2"   3"   4"   5"   6"

COMPLETED OVAL

OVAL QUARTER PATTERN

Shopping List

☐ R3 minibiscuits

☐ 2 bf of desired wood

☐ ¼-in. plywood or hardboard

☐ Wood glue

☐ Finishing materials

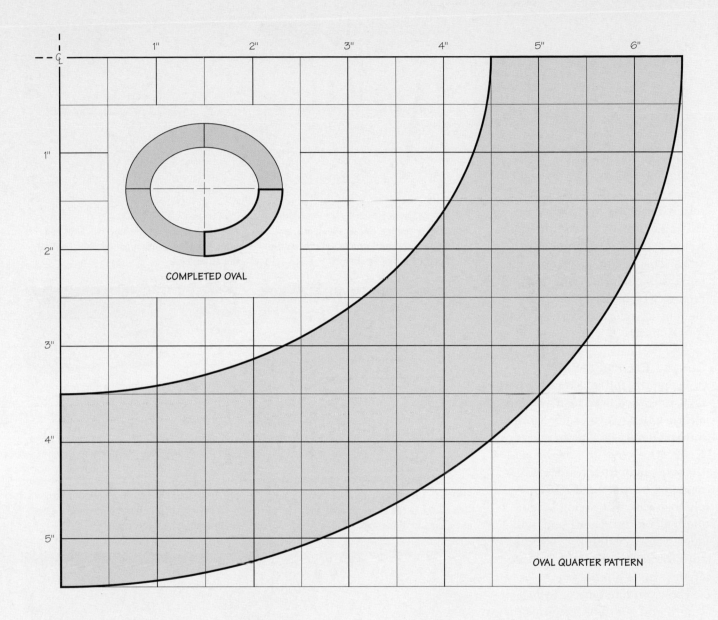

1" 2" 3" 4" 5" 6"

COMPLETED OVAL

OVAL QUARTER PATTERN

Making this oval frame is different than simply making a 45° mitered rectangular frame and cutting out an oval. That method would leave you with unequal sides. This frame has equal sides and complementary (but unequal) angles, which places the miters at six and 12 o'clock and at three and nine o'clock.

ELLIPSE LAYOUT

Using the full-size quarter patterns included here to draw your ellipse will save you some work, but you'll only be able to make frames the same size as the one that we made (this frame accommodates a trimmed 8 × 10-in. photograph). The string layout method, on the other hand, will allow you to customize your picture frame by plotting an ellipse of any size or shape.

First you must lay out the length and width of the ellipse (major and minor axes) for the inside of the frame on ¼-in. plywood or hardboard. Divide the length into four equal parts and drive brads, angled slightly toward the outside of the ellipse, at the quarter points. Then drive a brad at one end of the width of the ellipse.

Next, form a taut string loop around the three brads (**See Photo A**). Remove the brad at the end of the ellipse's width and take

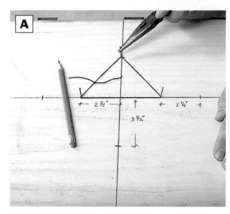

PHOTO A: Divide the ellipse's long axis into quarters and its short axis in half; then drive brads and tie string as shown.

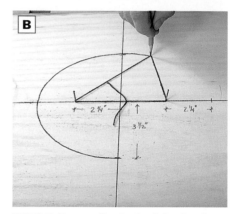

PHOTO B: Remove the short-axis brad and draw the ellipse with a pencil while holding the string taut.

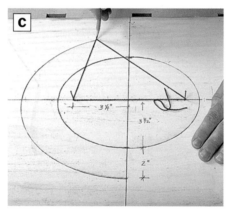

PHOTO C: Lay out and draw the frame's outside ellipse in the same manner; then cut out one quadrant of the pattern.

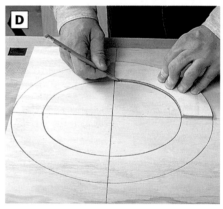

PHOTO D: Use the cut-out quadrant to trace a perfectly symmetrical oval onto a fresh piece of plywood; then cut it out.

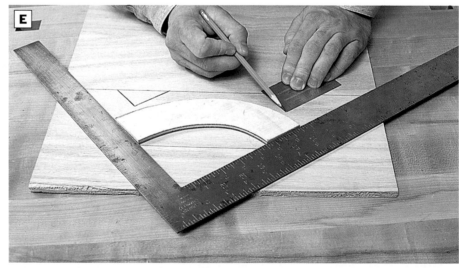

PHOTO E: Lay out the stock pattern with the quadrant pattern, a framing square and the corner of a straightedge.

up the slack in the string with a pencil point. While keeping the string taut, move the pencil around the center point to scribe the ellipse (**See Photo B**). Use the same methods and center point to draw the ellipse for the outside of the frame (**See Photo C**).

Because the pencil line can wander and the string can stretch, it's difficult to get a perfectly symmetrical ellipse using this method. You can fine-tune the ellipse by selecting the best quadrant and using it as a pattern for all four quadrants of a final plywood frame pattern (**See Photo D**). Then use a scroll saw to cut out this pattern.

It's important that the ends of the quadrant pattern be perpendicular to one another. If they're not, it will be difficult to make accurate miter cuts later. Cut the ends of the pattern stock square using a miter gauge or cutoff box on your table saw before you cut the curves.

SETTING UP THE CUTS

Before you do any cutting, determine the length and width of the stock. Make a plywood stock pattern (**See Photo E**) so you can set up the miter gauge angles and trace the clamp notches you'll cut in the stock. Use the quadrant pattern as a guide to ensure that there's enough room on the stock. Place the ends of the pattern flush with the edges of the stock to be sure there's enough stock to accommodate the pattern's arc.

Once you've laid out the pattern, use a T-bevel to transfer one of the miter angles (you'll need two) to a miter gauge (**See Photo F**). Screw a long fence to the gauge to stabilize the stock and to provide an attachment point for a stopblock. Attach a fence to

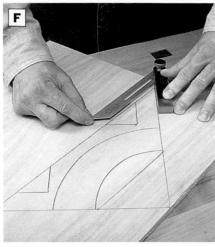

PHOTO F: Use a T-bevel to copy a corner angle from the stock pattern. Then transfer the angle to a table saw miter gauge.

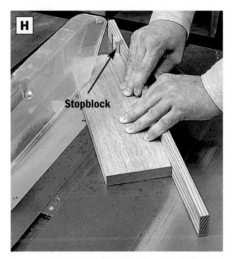

PHOTO H: Clamp a stopblock on the right side of the fence so a flat end remains on the stock after the cut is made.

the second miter gauge and use a framing square to set the 90° angle (**See Photo G**).

Slight deviations in miter cuts are magnified by the fact that there are four joints in a frame. Errors also become more noticeable with wider stock. To ensure that the length of each quadrant is identical to the others, I leave a flat end on the stock when I make the first miter cut (**See Photo H**). When placed against the stopblock for the second cut, the flat end guarantees that the workpieces will be a consistent length (**See Photo I**). A pointed end can

PHOTO G: After establishing one miter angle, use a framing square to set a second miter gauge perpendicular to the first miter gauge.

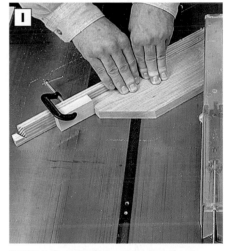

PHOTO I: Butt the flat end against the stopblock on the right miter gauge; then cut the complementary angle.

get crushed or find its way between the stopblock and fence, resulting in a piece that's too long.

FITTING & ASSEMBLY

After you've cut all of the miters, cut the clamp notches (one leg of each notch should be parallel with the miter). Test-fit the miters by clamping the workpieces together with hand screws (**See Photo J**) or C-clamps. Provided the pieces fit well, trace the outline of the frame pattern onto the stock. Be sure to align the joints with the axes of the ellipse.

If you need to adjust the fit of

the miters, use paper shims between the workpiece and the miter gauge fence. Remember, the error you'll see will be eight times larger than the correction needed—once for every miter cut.

Next, join the parts. Glue alone won't hold end grain on these miter joints, so you need to provide a long-grain connection between the parts. For a small frame such as this, I prefer minibiscuits **(See Photo K)**, but #0 or #10 biscuits work well for stock that's wider than 2¼ in. If you don't have a biscuit joiner in the shop, splines or dowels are the next best choices.

Cut the biscuit slots before cutting the inside curve on each piece. The extra stock gives you a little more to hold on to when doing the joinery. When cutting the curves, cut slightly to the waste side of the line to allow for variations in fit during assembly and so you can sand to the line afterward. Cut only the inside oval at first, then reassemble the frame. It's best to join the quarter sections into two separate halves, then assemble those pieces into the closed oval **(See Photo L)**.

After gluing and clamping the frame, cut out the oval **(See Photo M)** and sand the inside and outside edges. An oscillating spindle sander or drum sander mounted on a drill press works best. However, if you're making several frames, it's easier and faster to use the oval pattern as a template (it must be ¼ in. or thicker) by fastening it to the frame with double-stick tape, then routing the edges with a piloted flush-trimming bit. You'll still need to cut the frame to within ⅛ in. of the pattern line before routing.

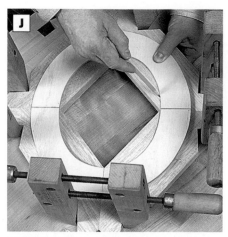

PHOTO J: After cutting the clamp notches, temporarily clamp the workpieces together and trace around the oval pattern.

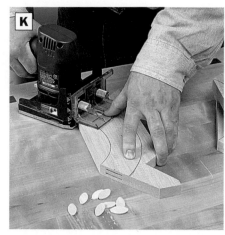

PHOTO K: Use double rows of minibiscuits, centered in the ends of the stock, to join the frame sections.

PHOTO L: Cut the inside curve before joining. Glue together two oval halves; then join the halves to complete assembly.

PHOTO M: Cut the outside of the frame with a band saw; then sand the inside and outside curves smooth.

DETAILING THE FRAME

You'll need to rout a rabbet in the frame back to hold the glass, photo, back, etc. Use a piloted rabbeting bit. Measure the thickness of these pieces and add about ⅛ in. to the depth of the rabbet if you use push points as retainers.

The frame edge detail allows you to customize the look of the finished project. I used common bearing-piloted, edge-profile router bits such as ogee, cove and chamfer to give my frames multiple appearances. Because the frames are small and the stock is narrow, it's best not to use a handheld router to mold the edges. The extra surface area of a router table provides

much better support and makes milling the profiles a lot easier.

The downside of custom frames is that appropriately sized glass will probably have to be cut. Since this operation can be difficult, I recommend that you have it done at a frame shop. Be sure to provide patterns of whatever sizes you need. A good alternative is to use sheet acrylic that you can purchase at any home center.

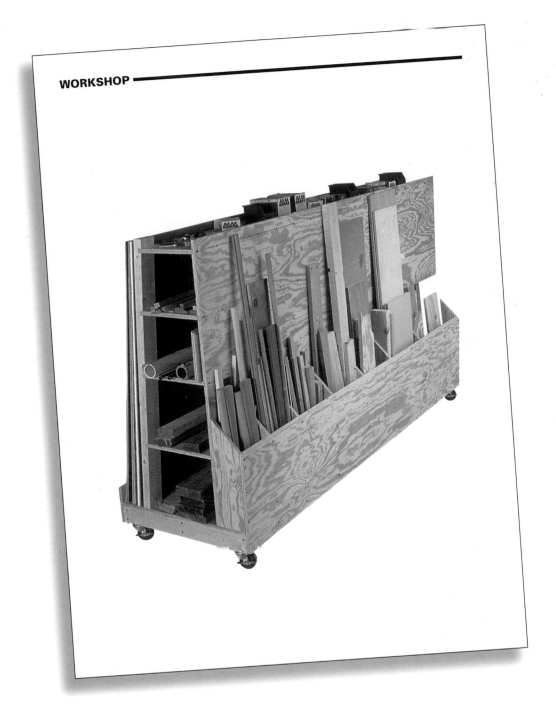

Materials Cart

Based on reports of do-it-yourselfers I've met, it's safe to say that many Club members keep quite an assortment of materials around their shops that are just waiting to find their way into future woodworking, remodeling or repair projects. Sheets of gypsum, extra plywood, hardwood cutoffs, sections of copper tubing, PVC pipe, expensive molding—all are valuable odds and ends that need the protected yet handy berth provided by this design.

Materials Cart

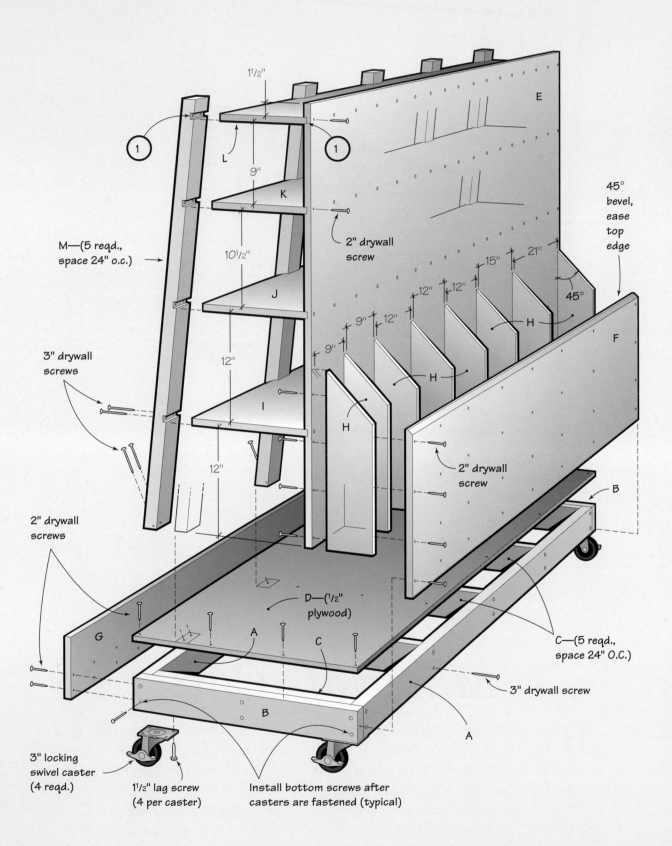

1½"

① 1

L

9"

M—(5 reqd., space 24" o.c.)

10½"

K

J

12"

I

12"

3" drywall screws

2" drywall screws

E

① 1

2" drywall screw

45° bevel, ease top edge

21"

15"

12"

12"

45°

9"

12"

9"

H

H

H

H

F

H

2" drywall screw

B

D—(½" plywood)

C—(5 reqd., space 24" O.C.)

G

A

C

B

3" drywall screw

A

3" locking swivel caster (4 reqd.)

1½" lag screw (4 per caster)

Install bottom screws after casters are fastened (typical)

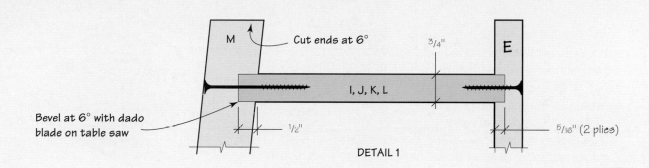

M

Cut ends at 6°

3/4"

E

I, J, K, L

Bevel at 6° with dado
blade on table saw

1/2"

DETAIL 1

5/16" (2 plies)

Shopping List

- ☐ (4) 3-in. locking casters
- ☐ (6) 10-ft. 2 × 4 studs
- ☐ (3) ¾-in. 4 × 8 BC plywood
- ☐ (1) ½-in. 4 × 8 BC plywood
- ☐ (16) ¼-in. × 1½ lag screws
- ☐ 3-in. & 2-in. drywall screws
- ☐ Construction adhesive

Materials Cart Cutting List

Part/Description		No.	Size	Material
A	Base front/back	2	1½ × 3½ × 93 in.	Stud
B	Base side	2	1½ × 3½ × 27 in.	"
C	Base stretchers	5	1½ × 3½ × 24 in.	"
D	Base top	1	½ × 27 × 96 in.	B/C plywood
E	Mid panel	1	¾ × 48 × 96 in.	"
F	Front panel	1	¾ × 18 × 96 in.	"
G	Back Panel	1	¾ × 7 × 96 in.	"
H	Dividers	8	¾ × 5¼ × 19¼ in.	"
I	Shelf 1	1	¾ × 14⁹⁄₁₆ × 96 in.	"
J	Shelf 2	1	¾ × 13³⁄₁₆ × 96 in.	"
K	Shelf 3	1	¾ × 12 × 96 in	"
L	Shelf 4	1	¾ × 11 × 96 in.	"
M	Shelf support	5	3½ × 48¼ in.	Stud

This project is the perfect solution to the problem of workshop organization. It takes up only 18 sq. ft. of floor space but holds a variety of tools, materials and accessories. Chances are you already have some plywood and 2 × 4 scraps lying around to get you started. If so, there will be that much less to buy (and store).

Although I initially designed the cart on paper, I verified the angles and measurements by drawing a full-size cross section on a sheet of plywood. Stability was one of my main concerns, so I made sure that the design would not be top-heavy or tippy.

ROUT RIGHT

Start by routing 5⁄16-in.-deep dadoes in the mid panel for the shelves **(See Photo A).** I used a straight 2 × 4 as a fence and simply screwed it to the plywood. With a carbide-tipped ¾-in. straight router bit and a 2-hp. router, I easily milled each groove in a single pass.

The spacing of the shelves is graduated to provide more room at the bottom for bigger, heavier lumber. Keeping heavy material low makes the cart more stable. In addition, there is also a shallow area at the top which is a perfect storage place for boxes of nails and screws.

PHOTO A: Cut dadoes, 5⁄16-in.-deep × ¾-in.-wide, in the mid panel using a router and a straight 2 × 4 for a fence.

CUT EFFICIENTLY

Using a table saw or a miter saw, cut the 2 × 4 shelf supports so the ends are beveled 6° and parallel. Once you cut the supports to length, you need to index the dadoes that will support the shelves. Use a table saw with a dado blade **(See Photo B).** Tilt the arbor of the saw to 6° and adjust the height so that the bearing (short) edge of the bevel is ½ in. deep.

Next you can rip all of the plywood for the shelves, bin dividers and base. Because it can be dangerous and difficult to rip full sheets on a table saw, I used a circular saw and a 2 × 4 fence **(See Photo C).**

Find the dimension to offset the fence by measuring from the edge of the saw's shoe to the far side of the blade. It is important to support the plywood so it doesn't fall away or bind as you cut. After years of framing, I prefer to saw with the blade side of the shoe riding the fence, but that minimizes the surface area the shoe has to ride on. If you prefer to cut the other way, with the larger side of the shoe against the fence, be sure to measure from that side of the shoe.

ASSEMBLING THE RACK

Once all your pieces are cut, begin the assembly. Start by laying the mid panel across a couple of sawhorses, grooved side down. Lay out the positions of the bin dividers as you want them. In hindsight, I wish I had left at least one bin large enough to accept 24-in.-wide cutoffs. Clamp

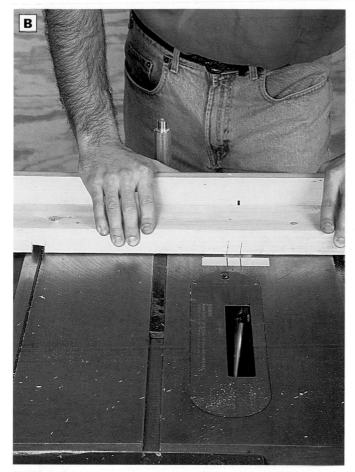

PHOTO B: Draw index marks on a piece of tape on the saw table to align the 6° dadoes in the shelf supports.

PHOTO C: Rip your panel stock with a circular saw and a straightedge. Support the workpiece, and set your blade to cut 1 in. deep.

the two end dividers in position and secure them with glue and 2-in. drywall screws (be sure to predrill to avoid splitting).

Next, clamp a couple of 2 × 4s across the dividers and install the other dividers with glue according to your layout marks. Tighten the clamps and, if necessary, slip shims under the 2 × 4s in order to stabilize each divider. Then continue your predrilling and screwing, using four screws per divider (**See Photo D**).

With the dividers in place, the mid panel should stand up on its own while you temporarily install the top shelf and the end shelf supports with clamps. This will brace the structure as you join the shelves to the mid panel. Work from the bottom up using glue and 2-in. screws at 6-in. intervals. As

you work your way up, you may need to jockey the clamps at the top to get everything to go together. Just be sure to keep the shelves supported throughout this assembly so that they don't tear out of their dadoes.

After all of the shelves are secured, you can permanently attach the five shelf supports. Start with the center one and apply glue to the dadoes. Then install the supports with two 3-in. drywall screws into the edge of each shelf (**See Photo E**).

BUILDING THE BASE

With the rack basically completed, you can turn your attention to the base. Start by cutting the 2 × 4s for the base. There are five stretchers spaced 24 in. on-center. They give you a place to

screw the shelf supports after the base is sheathed.

When you assemble the sides, don't put in the bottom screws right away. Rather, install the top with construction adhesive and screws. Then mount the four casters on the bottom, after predrilling, to avoid splitting the frame (**See Photo F**). This method guarantees that the frame screws will not get in the way when boring the larger-diameter holes for the caster screws.

FINAL ASSEMBLY

With the base completed, place the rack on the base, aligning the bin dividers with the sides and front of the base. Next, predrill and screw through the shelf supports and the base top and into the frame. To attach the front panel to the dividers, glue and clamp the

PHOTO D: Set the mid divider on sawhorses, and clamp the bin dividers in position during installation.

PHOTO E: Install the shelf supports with 3-in. screws and glue, starting at the center.

PHOTO F: For added strength, drive your lag screw at a slight angle when installing the casters.

front so it is flush with the sides of the base, making sure to check the alignment of the bevel on the top of the panel.

The beveled panel should follow the angle of the dividers and be flush with the bottom of the base. Make sure the panel is properly aligned by getting at least one screw into each divider. Then secure it with additional screws in the dividers and the base. Finally, attach the back panel to the base in order to prevent sheet goods from sliding off the cart as you roll it around your shop.

Since the cart is intended as a permanent shop fixture, and is therefore expected to take some abuse, applying a finish is not necessary. If, however, you'd like to increase its durability, several coats of polyurethane will help resist wear and tear. Exterior paint is another option that will add a little color to your shop and let you get creative with your cart's appearance.

Gardener's Bench

W hen gardening, there's nothing like working at a comfortable bench, especially when it's OK to make a bit of a mess in the process. This design cleverly combines many features other potting benches lack. The top is 36 in. high and supports a removable stainless-steel sink that drains into a plastic pail. The sink minimizes the mess when mixing potting materials and rinsing pots. Dry soil that's swept down the drain can be captured in a bucket for reuse. The crude "plumbing" also enables waste water to be recycled in the nearby garden. The sink is removable so it can be hosed down on the ground without soaking the rest of the bench. A simple side hook keeps the hose nozzle within reach (*Continued on page 120*).

Gardener's Bench

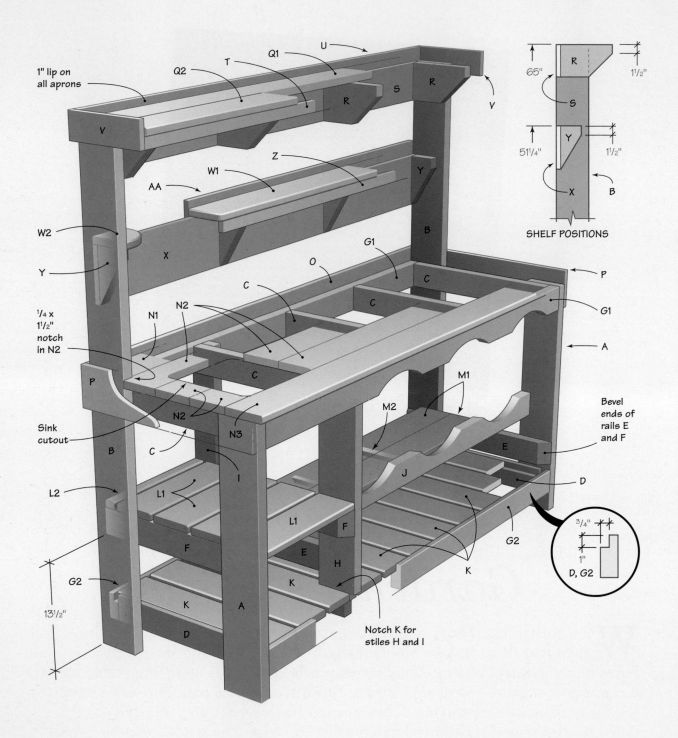

1" lip on all aprons

Q2

T

Q1

U

R

S

R

V

V

W1

Z

AA

Y

W2

X

B

Y

G1

O

C

C

C

N2

N1

C

P

N2

Sink cutout

B

C

N3

L2

B

I

L1

L1

F

F

G2

K

A

D

K

H

E

K

Notch K for stiles H and I

1/4 x 1 1/2" notch in N2

13 1/2"

G2

M1

M2

J

E

D

Bevel ends of rails E and F

A

G1

P

G1

G2

K

3/4"

1"

D, G2

SHELF POSITIONS

65"

R

S

Y

X

B

1 1/2"

51 1/4"

1 1/2"

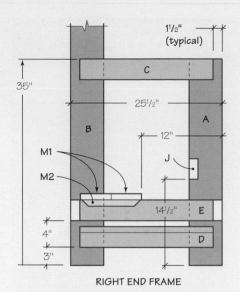

RIGHT END FRAME

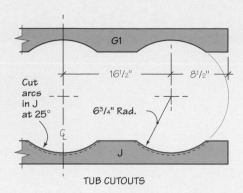

TUB CUTOUTS

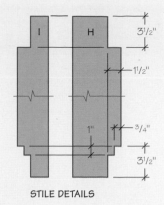

STILE DETAILS

Shopping List

- [ ] (2) 1 × 2 × 6-ft. cedar
- [ ] (1) 1 × 4 × 6-ft. cedar
- [ ] (1) 1 × 6 × 12-ft. cedar
- [ ] (1) 1 × 6 × 6-ft. cedar
- [ ] (1) 1 × 8 × 6-ft. cedar
- [ ] (1) 2 × 4 × 10-ft. cedar
- [ ] (2) 2 × 4 × 12-ft. cedar
- [ ] (3) 2 × 4 × 8-ft. cedar
- [ ] (1) 2 × 6 × 12-ft. cedar
- [ ] (1) 2 × 6 × 8-ft. cedar
- [ ] (1) 5/4 × 6 × 8-ft. cedar
- [ ] (1) 5/4 × 6 × 10-ft. cedar
- [ ] (7) 5/4 × 6 × 12-ft. cedar
- [ ] 2-, 2½- and 3-in. stainless-steel deck screws
- [ ] (4) 5/16 × 3½-in. carriage bolts with nuts and washers
- [ ] (4) 5/16 × 4-in. lag screws with fender washers
- [ ] (3) 10-gallon plastic tubs with lid
- [ ] Plastic storage box (as needed)
- [ ] (1) Plastic bucket
- [ ] Epoxy consolidant
- [ ] Finishing materials

Gardener's Bench Cutting List*

Part/Description		No.	Size
A	Legs (front)	2	1½ × 5½ × 35 in.
B	Legs (back)	2	1½ × 5½ × 65 in.
C	Rails (top)	5	1½ × 3½ × 22½ in.
D	Rails (bottom)	2	1½ × 3½ × 22½ in.
E	Rails (back tub support)	2	1½ × 3½ × 25½ in.
F	Rails (bucket shelf)	2	¾ × 3½ × 25½ in.
G1	Stretchers (top)	2	1½ × 3½ × 69 in.
G2	Stretchers (bottom)	2	1½ × 3½ × 69 in.
H	Stile (front)	1	1½ × 5½ × 32 in.
I	Stile (back)	1	1½ × 3½ × 32 in.
J	Tub cradle	1	1½ × 3½ × 50 in.
K	Bottom shelf	11	1 × 5½ × 24 in.
L1	Bucket shelf	4	1 × 5½ × 17¼ in.
L2	Bucket shelf	1	1 × 1½ × 17¼ in.
M1	Tub support shelf	2	1 × 5¼ × 50 in.
M2	Tub support cleats	2	1½ × 1½ × 10 in.
N1	Top	1	1 × 5¼ × 69 in.
N2	Top	3	1 × 5¼ × 72 in.
N3	Top	1	1 × 5⅜ × 72 in.
O	Aprons (top)	1	¾ × 5½ × 72 in.
P	Aprons (top)	2	¾ × 5½ × 26¼ in.
Q1	Top shelf	1	1 × 5¼ × 72 in.
Q2	Top shelf	1	1 × 5⅜ × 72 in.
R	Gussets (top shelf)	4	1½ × 5½ × 8¾ in.
S	Back panel (top shelf)	1	¾ × 5½ × 69 in.
T	Stiffener (top shelf)	1	¾ × 1½ × 72 in.
U	Apron (top shelf)	1	¾ × 3½ × 72 in.
V	Aprons (top shelf)	2	¾ × 3½ × 11¼ in.
W1	Middle shelf	1	1 × 5¼ × 51½ in.
W2	Middle shelf	1	1 × 5¼ × 4½ in.
X	Back panel (middle shelf)	1	¾ × 7¼ × 69 in.
Y	Gussets (middle shelf)	4	1½ × 3½ × 7¼ in.
Z	Stiffener (middle shelf)	1	¾ × 1½ × 50½ in.
AA	Apron (middle shelf)	1	¾ × 3½ × 51½ in.

*All parts cedar.

PHOTO A: Transfer the radius to a cardboard template to mark the cutouts on the cradle and the top stretcher.

Just below the benchtop are three 10-gallon plastic tubs for storing potting soil, peat moss and sand. They rest at an angle in a contoured cradle that distributes the weight evenly so their sides don't deform. The orientation keeps the tub openings high to minimize bending and makes it easy to scoop materials from each container, even when the supplies are getting low. Tight-fitting lids and cradles keep the containers watertight and tip-proof.

The bench offers plenty of room for temporary staging and long-term storage of gardening paraphernalia. The top and bottom shelves are good for large flats or small pots, while the middle shelf keeps soil additives handy. Shallow aprons prevent small objects from rolling off the backs of the shelves and top, and hand tools hang from hooks above the sink.

MATERIAL CHOICES

I built the bench from cedar because it is light, attractive and relatively rot-resistant. To improve the appearance and durability, I sealed the end grain of the feet with two-part epoxy consolidant before assembly and finished the entire bench with an oil-based, UV-resistant water-repellent finish before installing the towel ring, hose hook and sink. To prevent corrosion and staining, I assembled the lumber with stainless-steel screws and galvanized carriage bolts. The containers include commercial-grade plastic tubs and shallow plastic storage boxes.

I used ⁵⁄₄ × 6 deck boards for many of the parts because they are smooth on four sides and have radiused edges that do not need to be eased with a router. The 2 × 4 and 2 × 6 stock are smooth on all sides but have square corners. The 1× material had one rough side, which I smoothed with a thickness planer for better appearance. If you're unable to find ⁵⁄₄ cedar decking, substitute 2 × 6s for the top and 1 × 6s for the remaining parts that call for ⁵⁄₄ × 6 material. Either way, ease the exposed edges with a

PHOTO B: Assemble the right and left end panels. Be sure to square the pieces before driving screws.

router or a laminate trimmer after the project is fully assembled to prevent splinters. Switch to sandpaper to complete sanding where the tool won't reach.

MAKING THE CUT

Begin by cutting the legs, rails and stretchers to length. Then, cut rabbets along the edges of the lower rails and stretchers so the shelf slats fit flush with the top. That will save precious space above the shelf.

The cutouts in the front top stretcher and the tub cradle hold the tubs in place while they're being used

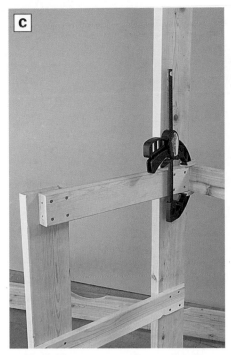

PHOTO C: Clamp the stretchers to the side assemblies for alignment before screwing them in place.

PHOTO D: Position the center assembly between the stretchers, but do not fasten it until the cradle (J) is installed.

PHOTO E: Rest the cradle (J) in position on clamps and attach it to the front stile (H) and the right front leg (A).

and allow them to be removed easily. To make the cutouts, first measure the inside diameter of the tubs below the handles; then add about ⅛ in. to compensate for the thickness of the tub walls. Use a trammel point to strike an arc on a piece of cardboard to make patterns for the barrel cutouts—one for the stretcher and one for the cradle **(See Photo A).**

I cut the cradle's angled curves on a band saw with the table tilted 25° and swung it back to 90° for the stretcher cuts.

SIMPLIFY ASSEMBLY

This project has 70 pieces of lumber. To simplify assembly, fabricate the critical subassemblies first. Then join them with temporary clamps and connecting components so you can square the structure before final assembly.

I put together the left end frame and the right end frame using 2½-in. screws **(See Photo B).** Substitute 2-in. screws in the rabbets and in the bucket shelf rail. Next, I supported the end frames using clamps as outriggers on the leg bottoms and secured the stretchers in place **(See Photo C).** Since the screws have to grab into end grain, make sure they are at least 3 in. long. Fasten the stretchers to the rails and the legs to the stretchers.

Cut notches in the stiles so they will fit between the stretchers; then attach a top rail and the tub support rail using 2½-in. screws. Fit this assembly in

position **(See Photo D);** use clamps to hold the panel in position, if needed. Mark the position of the tub cradle on the right front leg and the front stile; then place the tub cradle into position **(See Photo E).** When all the pieces are square, attach the stiles to the stretchers with 2½-in. screws.

I temporarily fastened the cradle to the stiles with screws. Then, I removed one screw at a time, bored through the joints and installed 5⁄16 × 4-in. lag screws. Next, I attached the bucket shelf rail and installed the remaining top rails with 3-in. screws.

Cut the slats for the bottom shelf and bucket shelf. Then, using 2-in. screws, install the slats so they are spaced about ¾ in. apart. This makes the shelves easier to keep clean. Note that one of the bottom shelf slats must be notched to fit around the stiles. You'll also need to cut a notch in the front bucket shelf to fit around the lag screw.

While the radiused edges of the decking boards work well for the spaced slats, they should be squared for the boards to butt tightly in the top and top shelf assemblies. I ripped ⅛ in. of each board on my table saw.

You need to rip one edge of the top, top shelf and middle shelf. Then you must square both edges of the remaining pieces.

Place the top pieces in position; then use clamps to draw them together. Attach them to the top rails with two 2-in. screws at each joint **(See Photo F).**

PHOTO F: Use clamps to draw the top shelf slats tightly together. Fasten them to the rails with 2-in. screws.

PHOTO G: Clamp the middle shelf in position. Fasten it in place with four 2½-in. screws driven into the gussets.

PHOTO H: Cut the opening so the self-rimming sink fits snugly against the sink tabs without retainer clips.

PHOTO I: To prevent splintering the edges, ease all exposed edges with a small router or laminate trimmer.

The top shelf fits on top of the back legs. Attach the top shelf pieces to the gussets; then add the back panel. For added strength, attach a 1 × 2 stiffener just under the front edge of the shelf. Fasten the shelf to the legs with two ⁵⁄₁₆ × 3½-in. carriage bolts. Then install the middle shelf the same way (**See Photo G).** Complete the top and shelves with their respective aprons.

Make the sink cutout with a jig saw so it fits snugly against the welded clip retainer slots, but do not install the clips (**See Photo H).** Before you install the sink basket, remove the strainer bands with tin snips so they don't catch debris. Fit the basket with a rubber stopper.

Since cedar has a tendency to splinter, it's a good idea to break all the edges of the bench with a router or laminate trimmer (**See Photo I).**

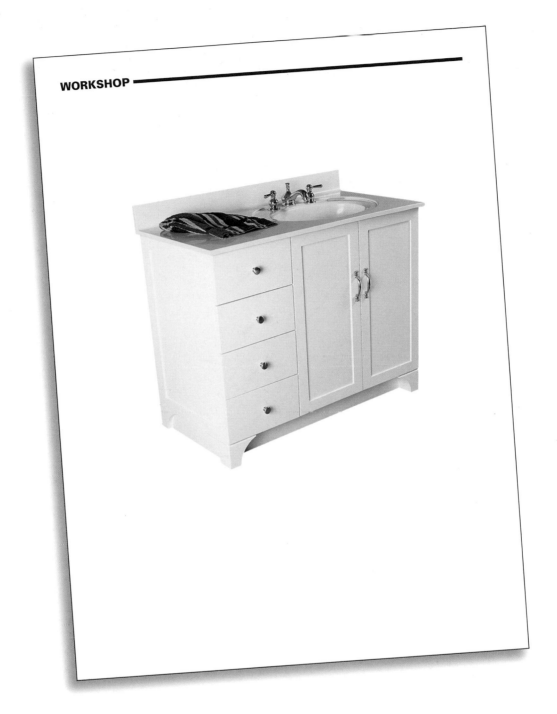

Bathroom Vanity

These days, it can be difficult to find suitable built-in furnishings for older home remodeling jobs. This project proves that you don't have to look any further than your local home center and your own workshop for an appropriate piece. I designed this traditional-looking vanity for a bathroom in a 70-year-old bungalow. It fits so well with its surroundings that you'd never know it's not original to the house.

Bathroom Vanity

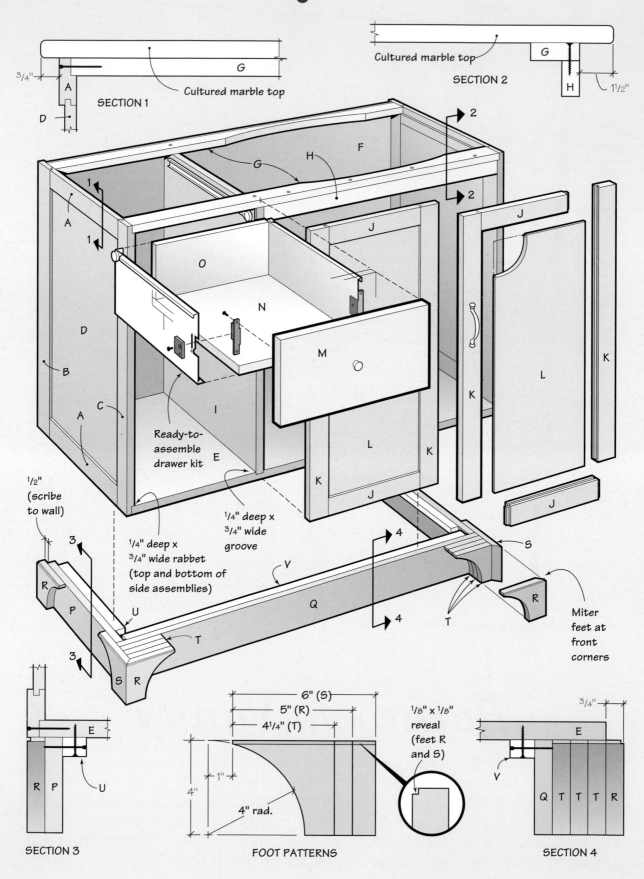

3/4"

A

D

SECTION 1

Cultured marble top

G

Cultured marble top

G

SECTION 2

H

1 1/2"

1

A

1

A

D

B

A

C

D

E

I

O

N

M

Ready-to-assemble drawer kit

F

G

H

J

J

2

2

J

L

K

K

K

L

K

J

1/2" (scribe to wall)

1/4" deep x 3/4" wide rabbet (top and bottom of side assemblies)

1/4" deep x 3/4" wide groove

V

Q

4

4

S

T

R

Miter feet at front corners

3

R

P

U

T

3

S

R

T

R

SECTION 3

E

R P

U

6" (S)

5" (R)

4 1/4" (T)

1"

4"

4" rad.

FOOT PATTERNS

1/8" x 1/8" reveal (feet R and S)

3/4"

E

V

Q T T T R

SECTION 4

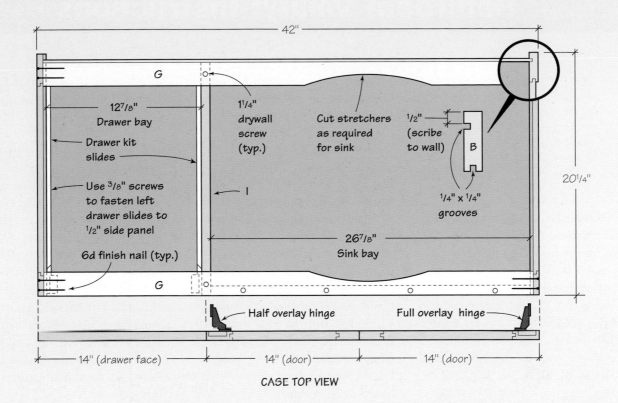

42"

G

12⁷⁄₈"
Drawer bay

Drawer kit
slides

1¹⁄₄"
drywall
screw
(typ.)

Cut stretchers
as required
for sink

½"
(scribe
to wall)

B

Use ³⁄₈" screws
to fasten left
drawer slides to
½" side panel

I

¼" × ¼"
grooves

6d finish nail (typ.)

26⁷⁄₈"
Sink bay

20¹⁄₄"

G

Half overlay hinge

Full overlay hinge

14" (drawer face)

14" (door)

14" (door)

CASE TOP VIEW

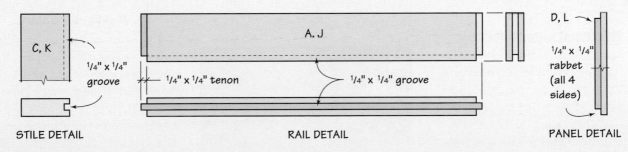

C, K

¼" × ¼"
groove

A, J

¼" × ¼" tenon

¼" × ¼" groove

D, L

¼" × ¼"
rabbet
(all 4
sides)

STILE DETAIL

RAIL DETAIL

PANEL DETAIL

Bathroom Vanity Cutting List

Part	/Description	No.	Size	Material
A	Side rail	4	¾ × 2 × 16¼ in.	MDF
B	Side stile (rear)	2	¾ × 2½ × 29¼ in.	"
C	Side stile (front)	2	¾ × 2 × 29¼ in.	"
D	Side panel	2	½ × 16¼ × 25½ in.	"
E	Bottom	1	¾ × 19½ × 41 in.	"
F	Back (birch ply)	1	¼ × 29¼ × 41 in.	"
G	Top stretcher	2	¾ × 2 × 41 in.	"
H	Top cleat	1	¾ × 26⅞ × 1½ in.	"
I	Divider	1	¾ × 19½ × 28 in.	"
J	Door rail	4	¾ × 2 × 10½ in.	"
K	Door stile	4	¾ × 2 × 29 in.	"

Part	/Description	No.	Size	Material
L	Door panel	2	½ × 10½ × 25¼ in.	MDF
M	Drawer face*	4	¾ × 7¹⁄₁₆ × 14 in.	"
N	Drawer bottom*	4	¾ × 11⅝ × 16⅞ in.	"
O	Drawer back*	4	¾ × 5⅞ × 11⅝ in.	"
P	Base side	2	¾ × 4 × 16½ in.	"
Q	Base front	1	¾ × 4 × 40½ in.	"
R	Foot (front, back side)	4	¾ × 4 × 5 in.	"
S	Foot (front side)	2	¾ × 4 × 6 in	"
T	Front leg fillers	6	¾ × 4 × 4¼ in.	"
U	Side cleat	2	¾ × 1 × 13 in.	"
V	Front cleat	1	¾ × 1 × 38¾ in.	"

Also required: (4) concealed hinges, (4) ready-to-assemble drawer kits, coarse-thread drywall screws, 6d finish nails, wood glue, finishing materials, cultured marble top, (4) knobs, (2) pulls.

*Used in conjunction with ready-to-assemble drawer kits.

To maintain a consistent style with the house, this vanity required recessed panels and arched feet. Standard vanities are 30 in. tall and typically 36 or 48 in. wide, but the interior designer for this project specified that the vanity be 34 in. tall for comfort and 42 in. wide to make the most of the available space. Without a doubt, a custom design was the only way to go.

MATERIALS PREPARATION

Nowadays, there's no reason why cabinets that look traditional can't use the latest materials and hardware. I specified medium-density fiberboard (MDF), ready-to-assemble drawer kits and concealed pocket hinges for this project. Each Blum Metabox drawer kit includes two metal sides and a pair of side-mounted glides. The drawer face, bottom and back must be cut to desired dimensions. Other ready-to-assemble systems are available in a wide range of sizes at local home centers.

MDF is a sheet material that has become quite popular with amateur woodworkers. The surface is smoother than the finest plywood, so it takes paint well. It's not veneered, so you don't have to worry about grain direction when you cut, rout or sand it. This minimizes waste and errors. And unlike plywood, it does not require edge-banding. I can get MDF for half the price of birch plywood and one-third the cost of clear pine on a square-foot basis.

Working with MDF does require a few special considerations. Because the cut edges are porous, you must sand and seal them before priming. The maker suggests "sizing" edges with thinned wood glue (one part glue, two parts water) applied with a brush and then sanded smooth when dry. But the glue mixture dries slowly and tends to gum up your sandpaper. I prefer to size the edges with two coats of water-based polyurethane. It dries very quickly and sands cleaner than the glue.

PHOTO A: An auxiliary top forms a gap-free base when mortising the narrow frame stock.

Since MDF is abrasive, use carbide-tipped saw blades and router bits, and always predrill before driving nails or screws to prevent the sides from bulging or splitting. Because of its composition, you will produce a lot of fine sawdust when you cut MDF. Be sure to wear a good particle mask during any milling operations. An efficient dust collection system is also a good idea. Although it's true that MDF is more moisture-resistant than particleboard, it isn't waterproof. Be sure to seal all edges inside and out, especially the bottoms of the feet, which will inevitably come in contact with damp floors.

PERFECT FRAMES

Use ¾-in. MDF for the stiles and rails and ½ in. for the panels. The drawer faces are small, so make each from a single piece of ¾-in. MDF. Determining the dimensions of the stiles is easy. They run the full height of the doors and the sides. The rails run horizontally between the stiles. To get their length, subtract the widths of stiles and add back the lengths of tenons. For instance, the 14-in.-wide doors called for 10½-in.-long rails (14-in. doors minus two 2-in.-wide stiles plus two ¼-in.-long tenons).

After ripping the rails and stiles to size for the sides and doors, fit your table saw with a dado blade and cut a ¼ × ¼-in. dado down the middle of one long edge of all the stile and rail stock (See Photo A). The slots will eventually house tenons on the ends of the rails, as well as the edges of the panels for the sides and doors.

To cut the tenons a uniform ¼ in. deep, clamp a short block to your table saw's rip fence and align it with the right edge of the ¼-in. dado blade. Then index each rail against the block before sliding it forward on the miter gauge to cut rabbets on both sides **(See Photo B).** Make sure the tenons are a bit short of the dado depth or they will hold the stile and rail joints open when glue is applied. The cut edges of the door frame components must be sealed before assembly. Apply two coats of water-based polyurethane with a small brush **(See Photo C).** This fast-drying sealer will sand much cleaner than any glue product.

GLUING PANELS

Your next step is to make the recessed panels. Wood expands and contracts across the grain, so panels usually must be allowed to float within the frame. Because it lacks directional grain, MDF expands and contracts equally in all directions. Since the doors and side panels are all made entirely of MDF, you can glue all of the joints.

Cut the panels from ½-in.-thick MDF and rabbet the back edges so they fit in the dadoes and are flush with the backs of the rails and stiles.

It's easier to sand the saw marks off the inside edges of the stiles and rails before you assemble the doors. But for a professional finish, sand the face joints and outside edges flush.

FRAMELESS CABINET

A cabinet is just a box (or carcase) with doors and drawers. This design has no face frame, and the top consists of two narrow stretchers that are trimmed as needed to make room for the sink. There is also a 1½-in. cleat under the front stretcher to strengthen it.

Make the rear stiles on the cabinet sides ½ in. wider than the others so you can scribe them to fit the wall. Use a table saw or a router to cut the dadoes and rabbets that hold the case together. First, cut ¼ × ¾-in. rabbets along the top and bottom edges of the sides to join them to the top stretchers and the bottom. Then cut a ¼ × ¾-in. dado in the bottom to house the vertical divider. Cut a ¼-in.-deep × ¼-in.-wide groove (inset ½ in.) in the sides to accept the ¼-in. plywood back.

Fasten the sides of the cabinets to the stretchers and bottom with wood glue and 6d finish nails. Use glue and 1¼-in.-long coarse-thread drywall screws to attach the divider to the stretchers, bottom and back for added strength. This extra support is a good idea since the fasteners won't show. When the glue dries, remove the clamps and sand the joints flush.

PHOTO B: For uniform tenons, index rails against a block clamped to the saw's rip fence.

PHOTO C: Size the porous MDF edges with two coats of water-based polyurethane before priming.

PHOTO D: Drawer faces are fully adjustable to the drawer kit's sides and mounting hardware to achieve a perfect fit.

127

PHOTO E: A spacer block ensures uniform height when installing pairs of drawer slides.

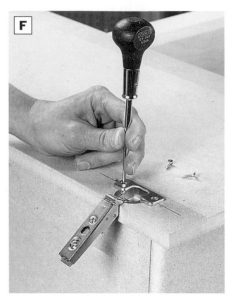

PHOTO F: Center punch, then predrill for screws to avoid splitting the MDF stiles.

PHOTO G: Make a template for the feet to ensure uniform arches.

QUICK, QUALITY DRAWERS

Begin by straight-cutting the drawer bottoms and backs from ¾-in. stock and attaching them to the epoxy-coated metal sides with screws. The drawer faces are attached with special adjustable brackets so you can move the faces up, down or side to side for a perfect fit (**See Photo D**). Then attach the side-mounted drawer slides (**See Photo E**). *CAUTION: You may need to substitute shorter (⅜-in.) screws when securing the left drawer slides to the ½-in.-thick side panel. Some standard drawer slide assembly screws will punch through the panel face.*

The left door is a half overlay and the right door is a full overlay. Both pocket hinges and mounting plates are concealed when the doors are closed. To install the hardware, drill 35mm holes for the hinge cups in the backs of the doors and secure the hardware to the doors and the case with screws (**See Photo F**). Separate adjustment screws let you shift the door in any direction for a perfect fit.

PRACTICAL BASE WITH FANCY FEET

While the cabinet looks like it is a chest resting on arched feet, it actually is supported by an MDF base frame that is recessed ¾ in. from the case on the sides and 3 in. from the front. This maintains the furniture look. It also provides a comfortable toe space, while sealing off the area under the cabinet to facilitate floor cleaning. The feet are flush with the door faces and the cabinet sides.

Between the vanity cabinet and the radiator frame, our project called for a dozen arched pieces. To make sure your feet match, make a template jig with MDF, using a compass to draw the arc (**See Photo G**). Then trace the form on the feet blanks and rough-cut the shapes with a band saw or jig saw. Finish the shaping using the jig and a router fitted with a flush-trimming bit (**See Photo H**). Secure the feet to the base from inside with glue and nails.

We finished the cabinet with an HVLP spray system. We applied one coat of alkyd enamel underbody and two coats of low-luster alkyd enamel paint. The

PHOTO H: Screw the rough-cut feet to the template and shape with a flush-trimming bit.

custom-sized cultured marble top is from a national marble supplier, while the faucet and drain kit were purchased from my local home center.

Corner Curio

Here's a corner cabinet that really fits. It fits the small corner of our dining room better than anything we could find in the furniture stores. And it fits our storage and display needs—to showcase some things, hide others and keep everything dust-free. And because I built it myself from affordable materials, it also fit within our budget. Compared to what you would pay for a similar piece in a furniture store, you could fill this cabinet with lead crystal and still be ahead.

Corner Curio

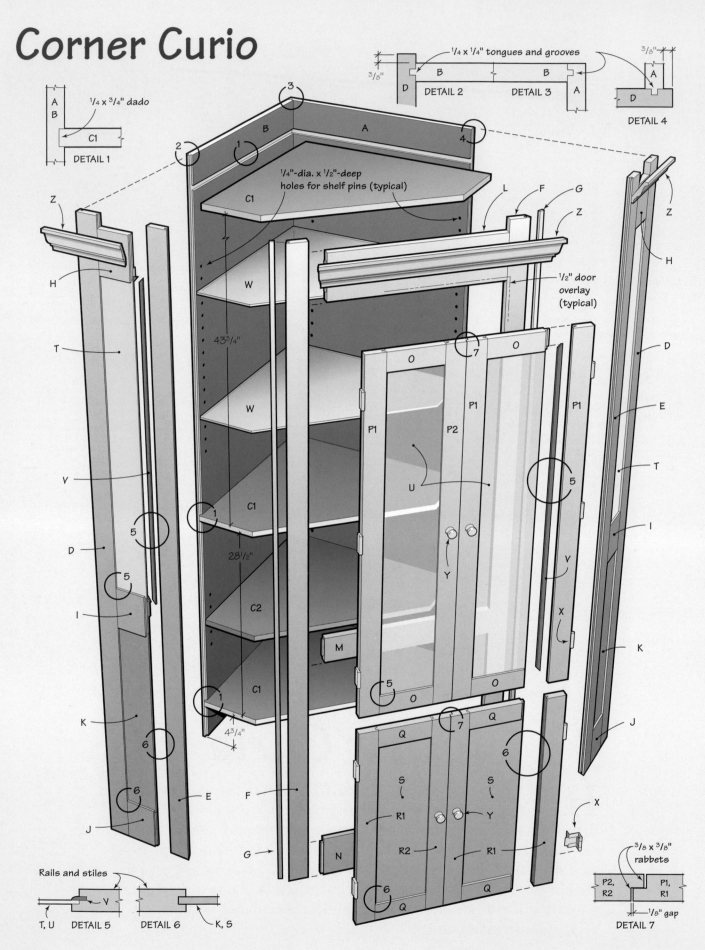

DETAIL 1
$1/4 \times 3/4$" dado
A B
C1

$1/4 \times 1/4$" tongues and grooves
DETAIL 2 B D
DETAIL 3 B A
$3/8$"

$3/8$"
A
D
DETAIL 4

3

B A

4

C1

$1/4$"-dia. x $1/2$"-deep
holes for shelf pins (typical)

L F G
Z

$1/2$" door
overlay
(typical)

Z

H
Z

T

W

$43^3/4$"

W

O O
7

P1

P1

P1
P1 P2

D

E

U

5

T

5

V

C1

X

28$1/2$"

Y

K

C2

M

5

O

I

O

J

C1

Q
7
Q

$43^3/4$"

Q

6

E

F

S S

R1
R2 R1

Y

G

N

X

6

Q

Rails and stiles
V
T, U   **DETAIL 5**   **DETAIL 6**   K, S

$3/8 \times 3/8$"
rabbets
P2,
R2   P1,
R1
$1/8$" gap
DETAIL 7

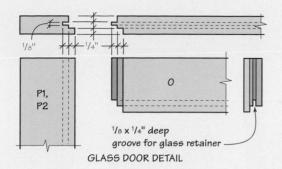

GLASS DOOR DETAIL

⅛ × ¼" deep
groove for glass retainer

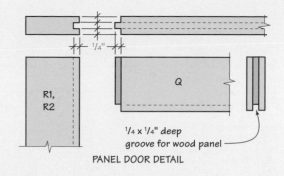

PANEL DOOR DETAIL

¼ × ¼" deep
groove for wood panel

Shopping List

- ☐ (3) ¾ × 49 × 97-in. MDF
- ☐ (6) 96-in. 1 × 6 red oak
- ☐ (1) ¼ × 24 × 48-in. oak plywood
- ☐ (1) 72 in. × 4-in. oak crown molding
- ☐ (2) ¼-in. glass shelves with polished edges
- ☐ (4) ⅛-in. tempered glass panes
- ☐ (10) Self-closing brass overlay hinges
- ☐ (4) Solid brass pulls
- ☐ (1) Plastic glass retainer
- ☐ (15) Shelf pins with rubber cushions
- ☐ (1) Light
- ☐ 1⅝-, 3-in. drywall screws
- ☐ Wood glue
- ☐ Finishing materials

Corner Curio Cutting List

Part/Description	No.	Size	Material
A Back panel (right)	1	¾ × 26 × 84 in.	MDF
B Back panel (left)	1	¾ × 25½ × 84 in.	"
C1 Top/bottom/ fixed shelves	3	¾ × 25½ × 25½ in.	"
C2 Adjustable shelf	1	¾ × 24¹¹⁄₁₆ × 24¹¹⁄₁₆ in.	"

Face Frame Cutting List

Part/Description	No.	Size	Material
D Stiles (outside)	2	¾ × 2⅝ × 84 in.	Oak
E Stiles (inside)	2	¾ × 2½ × 84 in.	"
F Stiles (center)	2	¾ × 2½ × 84 in.	"
G Splines	2	¼ × ½ × 84 in.	Plywood
H Rails (upper side)	1	¾ × 5½ × 4³⁄₁₆ in.	Oak
I Rails (center side)	2	¾ × 5½ × 4³⁄₁₆ in.	"
J Rails (lower side)	2	¾ × 5½ × 4³⁄₁₆ in.	"
K Panel (lower side)	2	¼ × 4⅛ × 26½ in.	Oak ply
L Rail (upper middle)	1	¾ × 5½ × 21 in.	Oak
M Rail (center middle)	1	¾ × 3½ × 21 in.	"
N Rail (lower middle)	1	¾ × 5½ × 21 in.	"

Doors, Etc., Cutting List

Part/Description	No.	Size	Material
O Rails (glass door)	4	¾ × 2¼ × 7⅜ in.	Oak
P1 Stiles (glass door)	3	¾ × 2¼ × 43 in.	"
P2 Stile (glass door)	1	¾ × 2⅝ × 43 in.	"
Q Rails (panel door)	4	¾ × 2¼ × 6¾ in.	"
R1 Stiles (panel door)	3	¾ × 2¼ × 27 in.	"
R2 Stile (panel door)	1	¾ × 2⅝ × 27 in.	"
S Door panels	2	¼ × 6⅝ × 22⅞ in.	Oak ply
T Side panes	2	⅛ × 4⅛ × 40⅜ in.	Tempered glass
U Door panes	2	⅛ × 6¾ × 39 in.	"
V Glass retainer		Cut to fit	
W Glass shelves	2	¼ × cut to fit	Glass
X Hinges	10	2¾ in.	Polished brass
Y Pulls	4	1½ in. dia.	Solid brass
Z Crown molding	1	4 in. × 72 in.	Oak

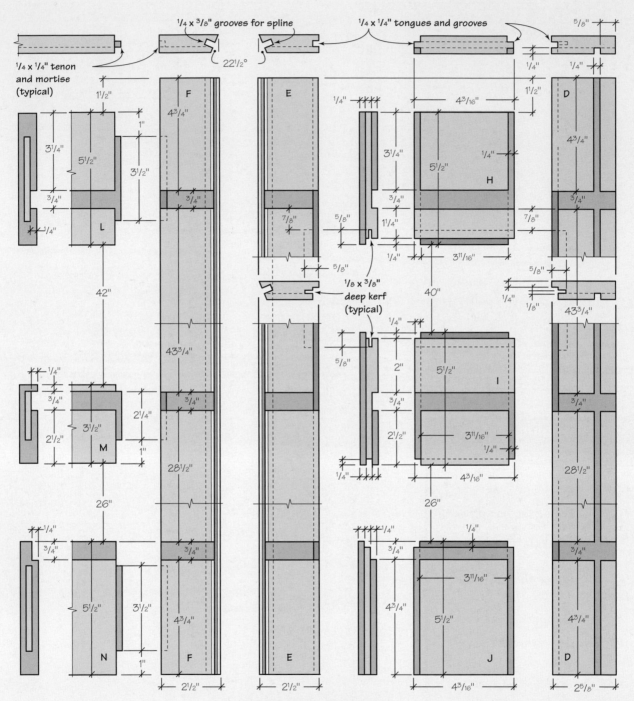

¼ x ⅜" grooves for spline

¼ x ¼" tongues and grooves

⅝"

¼ x ¼" tenon and mortise (typical)

22½°

¼"

¼"

DETAILS OF CABINET RAILS AND STILES

The face and sides of the corner curio are solid red oak. The lower panels are oak plywood. And the case and some shelves are medium-density fiberboard (MDF). I chose MDF for the case because it remains smooth when painted and is easy to mill. Be sure to store the oak in your shop for at least a week before you cut it so it can adjust to the temperature and humidity.

GETTING STARTED

Begin by cutting all the oak parts to size. First rip them ⅛ in. oversize, then joint them to the finished dimensions.

Large plywood and MDF panels are easy to rip to width on a table saw, but cutting them to length can be awkward. To make these cuts, I use a router jig that's simply a 1 × 2 hardwood fence glued to a ¼-in.-thick × 30-in.-long piece of plywood. The width of the plywood is determined by the size of your router base and the size of the bit you use initially. When you run the router with a straight bit along the fence, it will cut off the excess plywood. To use this jig, mark where you want to cut the panel, align the jig's plywood edge with the mark and then make the cut. Be sure to wear a dust mask during this operation; cutting the fine particles that make up MDF produces a large amount of dust.

PHOTO A: Cut dadoes in the back panels for the top, fixed shelf and bottom using a router fitted with a ¾-in. straight bit.

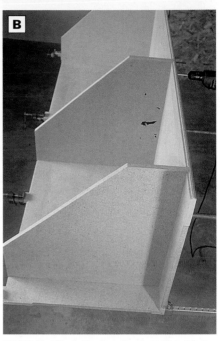

PHOTO B: Attach the top, fixed shelf and bottom to the back panels with glue and screws.

Now you need to cut three ¼-in.-deep, ¾-in.-wide dadoes in back panels A and B for the top, bottom and fixed shelf. Mark their positions, clamp the router jig in place and make the cuts (See Photo A). To prevent the cabinet from rocking on an uneven floor, make relief cuts along the bottom of each panel. Mark 1½ in. from each end, clamp your jig ¼ in. from the bottom, then remove the waste between the marks.

To reinforce the joint between the two back panels, I cut a tongue-and-groove joint. Use your router and a long straightedge to make both the tongue and the groove. Clamp a support behind the straightedge so that it won't flex. Also cut tongues on the front edge of each panel to fit into grooves in the back of the face frame.

The top, bottom and center fixed shelf are already cut to size as

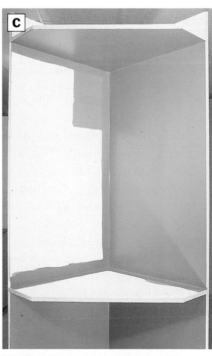

PHOTO C: Prime and paint the case interior before assembling the sides and face.

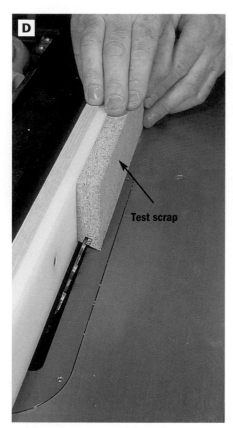

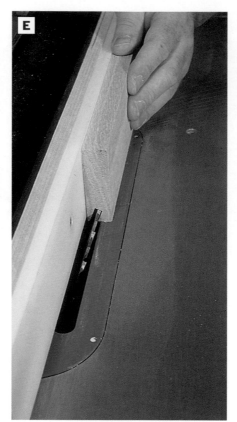

PHOTO D: Using scrap, set up spline-groove cuts with the blade angle set to 22½°.

PHOTO E: Move the fence and make a second cut so the spline will fit into the groove.

PHOTO F: After cutting the spline groove, adjust the fence and rip the stiles to wwidth.

squares and you can trim them to their final shape using the router jig. Glue and clamp the two back panels together. Use clamping blocks with grooves in them so you don't collapse the tongues. Then use glue and 1⅝-in. drywall screws to attach the top, the bottom and the fixed shelf **(See Photo B).** This will ensure that your cabinet is square.

Now make the adjustable shelf. It is the same size as the glass shelves, so make a cardboard pattern to take to the glass shop. Before you assemble the face, prime and finish the case interior and shelf **(See Photo C).** Be sure to leave the areas that will eventually be glued unfinished.

MILL THE BEVEL JOINTS

Making the beveled edges of the face frame stiles may seem intimidating, but they aren't that difficult if you follow these steps. First, set

your table saw blade to 22½° and rip a piece of ¾-in.-thick scrap so that the top face is 2½ in. wide. Now stand the scrap on edge and adjust the fence and blade height to cut the groove for the spline **(See Photo D).** Once the setup is correct, repeat the process with the good stock. Rip the groove in all four stiles. Move the fence ⅛ in. to complete the grooves and check this setup with your scrap piece **(See Photo E).** Move the fence back, lay the stiles flat on the table and rip the bevels **(See Photo F).** Make the splines from ¼-in. plywood, then check the fit of the parts.

MILL THE STILES

Cut ¼ × ¼-in. grooves lengthwise in the outside stiles for the MDF tongues on the back pieces. Use your router jig to cut the dadoes across all six stiles to accept the top, bottom and fixed

shelf. Mill two stiles at a time **(See Photo G).** To avoid tearout, put some ¼-in.-square scraps in the spline grooves **(See Photo H).** Cut a ¼ × ¼-in. groove in one edge of the four outside and inside stiles for the panels.

Because glass fits in the upper half of the cabinet, you need to cut away the inside wall of each of these grooves between the fixed shelf dado and the top dado. Set up and test with scrap before cutting the workpieces.

The glass is held in place by a continuous plastic retainer strip that fits into a ⅛-in.-wide kerf cut into the stiles. Make this cut, and limit it to the area between the fixed shelf and the top of the cabinet **(See Photo I).** Use your router table and a ¼-in. straight bit to cut ¼-in.-deep mortises in the center stiles for the three middle rail tenons.

PHOTOS G & H: Gang-cut the dadoes across two or more stiles with the router edge-guide jig clamped in place. Prevent router tearout by clamping ¼-in.-square scraps in the grooves and rabbets. Be sure the scraps are flush with the surface of the workpiece.

PHOTO I: Using the table saw, make a stopped-rabbet groove in the side stiles to accommodate the glass pane.

SIX SIDE RAILS

Cut ¼-in.-deep × ¾-in.-wide grooves in the backs of the upper and center side rails for the top and fixed shelf. Cut a rabbet in the lower side rail for the bottom. Next, cut the kerfs for the glass retainer strip in the bottom edge of the upper rail and in the top edge of the center rail. Now cut ½-in.-wide × ¼-in.-deep rabbets on the same edges. This leaves a ¼-in. lip to hold the glass.

Now make ¼ × ¼-in. grooves in the center and lower rails for the plywood panels (on the lower rail, the cut will look like a stepped rabbet because of the groove made for the bottom). Finally, cut the tongues on the ends of the rails using your router table. Move on to the three middle rails and cut the tongues on the ends and grooves in the back of each piece.

ATTACH THE FACE FRAME

Because this face frame is large and has some angled pieces, it's best to assemble it in stages. Start by gluing up the beveled stile joints **(See Photo J.)** To ensure a tight fit, I made five clamping fixtures out of scrap wood to draw the parts together. When the glue is dry, glue and nail one of the outside stiles in place, then work your way around to the other **(See Photo K).** Predrill the oak to avoid splitting. It's a good idea to use scrap and C-clamps to protect the beveled edges during this assembly **(See Photo L).** Set the nails and fill the holes after the glue dries. Sand any uneven joints flush, then finish-sand the frame.

MAKE THE DOORS

Start with the panel doors. Rout a ¼ × ¼-in. groove in the stiles and rails for the plywood panel. Note that one of the center stiles is wider to form an overlapping door closure. Next, cut ¼-in. tenons on the ends of the rails with the table saw and miter gauge. Use an auxiliary fence to avoid binding. Use your router table to cut the two rabbets for the door closure, then glue and clamp the doors together. Don't glue the panels into the grooves; they must float to accommodate wood movement.

Make the upper (glass) doors the same way, except that instead of cutting a panel groove, make a saw kerf for the retainer strip and a rabbet for the glass.

The tongue that locks into the stile on the ends of each glass door rail has a second ⅛-in.-wide tongue that seats into the kerf. You can cut this with your table saw, but set up the cut with scrap first. Glue and clamp the doors and, after the glue dries, sand them flush and smooth. You now can apply the finish to all the oak parts.

INSTALL YOUR CABINET

If you plan to put a light in your cabinet, install an outlet on the wall just above the cabinet, where it will be concealed by the crown molding. Set the cabinet (less doors and glass) in place and shim it, if necessary, so it is plumb. Then scribe and trim the back stiles so they fit snug to the walls. Secure the cabinet to the wall with 3-in. drywall screws that penetrate into the studs.

Install the glass side and door panes next. Just push the retainer strip into its kerf and miter the corners with a sharp knife. To install the doors, clamp a straight 2¼-in.-wide scrap piece ½ in. below the upper opening; then rest the doors on the scrap and center them. Bore holes for the hinge screws, then install the doors. Butt the lower doors against the scrap and repeat the process.

Using your drill press, bore holes every 2 in. along the scrap piece to make a guide for drilling shelf pin holes. Drill one set of holes in the back corner of each compartment, another set at the outside edge of each back panel close to where it meets the face frame and a third set on the inside of each center stile. Use brass shelf pins with rubber cushions for the glass shelves and regular brass pins for the adjustable shelf.

Center the pulls on the stiles and install them. Now you only

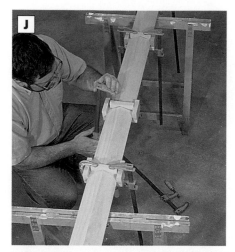

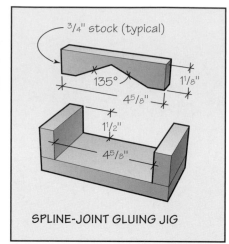

SPLINE-JOINT GLUING JIG

PHOTO J: Use a spline-joint gluing jig (see drawing, right) to draw together the beveled stiles (E, F). Make a 135° fixture to hold the beveled spline joints together for gluing.

PHOTO K: Check the fit of all the pieces, then glue the face frame to the case.

PHOTO L: When clamping, use C-clamps and scrap to protect beveled edges from damage.

need to install the crown molding around the top of the cabinet and the baseboard around the bottom. Then, attach the light as close as possible to the front.

Building Custom Cabinets

Most base cabinets are built the same way whether they are to be exposed on the sides or fit into a narrow alcove. That not only wastes time and materials, but also results in some cabinets that are less functional and more difficult to install than they should be. This custom cabinetry project highlights several tips and techniques to help you avoid the usual pitfalls and develop the perfect cabinet for your space.

137

Building Custom Cabinets

Our remodeling project called for an odd-sized cabinet to fit an opening that was roughly 15 in. deep, 45 in. tall and 92 in. wide. Because stock cabinets wouldn't fit, this situation presented the perfect opportunity to build a custom cabinet that not only performs well but is also a breeze to install.

CASE CONSTRUCTION

Although I appreciate fine woodworking, I also believe it's unnecessary to make anything more complicated than it needs to be. Since the case would be completely enclosed by walls, I built it with butt joints. I relied on plate-joining biscuits for alignment of the pieces and a combination of screws, nails and glue for fastening.

The case and the shelves are made with white, melamine-coated particleboard because it is affordable, easy to clean and bright (no one likes a dark cabinet interior). Best of all, it does not require finishing, unless you count ironing on edging tape to finish the edges of the shelves.

Granted, particleboard is heavy and weaker than plywood, but that hardly matters for a captured base cabinet like this. Actually, this base cabinet is rock solid because the case is a complete box with a solid back, sides, base and top. With its melamine skin and tight joints, the case leaves no openings for crumbs to collect or ants to sneak in. That's much better than the typical backless base cabinet.

A few operations must be performed before assembly. After cutting all parts to size, drill shelf pin holes into the sides using a jig that ensures proper depth and spacing (**See Photo A**). Biscuit slots must then be cut along all of the sides in order to aid in alignment (**See Photo B**).

This case is easy to assemble because it requires no clamps: the screws hold the joints tight while the glue dries. Still, with a large case like this, it pays to be methodical (and to test fit) so assembly doesn't

PHOTO A: Drill shelf pin holes in the sides using a jig to guide hole spacing, depth and alignment. Anchor the jig at each end with ¼-in. drill bits.

become a mad race. Predrill all of the screw holes and assemble the case without glue to make sure all the parts fit and to work out the assembly sequence (**See Photo C**). When you are ready to permanently assemble the case, have all the parts laid out in place. Glue all of the biscuits in one side of each joint. Then glue the other halves and run a bead of glue along the edges before you join the pieces with screws (**See Photo D**). Keep in mind that you will need to use a thin bead of polyurethane glue rather than wood glue where the melamine faces butt against the particleboard edges (**See Photo E**), but don't use the polyurethane glue on the biscuits themselves. Iron-on tape is a simple solution for covering the exposed edges of the melamine shelves (**See Photo F**).

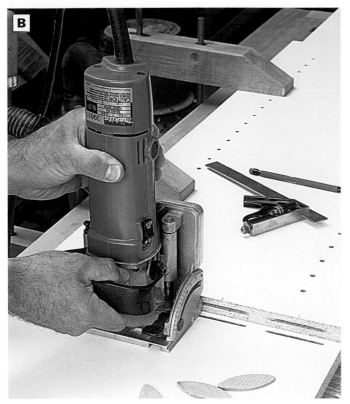

PHOTO B: To cut biscuit slots in the middle of a workpiece, clamp the mating piece along the edge mark. Then center the tool on the corresponding biscuit slot.

PHOTO C: Dry-fit the case sections with biscuits and predrill all screw holes to ensure a good fit before permanently assembling them.

FACE IT

The ¾-in. particleboard case with its ½-in. particleboard back would have been sturdy enough on its own, but I finished the front with an oak face frame for a more traditional look. The face frame is made of ¾-in.-thick stock that is joined with biscuits, glue and brads. Biscuits along the top edge of the frame ensure a flush relationship with the top of the case **(See Photo G)**. A pneumatic nailer makes easy work of attaching the face frame to the case **(See Photo H)**.

While I took a utilitarian approach to building the case, I put a lot of thought into the aesthetics of the face frame and doors because they're the only parts of the cabinet that would show.

DOOR CONSTRUCTION

You don't need a lot of expensive tools to make strong, attractive doors. To simplify construction, I bought 1 × 3 (¾ × 2½ in. actual size) face-frame stock from the lumberyard so I didn't have to mill my own rails and stiles.

Because all the door frame parts are the same width, organizing them was simple. Instead of using a shaper and door set to produce traditional coped joints, I used a plate joiner and cut double biscuit slots for each rail/stile joint **(See Photo I)**. The fin-

PHOTO D: Glue all of the biscuits in one side of the joint. Then glue the other half just before joining the pieces with screws.

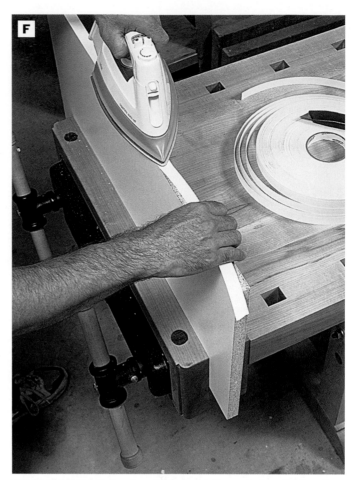

PHOTO E: Use polyurethane glue and screws to attach the back. Poly glue sticks well to melamine and particleboard.

PHOTO F: Cut the shelves from ¾-in. melamine-coated particleboard; then finish the edges with iron-on tape.

PHOTO G: Use biscuits along the top edge of the assembled face frame to align it flush with the top of the case.

ished joints are tight and flush and they probably are stronger than coped joints. Two straight boards clamped perpendicularly on your workbench make a handy jig to facilitate square door frame assembly **(See Photo J).** Apply even pressure during the glue-up, being careful not to elevate the frame above the bench **(See Photo K).**

Rather than try to cut stopped grooves for the recessed panels, I routed a rabbet in the back of the assembled door frame **(See Photo L).** This technique simplifies door assembly because you can glue up the rails and stiles without worrying about getting glue in the loose-panel grooves. Keep in mind that when you rout a rabbet in the back of the door frames to accept the panels, you need to square the corners with a chisel (or radius

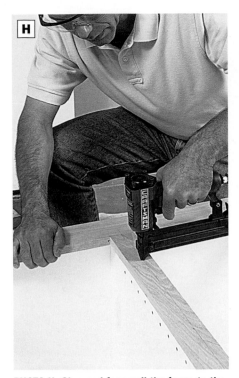

PHOTO H: Glue and face-nail the frame to the case. Nail along a pencil centerline on the frame stock.

PHOTO I: Use double rows of biscuits to join the door rails and stiles. Center the slots so they don't break out the ends.

PHOTO J: To assemble square door frames, square, then clamp a two-board jig to your benchtop.

the square corners of the panels). The panels are installed afterward using screw-mounted retainer clips for fastening.

Keeping the panels separate greatly improves finishing because you can stain and finish the panels and the door frames separately. This way, you don't end up with a strip of unfinished wood showing if the panel happens to shrink over time. It also enables you to substitute glass or panels that are stained or painted a different color.

To mount the doors to the cabinet, I used ¾-in.-overlay, concealed face-frame hinges. These hinges are easy to install provided you have a drill press and a 35mm (1⅜-in.) hinge-boring bit. Because they are adjustable in two directions, you can align the doors perfectly as long as the frames are square.

DESIGN TO FIT

It may seem odd, but installa-tion is one of the first and most important things you should think about when designing and constructing a built-in cabinet. The case should not completely fill its allotted space, because walls sel-dom are built with the same preci-sion as a cabinet. You should allow enough room around the case so it can be installed plumb and square in what's often an out-of-square space.

In this instance, the cabinet fit in a cove so only its front showed. I made the case 1 in. narrower than the opening and let the face frame project ½ in. on both sides so it could be scribed to fit the walls after leveling and plumbing the cabinet. I also made the cabinet 1 in. shallower than the space so I could match the reveals on both ends if the two walls were not perfectly aligned.

Normally, I would rabbet the end stiles (the vertical members of the face frame) and fit them with narrow scribe strips so I could fit the frame tight to the walls. This time, I tried a new technique recommended by a professional trim carpenter (See *Pro Tips for a Perfect Installation*, page 144). By leaving the right stile loose, we were able to fit the cabinet into the space and scribe both ends without the need for separate scribe strips.

Most base cabinets are leveled and plumbed with shims. Since this cabinet was huge and heavy and the space offered no access from the sides or the back, I fitted it with leveling legs. They are installed under the base when you build the case. Then they can be raised or lowered from inside the cabinet using a screwdriver **(See Photo M)**. The base cavity needs to be at least 3½ in. tall to accommodate the adjustable supports. The supports were particularly useful in this project because the floor was uneven after the old wall plate was removed.

Once the unit is sufficiently level, scribe the stile with a pencil and a shim **(See Photo N)**. With the cabinet lying on its back, plane down to the scribed line and cut a back bevel **(See Photo O)**. Put the cabinet back in place and refit the loose stile after ripping it with a 5° bevel that's ⅛ in. wider than needed to provide a tight fit

PHOTO K: Tighten bar clamps until the joints just close. Be sure the frame does not lift off the bench top.

PHOTO L: Secure the door frame on all four sides; then use a piloted rabbeting bit to cut the rabbet for the door panel.

(See Photo P).

After the stile has been scribed, remove it and plane to the mark, refitting to check your progress **(See Photo Q).** When everything fits, secure the cabinet to the wall with screws through the back

(See Photo R). Next, hang the doors by slipping the hinges into the brackets previously installed on the face frame **(See Photo S)**, adjusting for even margins with a screwdriver **(See Photo T).**

(*Continued on page 144*)

PHOTO M: With the loose stile off, position and level the cabinet in all directions. Use adjustable supports or shims to level.

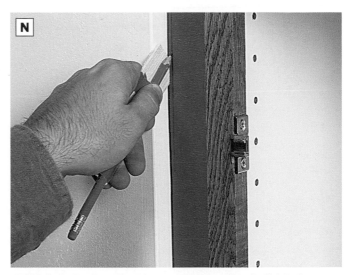

PHOTO N: Scribe the stile with a pencil and a shim. On finished surfaces, low-tack masking tape makes your line visible.

PHOTO O: Lay the cabinet on its back and plane to the scribe line. Cut a back bevel for a tight fit.

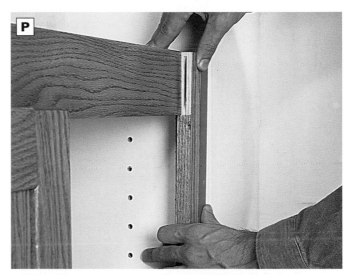

PHOTO P: Reposition the cabinet and fit the loose stile. Rip it with a 5° bevel ⅛ in. wider than needed, then scribe the wall.

PHOTO Q: Clamp the stile securely and plane with the grain until you hit the line. Check progress by fitting the stile often.

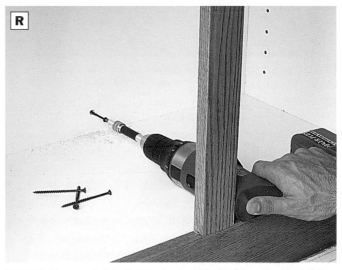

PHOTO R: To prevent distorting the back, drill pilot holes; then install the cabinet with 2½-in. screws.

PHOTO S: Install the cabinet with the doors off, then slip the hinges into the mounting bracket on the face frame.

PHOTO T: Adjust the doors so the margins are even, then tighten the screws by hand. Don't use a drill; it will strip the heads.

COUNTER POINT

The countertop, although not an integral part of the cabinet, is a vital element that physically and visually bridges the walls and cabinet. We chose a cultured marble top with a matte finish from a national marble supplier. We sized the counter ¼ in. smaller than the opening so it would fit between the walls without binding. The counter is bound to the cabinet and wall with silicone adhesive; then it's caulked around the ends to hide the seams.

Pro Tips for a Perfect Installation

As a professional trim carpenter, I rely on loose stile cabinet installation for the best possible fit. In cases where the cabinet fits a specific opening, I ask the cabinet shop to leave one stile loose for easier double-scribed cabinet installation.

Instead of trying to fit two sides of the cabinet at once, I remove the loose stile of the cabinet, fit the fixed stile, then complete the installation. Since my cabinets are always finished on-site, my approach to installing the loose stile involves cutting out the back side of the mortise so it slips in from the front of the cabinet. After the glue dries, I touch up the joinery with a bit of sanding.

However, that approach wouldn't have worked with a pre-finished cabinet like the one shown here. In this case, it's necessary to fit the two sides of the cabinet, reinstall the stile, then push the entire unit into place at once. The fitting process is basically the same, except the cabinet has to be removed from the opening to attach the stile before permanent installation. Since biscuits were used to assemble the face frame, aligning the rail and stile is automatic. Ordinary wood glue and face nails keep the stile in place during installation.

Each system has its advantages. The loose stile is faster, but may require some time-consuming touch-up sanding. You'll also need to consider the opening's width. In many cases, corner bead makes openings too narrow at the front for the cabinet's width. In this case, you have no choice but to install the stile with the cabinet already in place.

—Blake Stranz

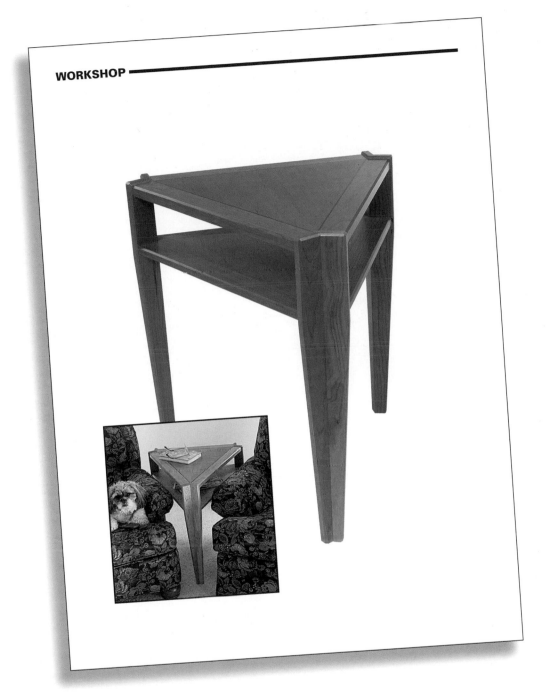

Triangular Table

The old adage that square pegs don't fit into round holes has a special meaning when it comes to arranging furniture. Try to make a square end table fit between chairs that are slightly angled in front of an entertainment center or next to a bed that's angled into a corner. It doesn't work visually or functionally because there are always awkward gaps left between the furniture pieces or along the walls. Here's a stylish triangular design that solves all those arrangement problems.

Triangular Table

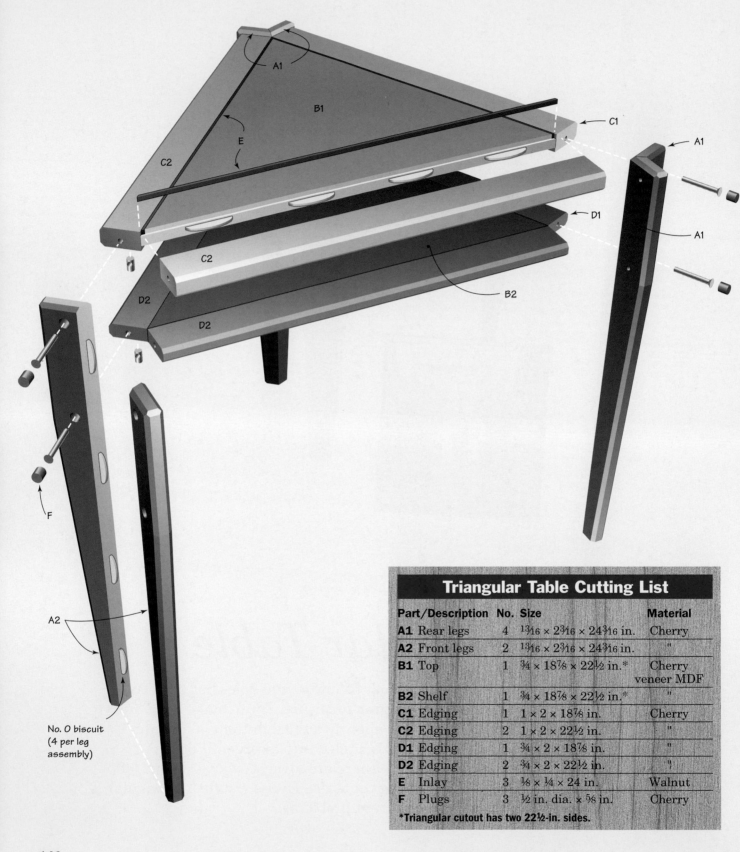

Triangular Table Cutting List			
Part/Description	No.	Size	Material
A1 Rear legs	4	1¾₁₆ × 2³₁₆ × 24³₁₆ in.	Cherry
A2 Front legs	2	1¾₁₆ × 2³₁₆ × 24³₁₆ in.	"
B1 Top	1	¾ × 18⅞ × 22½ in.*	Cherry veneer MDF
B2 Shelf	1	¾ × 18⅞ × 22½ in.*	"
C1 Edging	1	1 × 2 × 18⅞ in.	Cherry
C2 Edging	2	1 × 2 × 22½ in.	"
D1 Edging	1	¾ × 2 × 18⅞ in.	"
D2 Edging	2	¾ × 2 × 22½ in.	"
E Inlay	3	⅛ × ¼ × 24 in.	Walnut
F Plugs	3	½ in. dia. × ⅝ in.	Cherry

*Triangular cutout has two 22½-in. sides.

No. O biscuit
(4 per leg
assembly)

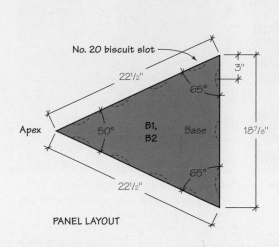

No. 20 biscuit slot

22½"

3"

65°

Apex

50°

B1,
B2

Base

18⅞"

65°

22½"

PANEL LAYOUT

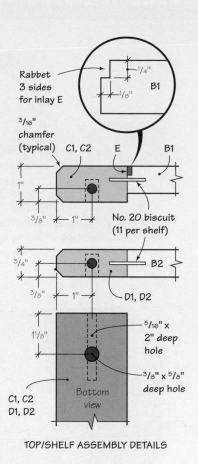

Rabbet
3 sides
for inlay E

¼"

B1

⅛"

³/₁₆"
chamfer
(typical)

C1, C2

E

B1

1"

⅜"

1"

No. 20 biscuit
(11 per shelf)

¾"

B2

⅜"

1"

D1, D2

1⅛"

⁵/₁₆" x
2" deep
hole

⅜" x ⅝"
deep hole

C1, C2
D1, D2

Bottom
view

TOP/SHELF ASSEMBLY DETAILS

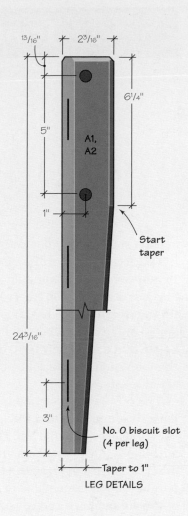

¹³/₁₆"

2³/₁₆"

6¼"

5"

A1,
A2

1"

Start
taper

24³/₁₆"

3"

No. 0 biscuit slot
(4 per leg)

Taper to 1"

LEG DETAILS

Shopping List

- [ ] 1¼ bf ⁵/₄ cherry (edging)
- [ ] 5 bf ⁴/₄ cherry (legs, edging)
- [ ] ¾ × 48 × 48-in. cherry-veneer MDF
- [ ] ¾ × 2 × 24-in. walnut
- [ ] (12) ¼-20 × 2-in. flathead machine screws
- [ ] (12) 16 × 10 mm steel cross dowels
- [ ] Drilling jig
- [ ] (12) #0 plate-joining biscuits
- [ ] (22) #20 plate-joining biscuits
- [ ] 120- and 220-grit sandpaper
- [ ] Finishing materials

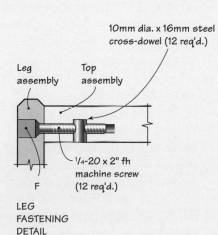

10mm dia. x 16mm steel
cross-dowel (12 req'd.)

Leg
assembly

Top
assembly

¼-20 x 2" fh
machine screw
(12 req'd.)

F

LEG
FASTENING
DETAIL

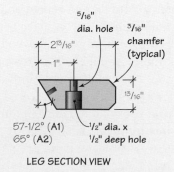

⁵/₁₆"
dia. hole

³/₁₆"
chamfer
(typical)

2¹³/₁₆"

1"

¹³/₁₆"

57-1/2° (A1)
65° (A2)

½" dia. x
½" deep hole

LEG SECTION VIEW

This small triangular end table fits perfectly in awkward spots. In addition to its adaptability, it also has a smooth top (there's no lip that might cause beverage spills) and a convenient shelf below that's ideal for magazines, the television remote control or a set of coasters.

The table's construction is wonderfully simple because the legs are attached to the top and shelf with mechanical fasteners and the other joints are made with plate-joining biscuits. An added benefit of the simple lines and construction is that it's easy to modify details or even change the style of the table.

I used solid cherry to make the legs and cherry-veneered MDF-core plywood with solid cherry edging for the top and shelf. The MDF core provides a more stable substrate for the veneer than common veneer-core panels. You can buy it at hardwood-plywood and lumber suppliers. To dress up the top, I added a contrasting walnut inlay between the veneered panel and the solid edging. The inlay technique isn't too difficult and the contrasting band provides the table with an elegant detail.

MAKING THE LEGS

The angled legs are made by gluing together two beveled strips. Note that the two legs at the base

PHOTO A: Bevel the leg stock before you rip it to width and taper it.

PHOTO B: Rough cut the leg tapers just outside the line using a jig saw. Then smooth and straighten with a block plane.

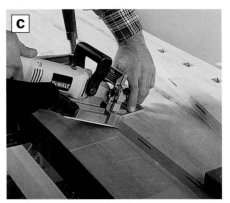

PHOTO C: Join leg halves with #0 biscuits. Be sure to set the fence on the plate joiner to the proper angle for each leg.

PHOTO D: Use two shaped blocks to help draw the leg joints tight and clamp them at each end of the leg with gentle pressure.

of the triangle are joined at one angle and the leg at the apex of the triangle is joined at a different angle. The only difference in construction, however, is the angle at which you rip the bevel on the strips for the legs.

Rip and crosscut a 5 × 26-in. blank for each leg section. Set the table saw to the appropriate bevel angle for the leg, then cut the bevel along the outside edges of the blank (**See Photo A**). It's safer and easier to cut the bevels on the larger blanks than the smaller leg halves. After you've beveled all the leg blanks, reset the saw to 90° to rip the strips to

width; then crosscut each to the finished length.

Lay out the tapered profile of each leg half. Note that the taper begins 6¼ in. from the top of each leg. Use a jig saw to make the tapered cut, sawing on the waste side of the layout line (**See Photo B**). Use a sharp block plane to remove the saw marks and refine the profile.

Mark the location of the #0 plate-joining biscuits that strengthen and align the legs' bevel joint. Set the fence on the plate joiner to the appropriate angle for each bevel and make a test cut on a scrap piece before cutting the slots on the leg halves. Because the leg parts are rather narrow, it's best to clamp them to the workbench before cutting the slots (**See Photo C).** You can then use both hands to control the plate joiner, and keep your fingers safely out of the path of the cutter.

Apply glue to both halves of the leg bevel joint, the biscuit slots and the biscuits; then assemble a leg. Use clamps to pull the joint tight, but don't apply too much pressure. Because of the angled nature of the joint, the clamps will tend to pull the top of the bevel open. To counteract this, make two shaped blocks and clamp them over the leg securely, closing any visible gap (**See Photo D).**

Let the glue set for about 45 minutes, then scrape off any squeeze-out from the leg joints. Chamfer the leg edges with a block plane or use a chamfer bit and router mounted in a router table. However, to chamfer the top of each leg, you must use a razor-sharp chisel to avoid tearing the end grain. Mark guidelines around the top of the leg and gradually remove material until you reach the line.

TOP & SHELF

Cut the panels for the top and shelf from ¾-in.-thick MDF-core cherry plywood. Use either a band saw or a jig saw to cut the pieces. Or you can cut the pieces to rough size, then use a router and straight-edge to trim them to size. Whatever method you use, just be sure that the two panels are identical in size and shape, and that the angles are accurate.

The walnut inlay on the top is glued into a rabbet cut around the top edge of the panel. It's best to first cut the ⅛ × ¼-in. inlay strips; then size the rabbets to fit them exactly. Leave the inlay strips long at this point and trim them to length after glue-up.

Use the router table and a straight bit to cut the rabbet for the inlay. Test the setup on scrap pieces until it's exactly right, then make the cuts in the panel (**See Photo E).**

Apply glue to the rabbet on one edge of the panel and place the strip; then secure it with masking tape until the glue sets (**See Photo F).** Because the strip is so small, the tape applies sufficient pressure to form a good bond to the panel. Use a dovetail saw to trim the ends of the inlay strip close to the rabbet (**See Photo G).** Once the other inlay strips have been installed, pare them flush to the edge of the rabbet with a sharp chisel (**See Photo H).**

Next, cut the edging strips to their finished dimension. Note that the top edging is 1 in. thick and the shelf edging is ¾ in. thick. Cut matching biscuit slots

PHOTO E: Use a straight bit in the router table to cut the ⅛ × ¼-in. rabbet for the walnut inlay in the plywood top.

PHOTO F: Glue the inlay strip in the rabbet and use masking tape every inch along the length of the edge to clamp.

PHOTO G: Use a fine-tooth dovetail saw to trim the ends of the inlay strip close to the rabbet on the adjacent edges.

PHOTO H: Trim the inlay strip flush with the edge of the rabbet by making a series of fine, paring cuts with a razor-sharp chisel.

PHOTO I: Attach the edges to the top and shelf with plate-joining biscuits; then secure them with edging clamps.

PHOTO J: Use a doweling jig to bore holes for the ¼-20 machine screws in the ends of the edging to attach the legs.

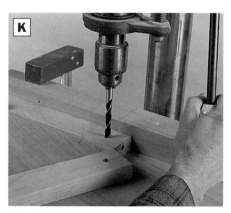

PHOTO K: Bore the cross dowel holes in the bottom of the edging. Use the drill press depth stop to ensure the proper depth.

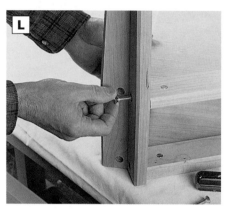

PHOTO L: To fasten a leg to the shelf, run the screws through the leg holes and into the threaded cross dowels.

in the edging and panel; then glue the edging in place. Use specially designed 3-way edging clamps to pull the joints tight **(See Photo I).**

ATTACHING THE LEGS

Bore the required holes in the edging for the machine screws and cross dowels. To drill the holes into the ends of the solid edging, you should use a drilling jig. If you have a doweling jig, you could use it to guide the drill. As an alternative, some woodworking stores offer an inexpensive drilling jig for Minifix fasteners that can be used for the holes **(See Photo J).** If you use this jig, you will need to trim about ½ in. off each end of the wooden guide block.

Install the cross dowels in the bottom of the shelf and top after drilling the appropriate holes on the drill press **(See Photo K).** Then drill and counterbore the holes through the legs. Before assembly, sand all table parts first with 120- and then 220-grit sandpaper. Be sure to dust off the legs thoroughly.

Fasten the legs to the shelves with 2-in.-long, ¼-in.-dia. × 20 thread machine screws **(See Photo L).**

Use a plug cutter in a drill press to cut ½-in.-dia. plugs from scrap cherry blocks. Choose material that matches the color and grain of the table legs. Apply glue to the plugs and holes with a small brush, then position the plugs to cover the screw heads. Be sure to align the grain of the plugs with that of the leg as you install them. When the glue sets, use a sharp chisel to trim the plugs flush to the leg surface, then do any required touch-up sanding.

Because the table is likely to be subjected to moisture, cold and heat from drinks placed on it, I applied three coats of polyurethane varnish. Short of using coasters on the tabletop, this finish affords the best possible protection.

Treasure Chest

The traditional blanket chest is more than just a place to store blankets. It's become the standard place where many Americans accumulate life's treasures and in the process, it has become a treasure in its own right. For hundreds of years, people have handed down dovetailed chests like this one from one generation to the next. Now, with this handsome design, you too can start your own family tradition.

Treasure Chest

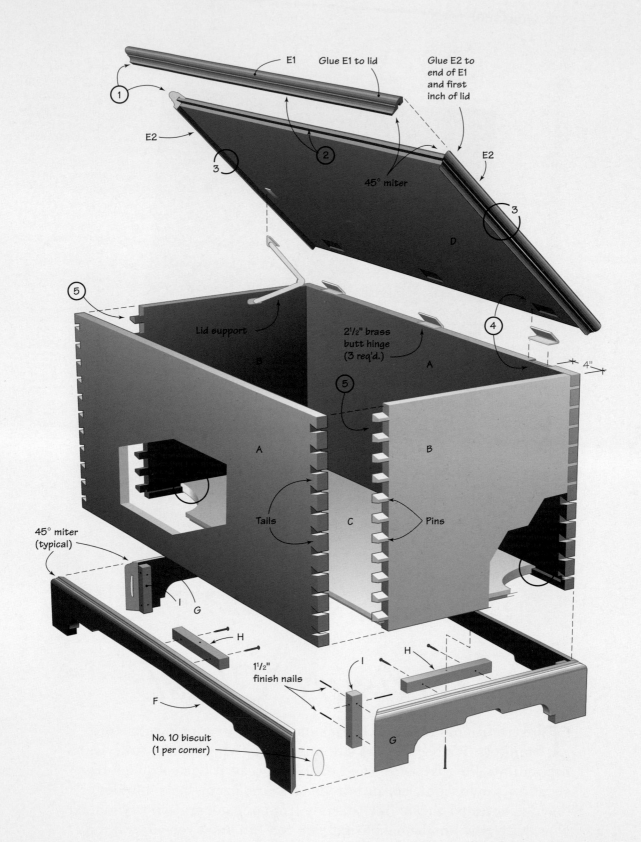

E1

Glue E1 to lid

Glue E2 to end of E1 and first inch of lid

(1)

E2

2

3

45° miter

E2

E2

3

D

5

Lid support

2½" brass butt hinge (3 req'd.)

A

4

4"

B

5

B

A

C

Tails

Pins

45° miter (typical)

I

G

H

I

1½" finish nails

H

F

G

No. 10 biscuit (1 per corner)

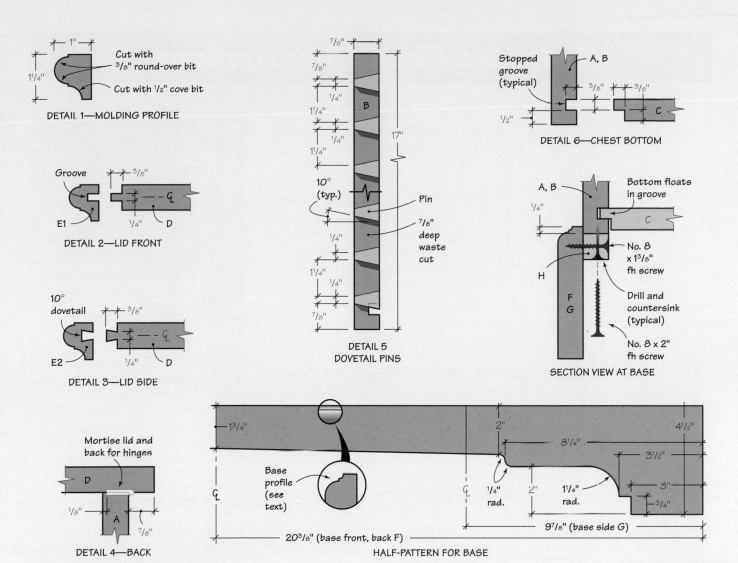

DETAIL 1—MOLDING PROFILE

Cut with 3/8" round-over bit
Cut with 1/2" cove bit
1"
1 1/4"

DETAIL 2—LID FRONT

Groove
E1
3/8"
1/4"
D
G

DETAIL 3—LID SIDE

10° dovetail
E2
3/8"
1/4"
D
G

DETAIL 4—BACK

Mortise lid and back for hinges
D
1/8"
A
7/8"

DETAIL 5 DOVETAIL PINS

7/8"
7/8"
1/4"
1 1/4"
1/4"
1 1/4"
10° (typ.)
1/4"
1 1/4"
1/4"
1 1/4"
1/4"
7/8"
B
17"
Pin
7/8" deep waste cut

DETAIL 6—CHEST BOTTOM

Stopped groove (typical)
A, B
3/8"
3/8"
1/2"
C

SECTION VIEW AT BASE

A, B
Bottom floats in groove
1/4"
C
H
F
G
No. 8 × 1 3/8" fh screw
Drill and countersink (typical)
No. 8 × 2" fh screw

HALF-PATTERN FOR BASE

1 3/4"
Base profile (see text)
2"
8 1/4"
4 1/2"
3 1/2"
1/4" rad.
2"
1 1/4" rad.
3"
3/4"
20 3/8" (base front, back F)
9 7/8" (base side G)

Shopping List

- [ ] 50 bf of 5/4 cherry
- [ ] 5 bf of pine
- [ ] (3) 2 1/2-in. brass butt hinges
- [ ] (1) lid support
- [ ] (8) #8 × 1 3/8-in. flathead wood screws
- [ ] (4) #8 × 2-in. flathead wood screws
- [ ] #10 plate-joining biscuits
- [ ] 1 1/2-in. finishing nails (or pneumatic brads)
- [ ] Wood glue
- [ ] Polyurethane glue
- [ ] Finishing materials

Treasure Chest Cutting List

Part/Description		No.	Size	Material
A	Front/back*	2	7/8 × 17 × 39 in.	Cherry
B	Sides*	2	7/8 × 17 × 18 in.	"
C	Bottom*	1	3/4 × 16 7/8 × 37 7/8 in.	Pine
D	Lid*	1	7/8 × 19 1/4 × 39 3/4 in.	Cherry
E1	Front molding	1	1 × 1 1/4 × 41 in.	"
E2	Side moldings	2	1 × 1 1/4 × 19 7/8 in.	"
F	Base front/back	2	7/8 × 4 1/2 × 40 3/4 in.	"
G	Base sides	2	7/8 × 4 1/2 × 19 3/4 in.	"
H	Cleats	4	7/8 × 7/8 × 8 in.	"
I	Corner blocks	4	7/8 × 7/8 × 4 1/4 in.	"

*Must be assembled from narrower stock.

WHY DOVETAILS?

Before the advent of central heating and air conditioning, the dovetail was the woodworker's joint of choice for building cases because furniture had to endure a wide range of temperature and humidity. Dovetailed cases continued to hold together even after expansion and contraction caused glue failure. With modern climate control and superior glues, dovetails are no longer a structural imperative, but there is no denying they can transform an ordinary chest into an heirloom-quality treasure.

If you're intimidated by doing this seemingly precise work by hand, remember that until just a few generations ago woodworking was done only with hand tools. Practice on some scrap pieces first and you'll find that it takes more patience than skill to chop a dovetail by hand. And if you're still not sold on doing the work with hand tools, but you like the look of dovetails, there are a number of commercially available through-dovetail jigs for routers that will dramatically speed up your work. The down side is that these jigs can cost a hefty sum, making them impractical unless you cut dovetails with some regularity.

DEALING WITH STOCK

I used cherry to build this chest, but you can use almost any furniture-grade wood. You'll get the best results if you mill your own stock (if you can't, it's okay to use ¾-in. stock, but you'll have to modify the dimensions of the bottom and base). Start with 5⁄4-in. (1¼-in.) rough stock to ensure that you'll wind up with 7⁄8-in.-thick milled stock. Let the wood acclimate to your shop's environment for about a week before you start milling. Be sure to mill extra pieces to set up cuts.

When gluing up the top, front, back and side panels, use plate-joining biscuits to help align and join the boards. And to minimize the visual transitions between boards, try to match the grain at the joint line. Also, be aware of wood color and avoid defects such as knots and pitch pockets.

You might also consider making a drop-in aromatic cedar bottom out of ¼-in. tongue-and-groove cedar closet liner, which is available at home centers.

MARK & CUT DOVETAILS

One of the first and most important steps when cutting dovetails is to label all of the case parts to avoid confusion. Corners must mate perfectly, so you can't mix them up. I make masking tape labels (front, back, up, left, right, etc.) and leave them on until the case is fully assembled. You can use the pin layout in the drawing or figure out your own spacing. For instance, if you don't want to do quite so much cutting, increase the spacing between pins (to make larger tails) or vary the size of the pins or tails for a random appearance. However, the tails on the top

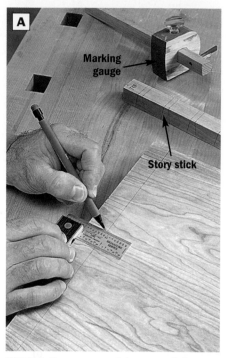

PHOTO A: To ensure consistency, mark the pins using a story stick (in background); then extend the layout marks with a square.

and bottom should be one-half to three-quarters the width of the rest of the tails. If you make them too wide, they'll look clumsy; if they're too narrow, they can break off easily when you assemble the chest. When in doubt, don't make them any less than ¾ in. wide.

I made the narrowest part of the pins ¼ in. wide so it would be practical to remove the waste between the tails (where the pins fit) with a ¼-in. chisel. Some woodworkers like smaller pins because they look more refined, but they're more prone to breaking, and removing the waste between the tails is sure to try your patience.

I've found that one of the best ways to ensure accurate and consistent joints is to use a story stick (See Photo A). This is simply a piece of stock that's the same width and thickness as the panels and has the dovetail layout drawn on it. To use it, just transfer the marks on the stick directly to the workpiece—no measuring, no mistakes.

It's a good practice to lay out the joinery so the ends of the pins and tails protrude about 0.001 in. after assembly. This is so you can sand or plane the end grain perfectly

PHOTO B: Extend the pin marks on the end grain by setting a T-bevel to 10°. Mark with a fine pencil or a utility knife.

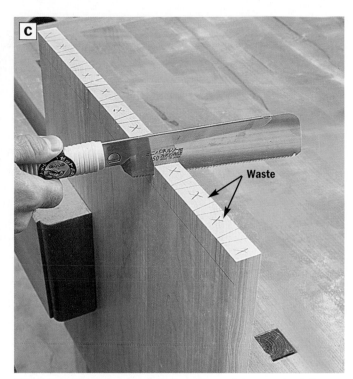

PHOTO C: Cut on the outside of the line with a pull saw or a dovetail saw. Mark the waste with an "X" to prevent mistakes.

smooth and flush with the front of the panels. To get the right amount of projection, set up the mark for the shoulder line with a piece of stock that's the same thickness as the panel stock. Then add the width of a .05 pencil line (the line is always smaller than the diameter of the lead). Mark the shoulder line with a combination square and pencil or with a marking gauge. When you begin cutting the shoulders with a chisel, be sure to cut to the outside of the line (See Photo D).

Cutting the cheeks of the pins and tails requires the greatest amount of skill and patience. You'll get a lot of practice cutting pins first (See Photo C), but cutting between the tails (where the pins go) is where accuracy really counts. I use a small Japanese panel saw to make the cuts. A good European-style dovetail saw will also do the job. These specially designed back saws make quick work of the task at hand.

Fine, crosscut teeth and minimal tooth set produce smooth, even cuts with very little tearout. Be sure the workpiece is securely clamped, and try to keep the saw perpendicular to the edge of the work. Once the cut is started, let the saw find its own path. Careful, controlled strokes, rather than heavy downward pressure on the blade, will yield the best results. If the blade wanders, don't try to force it back onto the line. A sharp chisel works well to straighten any crooked pin cheeks after you've chipped away all the waste and before you lay out the tails (See Photo E).

Use the pins to determine the position of the tails by laying out mating parts. First, use the inside of the pins to mark the tail locations on the outside of the front (See Photo G). After the edges have been marked, connect them and the inside marks with a pencil line (See Photo H).

Next, stand the side piece on

edge in its correct orientation in order to mark the inside of the front and to trace fully around the pins (See Photo I). Be sure to keep the workpieces properly aligned throughout the layout, as even the slightest shift will cause mismatched joints down the road.

Cutting the cheeks of the tails is one of woodworking's more tedious and time-consuming techniques. Take extra care to cut precisely along the layout lines in order to give your joints the most refined appearance possible. Don't get frustrated with the process; remember that the result will be one of the most attractive, secure styles of joinery available.

Once you've cut all the tails and pins, you'll probably need to adjust the fit. The joints should slide together easily without being forced. If a few of the parts require some fine-tuning, pare pins and tails as necessary with a sharp chisel. Don't worry if you remove a little too much. You can always

155

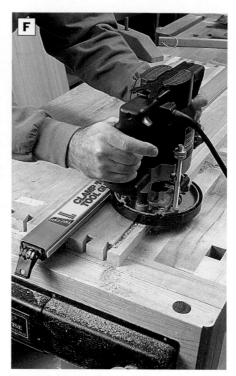

PHOTO D: Make shallow cuts on the shoulder lines. Don't cut too deep or the chisel will drift off the line.

PHOTO E: Alternately chisel on the line and chip out the waste (shown) until you're about two-thirds through. Finish from the other side.

PHOTO F: The bottom requires a stopped groove in all four case sides. If you rout through, the groove will show on the outside.

glue slivers or a piece of veneer back on before the final assembly.

MORE JOINERY

Rout the stopped grooves for the bottom in the front, back and sides **(See Photo F).** To make setting up the fence for the router easier, use a ¼-in.-thick hardboard spacer cut to a width that's equal to the distance from the edge of the workpiece to the fence. For consistent spacing, hold the spacer against the fence and the edge of the work, then lock down the fence. Be careful not to rout through the ends of the workpiece, which would expose the dado on the outside of the chest.

Cut the bottom ⅟₁₆ to ⅛ in. smaller in length and width than the size of the opening (in the grooves) to allow for seasonal wood movement. Cut it for a tighter fit in the summer and a looser fit in the winter.

Trim the lid to size only after fitting the case together (without

glue) to determine its exact size. Allow ⅟₁₆ in. overhang on each side and ⅛ in. on the front edge. Remember to add to your dimensions the tongue for the front molding and the dovetail for the side moldings.

LID MOLDINGS

Make the lid moldings with a router table or a shaper if you have one. Don't attempt to make these cuts with a handheld router. Set up your router table with appropriate guards and featherboards. Be sure to have extra stock, because you'll probably need to make several practice cuts when setting up. First, cut the lower ⅜-in. radius (middle cut); then make the bottom ½-in. cove cut; finally, cut the top ⅜-in. radius (See *Detail 1,* page 153).

Note that there's a difference in how the front molding and side moldings are attached to the lid. The molding on the front is attached with a tongue-and-groove

joint and glue. However, the moldings on the sides run perpendicular to the lid's grain, so they must allow for the lid's expansion and contraction. Any molding that is solidly glued, screwed or nailed to the lid can cause it to split. To prevent this, I used a sliding dovetail to attach the side moldings. The joint is glued only at the front miter and about 1 in. behind it (apply glue only on the lid side of the joint or glue will be spread along the entire length of the molding). This allows the lid to slide freely in the molding.

You can use a table saw (as I did) or a router table to cut both sides of the joint. Practice with scrap first to get the fit right. The molding should fit snugly but slide easily on the lid dovetail. When making the groove, first cut it straight in order to remove most of the stock and to establish the depth; then tilt the blade (or change the bit) to cut the 10° angle on both sides of the groove.

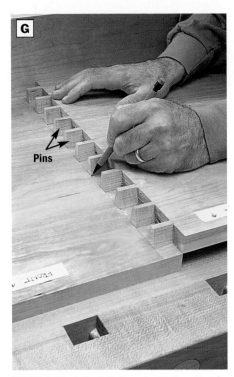

PHOTO G: Mark the tails layout with the pins of the mating part. First, mark the outside of the front with the inside of the pins.

PHOTO H: Keep the workpieces aligned and mark the edges; then connect the edge and inside marks with pencil lines.

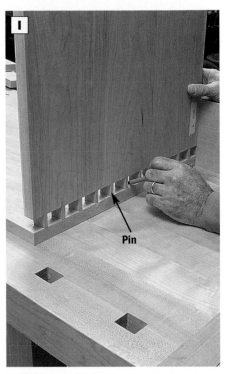

PHOTO I: Mark the inside of the front by standing the side on its edge (oriented correctly); then trace around the pins.

Now you're able to cut the lid dovetail to fit.

MAKING THE BASE

As with the lid, you should wait until you've assembled the case (either glued or not) before you size the base parts. The front, back and sides can fit tightly against the case because there's no cross-grain wood movement to worry about.

When making the parts, rout the top profile first on your router table. Any piloted edge-forming bit such as a cove-and-bead or an ogee bit will work. Next, cut the miters. You'll need a miter saw with a fairly substantial capacity or a table saw and a cutoff box.

Make a hardboard half-pattern for the base relief cuts; then use it to trace the design onto the workpieces (the pattern is the same for the front, back and sides). Cut out the pattern on the workpieces with a band saw or jig saw and sand the edges smooth. Because

of the shape of the decorative contours, an oscillating spindle sander works particularly well for this job.

ASSEMBLY & FINISHING

I used polyurethane glue to assemble the case because it has a long open time and it only needs to be applied to one side of the joint **(See Photo J).** Also, it has very little tack, which is key in getting the dovetails to slide together easily.

Because the bottom is held in a stopped groove, the assembly sequence is very important for the case to go together properly. First, attach the bottom to the sides (standing all three pieces on edge works best); then slip on the front, followed by the back. Tapping the joints together lightly with a soft mallet and a scrap block will secure the fit and further distribute the glue within the dovetails **(See Photo K).** Plywood cauls at each joint will apply even pressure after clamping up the case, while

measuring the diagonals of the assembly is a good way to check for square **(See Photo L).** Once the glue has cured, you can trim the protruding ends of the pins and tails with a hand plane or sand them flush.

Install all of the hardware before finishing to check the fit and make adjustments. Be sure to remove the hardware before finishing, though. If you plan on installing a lock, keep in mind that the lid will expand and contract, so the latching mechanism must accommodate this play.

Though cherry is a wood that's prone to blotching when stained, thorough sanding and careful stain application will help to prevent it. In order to properly prepare the surface, I sanded with progressively finer grits up to 220. Instead of staining the entire chest at once, I applied oil-based pigment stain to one surface at a time and quickly wiped off the excess. This piecemeal technique

PHOTO J: Use a brush to apply polyurethane glue to the mating surfaces of the pins (apply glue to all surfaces if you use wood glue).

PHOTO K: Lightly tap the sides together with a mallet and block, but be careful to keep the pieces from jamming.

PHOTO L: Clamp the case behind the joints using plywood cauls. Check for square by measuring the case diagonally.

helped prevent pools and runs that can cause blotching.

For adequate protection, a project like this needs a film finish; avoid using an oil finish. I applied six coats of semi-gloss wiping varnish to all the surfaces of the chest. Wiping varnish is simply regular alkyd or polyurethane varnish that's been thinned with mineral spirits. You can either buy it mixed or make your own in the shop, as I did. The advantage of wiping rather than brushing is that you'll get a finish that looks like it's been sprayed. To remove dust nibs and achieve the smoothest possible finish, sand with 320-grit or finer paper between coats and rub out the final coat with 0000 steel wool. After both the base and case have been finished to a desirable look and texture, join the two pieces with screws through the cleats previously attached to the base **(See Photo M).**

PHOTO M: Finish the case and base separately before joining them with 2-in. wood screws.

Index

A

Arc,
  laying out, 8, 34, 35, 120, 121

B

Bathroom vanity, 123-128
  cutting list, 125
  detailed drawings, 124, 125
  step-by-step, 126-128
Bed-rail fasteners,
  machining for, 29, 30
Bench (see *Entry bench*)
Bench dogs, 29
  drilling holes for, 30
Bevel,
  ripping, 48, 49, 66, 134, 148
Beverage bar, 45-50
  cutting list, 47
  detailed drawings, 46, 47
  shopping list, 46
  step-by-step, 48-50
Biscuit jointing, 22, 23, 54-56, 84,
  85, 103, 104, 110, 139
  offset, 41, 84, 85, 148, 149
Booth (see *Kitchen nook*)
Building custom cabinets,
  137-144
Butcher block (see *Sink board*)

C

Casters,
  mounting, 30, 50, 74, 115, 116
Chamfering, 92, 102, 149
Chest (see *Treasure chest*)
Climb cutting,
  with router, 85
Computer desk, 75-80
  cutting list, 77
  detailed drawings, 76, 77
  step-by-step, 78-80
Corner curio, 129-136
  cutting list, 131
  detailed drawings, 130-132
  installing, 136
  shopping list, 131
  step-by-step, 133-136
Curio (see *Corner curio*)
Curved contours,
  laying out, 90, 91
Custom cabinets, (see also

Bathroom vanity)
  building, 137-144
  installing, 140-144
Cutting board (see *Sink board*)

D

Dado,
  cutting on table saw, 54, 55, 72,
  114, 115, 126
  gang routing, 28, 134, 135
  routing, 8, 114, 115, 131, 156
Desk (see *Computer desk* &
  Portable desk)
Display coffee table, 19-24
  cutting list, 20
  detailed drawings, 20, 21
  shopping list, 21
  step-by-step, 22-24
Door frame assembly, 141
Double rocker, 31-36
  cutting list, 32,
  detailed drawings, 32, 33
  hardware list, 32
  shopping list, 33
  step-by-step, 34-36
Dovetail joints,
  about, 154
  marking & cutting, 154-157
Drawer,
  face attachment, 18
  ready-to-assemble kit, 126, 128

E

Edge-banding,
  applying, 78, 140
  trimming, 78
Ellipse,
  laying out, 108, 109
Entry bench, 5-10
  cutting list, 6
  detailed drawings, 6, 7
  shopping list, 7
  step-by-step, 8-10

F

Figure-8 fasteners,
  machining for, 66, 67
Fillets,
  about, 9
  installing, 102
Finishing tips, 18, 157, 158
Fireplace surround (see *Mantel*)
Flower bed, 87-92
  cutting list, 88
  detailed drawings, 88, 89

shopping list, 89
  step-by-step, 90-92
Flush trimming, 16, 97, 98
Frame (see *Oval frame*)

G

Gardener's bench, 117-122
  cutting list, 119
  detailed drawings, 118, 119
  shopping list, 119
  step-by-step, 120-122
Glass stops,
  installing, 24
Grain matching, 15
Grates,
  milling, 10

H

Hinges,
  installing, 23, 24, 55, 56

I

Inlay,
  installing, 149

K

Kitchen nook, 37-44
  detailed drawings, 38, 39
  determining dimensions, 40
  installing, 42, 44
  step-by-step, 40-44
  tools needed, 40
  upholstering, 42-43
Knock-down (KD) fasteners,
  about, 78
  assembling with, 80
  diagrams, 77
  installing 78, 79

L

Laminate,
  attaching, 79
Laminating, 96-98
Lap desk (see *Portable desk*)
Leveling legs, 142, 143

M

Mantel, 81-86
  cutting list, 83
  detailed drawings, 82, 83
  step-by-step, 84-86
Materials cart, 111-116
  cutting list, 113

detailed drawings, 112, 113
shopping list, 113
step-by-step, 114-116
Medium-density fiberboard
(MDF),
characteristics, 126
expansion & contraction, 127
working with, 126
Metabox drawer kit, 126, 128
Minifix-brand fasteners,
assembling with, 80
diagram, 77
installing, 79
machining for, 78, 79
Mission table, 11-18
cutting list, 13
detailed drawings, 12, 13
shopping list, 13
step-by-step, 14-18
Miter cutting, 62, 68, 109
compound, 86
Molding,
making, 22, 156, 56
miter cutting, 68
Mortising,
for hinges, 23, 24
for tenons, 8, 14, 15, 90

N

Nook (see *Kitchen nook*)

O

Oval frame, 105-110
detailed drawings, 106, 107
shopping list, 106
step-by-step, 108-110

P

Panels, door,
making, 127
Picture frame (see *Oval frame*)
Plugging screw holes, 150
Plunge routing, 14, 15, 17, 49, 50,
55, 56, 92
Pocket screws, 73
Polyurethane glue,
caution, 97
characteristics, 48, 96
Portable desk, 51-56
cutting list, 52
detailed drawings, 52, 53
step-by-step, 54, 56
tools needed, 54
Profile routing, 67, 68, 85, 86, 102

Q

Quilt rack, 63-68
cutting list, 64
detailed drawings, 64, 65
shopping list, 64
step-by-step, 66-68

R

Rabbeting,
for door panels, 140-142
for glass, 23, 110, 135
for shelves, 134, 135
Radiator cover, 99-104
cutting list, 101
detailed drawings, 100, 101
installing, 104
shopping list, 101
step-by-step, 102-104
tools needed, 102
Ready-to-assemble (RTA),
computer desk, 75-80
drawer kit, 126, 128
Resawing, 15
Ripping sheet goods, 114
Rocker (see also *Double rocker*),
laying out, 34, 35
Rolling island (see *Mission table*)

S

Scribes,
marking, 42, 44, 142, 143
Sheet goods cart (see *Materials
cart*)
Sheet goods,
cutting to length with router,
133
ripping, 114, 115
Shelf pin holes,
drilling, 73, 74, 138
Sink basket,
installing, 122
Sink board, 93-98
care, 98
detailed drawings, 94, 95
determining dimensions, 97
shopping list, 95
step-by-step, 96-98
tools needed, 96
Sizing MDF edges, 126
Slide-fitting biscuit connectors,
diagram, 77
installing, 80
Spline gluing jig, 135, 136
Spline-groove cutting, 134
Stiles,

determining dimensions on
custom cabinetry, 126
ripping to width, 134
scribing for cabinet installation,
142, 143
Story stick, 154, 155

T

Tenon cutting, 15, 16, 127
Toggle clamp casters, 30
Tool cart, 69-74
cutting list, 71
detailed drawings, 70, 71
shopping list, 71
step-by-step, 72-74
Treasure chest, 151-158
cutting list, 153
detailed drawings, 152, 153
shopping list, 153
step-by-step, 154-158
Triangular table, 145-150
cutting list, 146
detailed drawings, 146, 147
shopping list, 147
step-by-step, 148-150

U

Upholstering, 42, 43
materials needed, 42

W

Wainscot, 57-62
cutting list, 58
detailed drawings, 58, 59
determining dimensions, 60, 61
installing, 62
step-by-step, 60-62
Water-based polyurethane,
sizing MDF with, 126, 127
Wood,
characteristics when wet, 48
examining, 34
expansion & contraction, 127
for food surfaces, 96
Workbench, 25-30
cutting list, 27
detailed drawings, 26, 27
determining dimensions, 28
hardware list, 27
step-by-step, 28, 30
Workstation (see *Computer desk*)